Knowledge and Action

Knowledge and Action

Edited by

Dieter Frey
Heinz Mandl
Lutz von Rosenstiel

Department of Psychology
Ludwig-Maximilians University Munich

HOGREFE

Library of Congress Cataloging-in-Publication Data

is available via the Library of Congress Marc Database under the
LC Control Number 2006920398

Library and Archives Canada Cataloguing in Publication Data

Knowledge and action / Dieter Frey, Heinz Mandl, Lutz von Rosenstiel, editors.

Includes bibliographical references.
ISBN 0-88937-299-3

1. Cognitive psychology. 2. Human behavior. I. Frey, Dieter, 1946-
II. Mandl, Heinz III. Rosenstiel, Lutz von, 1938-

BD161.K564 2006 153.4 C2006-900170-7

PUBLISHING OFFICES

USA: Hogrefe & Huber Publishers, 875 Massachusetts Avenue, 7th Floor, Cambridge, MA 02139
Phone (866) 823-4726, Fax (617) 354-6875, E-mail info@hhpub.com

EUROPE: Hogrefe & Huber Publishers, Rohnsweg 25, D-37085 Göttingen, Germany,
Phone +49 551 49609-0, Fax +49 551 49609-88, E-mail hh@hhpub.com

SALES & DISTRIBUTION

USA: Hogrefe & Huber Publishers, Customer Service Department,
30 Amberwood Parkway, Ashland, OH 44805,
Phone (800) 228-3749, Fax (419) 281-6883, E-mail custserv@hhpub.com

EUROPE: Hogrefe & Huber Publishers, Rohnsweg 25, D-37085 Göttingen, Germany,
Phone +49 551 49609-0, Fax +49 551 49609-88, E-mail hh@hhpub.com

CORPORATE OFFICE (USA)

Hogrefe & Huber Publishers, Inc., 218 Main Street, Suite 485, Kirkland, WA 98033

OTHER OFFICES

CANADA: Hogrefe & Huber Publishers, 1543 Bayview Avenue, Toronto, Ontario M4G 3B5

SWITZERLAND: Hogrefe & Huber Publishers, Länggass-Strasse 76, CH-3000 Bern 9

Hogrefe & Huber Publishers
Incorporated and Registered in the State of Washington, USA, and in Göttingen, Lower Saxony, Germany

Printed and bound in the USA
ISBN 0-88937-299-3

Table of Contents

Introduction

Dieter Frey, Heinz Mandl, & Lutz von Rosenstiel

In this volume, we summarize the findings of a research group on the topic of knowledge and action, supported by the German Science Foundation, at the University of Munich. The joint endeavor of the research group was to investigate the action-relevant function of knowledge in different areas, as well as to investigate the effect that the acquisition of knowledge has on action in certain fields. The disciplines involved were social psychology, cognitive psychology, work and organizational psychology, educational psychology and developmental psychology.

The relationship between knowledge and action is highly important for the following reasons:

(1) without knowledge, there is often no action, and

(2) knowledge can highly influence the action taken.

However, there are high levels of inconsistency between knowledge and action and little research is available on this relationship.

Knowledge and action: How these concepts are used

Differentiation is made between declarative and procedural knowledge about a certain field. For example: Knowledge about leadership strategies (Kehr & von Rosenstiel), knowledge about aspects of decision cases (Jonas, Schulz-Hardt, & Frey), functional knowledge about language in use (Henninger, Mandl, & Hörfurter), and knowledge about nursing (Büssing, Herbig, & Latzel). Knowledge is used in the sense of "self-relevant knowledge," for example, concerning one's own performance in certain school subjects (Ziegler, Heller, Schober, & Dresel), knowledge about one's own goals (Brandstätter & Frank), and knowledge about action results (Försterling); see Figure 1.

On the other hand, action (as shown in Figure 2) also relates to various action processes, such as the integration of learned self-management strategies into one's own leadership behavior (Kehr & von Rosenstiel). The particularities of the concept of action differ in each of the individual projects. Some are based on the Rubicon Model (such as the Brandstätter project), which encompasses the whole action process, whereas others, such as Frey's project, focus on decision processes and cognitive processes.

Figure 1. Fundamental factors relating to knowledge and action.

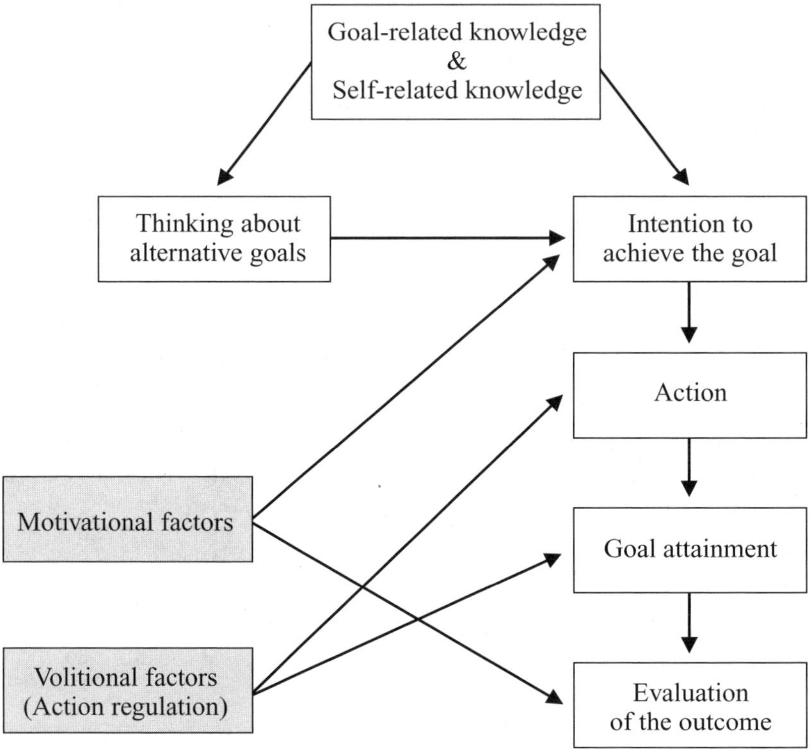

Goal-related knowledge is understood in the sense of desirability/value/incentive of the specific goal. Self-related knowledge means beliefs concerning the realization of the specific goal (e.g., self-efficacy, outcome-expectancy, independence of proceeding action results and their attribution).

The process of converting knowledge into action can be seen as a dynamic process. Therefore, emotional, cognitive, motivational, volitional, and action-regulating processes should be investigated. Because of the complexity of the processes involved, it is not yet possible to have one single knowledge or action theory that sufficiently describes the whole dynamic. However, it is necessary to investigate the different processes involved.

In the following section, we provide an overview of the research questions. These encompassed, for example:

- In which ways does knowledge about end goals affect the persistence of intentional and motivated action and the process of abandoning certain actions or goals? (Brandstätter & Frank)
- How do different degrees of freedom in the workplace relate to different levels of work satisfaction? (Büssing, Herbig, & Latzel)
- How do actual behavior or decisions influence the subsequent search for information? Can selectivity in the search for information impair subsequent decisions? (Jonas, Schulz-Hardt, & Frey)

Figure 2. The two main aspects of transforming knowledge into action: Knowledge and motivation/volition.

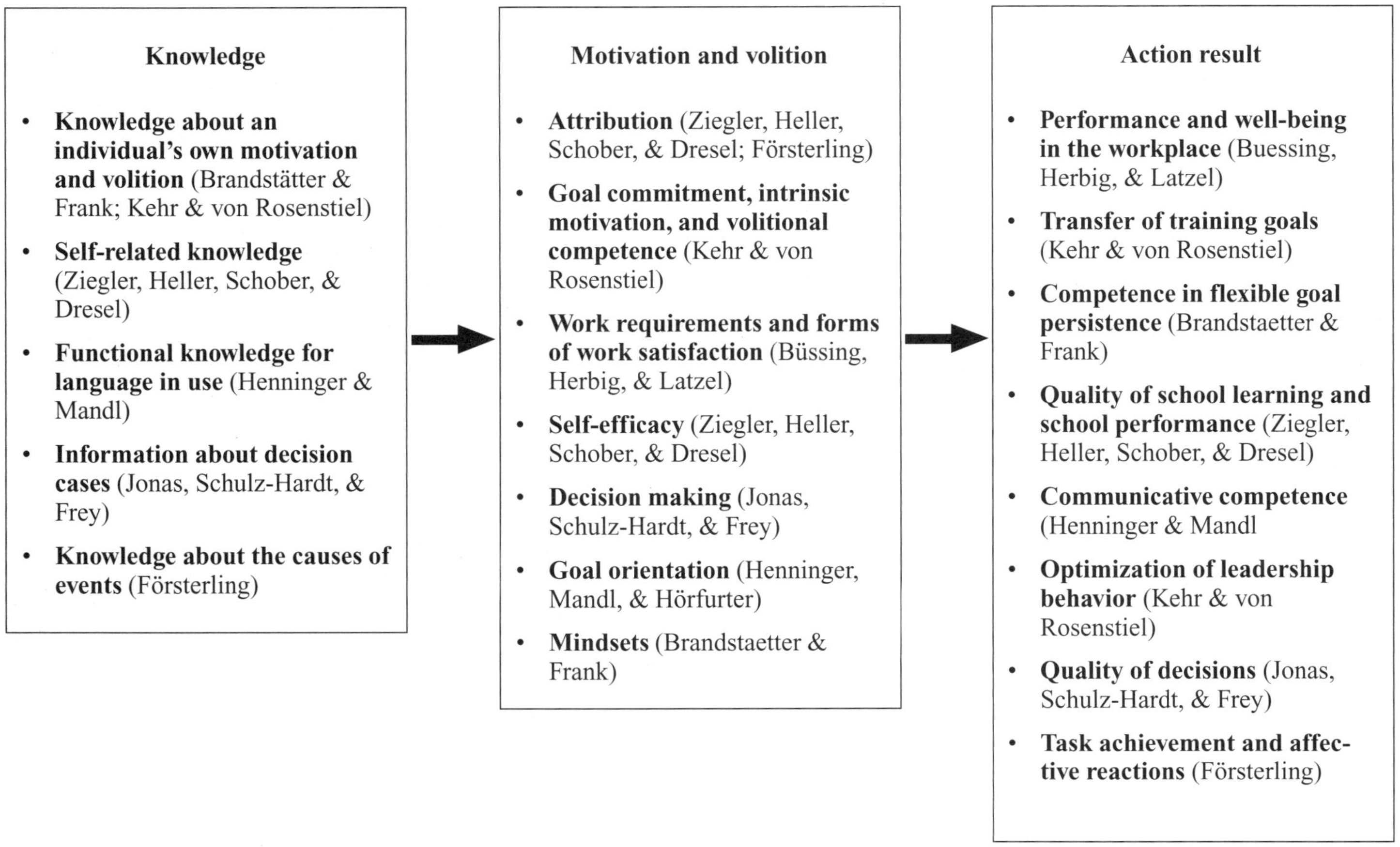

- Which facets of the self-related and action-related knowledge of students are crucial for adequate learning processes and school performance? Can improvements in self-related and action-related knowledge (attained, e.g., with cognitively oriented attributional retraining) boost school learning and performance in different domains? (Ziegler, Heller, Schober, & Dresel)
- Do more authentic learning environments lead to better learning result in the field of communicative competence? How can the acquisition of transferable communication knowledge be fostered? (Henninger & Mandl)
- How does motivational and volitional knowledge influence the process of leadership behavior? Under which conditions will intentions concerning new behavior be translated into action? (Kehr & von Rosenstiel)
- How can we define and measure realistic und unrealistic attributions and what are the emotional and behavioral consequences of causal ascriptions differing in veridicality (Försterling)?

All of the projects of the research group investigated goal-directed action and behavior; i.e., our research did not involve reflexes, automatic motor actions, or habitual actions.

In these articles, knowledge and action are viewed not as a unidirectional process, but as an interaction. Transforming knowledge into action is not the only focus; some projects investigate how action (in the sense of decisions) influences ongoing information seeking, and how this information and knowledge seeking influences ongoing actions.

Knowledge alone is not sufficient for action to take place, as no one will act in a way he or she does not want. Therefore, it is important to also consider motivational and volitional factors. Knowledge is only the first step in the process of action. The second step comprises motivational and volitional processes. A certain action will be carried out only if motivation/volition is adequate. Therefore, a scientific investigation of the process of knowledge and action should consider:

- knowledge about goals and actions
- motivational processes of goal choice
- volitional processes of goal-directed action
- evaluative processes of action results.

As the different articles show, goal-oriented action always relates to an action's results. There is also evidence of universal relevance in different fields of application: School performance in physics and chemistry, linguistic communicative competence, optimizing one's own leadership behavior, quality of decision making, competence in flexible goal persistence, performance and well-being at the workplace, and attribution.

The articles in this book are concerned either with the acquisition of knowledge or with the motivational/volitional conditions which promote the transformation of knowledge into action. The following questions relate to knowledge acquisition:

- How must learning environments be structured to ensure that knowledge can be acquired effectively and in a sustainable way?
- How do people behave when searching for sufficient knowledge in order to make a decision (information seeking)?

The motivational and volitional basis of action encompasses aspects such as:

- What are the person's aspirations?
- What motivational and volitional competencies does a person have?

- What role does self-efficacy play?
- Which attributions are made after certain results?

Our empirical research can also be applied to the field of intervention. For example, Kehr & von Rosenstiel's project developed an innovative approach to self-management training for leadership behavior in order to strengthen the transfer of knowledge.

Ziegler et al. show with a series of intervention studies that attributional retraining can be applied successfully to enhance self-related knowledge, motivation, action, and performance also in the ecologically valid setting of regular school classes. Furthermore, they showed that the effectiveness of attribution retraining can be enhanced if the content and sequence of the attributional feedback is concordant with an incremental view of an individual's own competences. In addition, by applying the newly developed Munich Motivational Training (MMT), a fully integrated concept of all facets of self-related knowledge and motivation, they were able to observe training effects on motivation and school action that are larger than those of previous training attempts.

Mandl & Henninger showed that multimedia training enables participants to reflect their behavior more accurately and to perform better subsequently, when they find themselves in difficult communication situations.

Frey et al. specified how to reduce the number of incorrect decisions by identifying the personal and situational factors that distort knowledge seeking after tentative decisions. Incorrect decisions are a costly factor and may have serious consequences on subsequent actions in politics and economics, as well as in private life.

Summary

All of the projects undertaken by the research group "Knowledge and Action" at the University of Munich dealt with goal-oriented, intentional actions.

In order to "act" in the sense of the above definition, an individual has to

- *know* how the action can be carried out (in all its different stages, e.g., beginning, middle, and end)
- *manage* the whole process of intentionally acting, i.e., the individual has to coordinate decision processes, planning his or her actions, acting, and evaluating the process (i.e., what the individual has achieved).

Through our analyses, we are able to better explain how learning takes place, i.e., how new behavior can be learned (step one), converted into action (step two), and maintained on a regular basis (step three).

These theoretical insights can be important in different fields, for example:

- transfer of knowledge after training programs
- improving teaching within schools
- enabling employees to continuously learn
- establishing means and institutions in our societies that help educate people so that they will be able to better handle the global changes in many different areas and on many different levels in the future.

The Role of Implemental Versus Deliberative Mindsets in Goal-Setting and Goal-Directed Persistence

Veronika Brandstätter & Elisabeth Frank

The interface between cognition and action is a classic topic in motivation and social psychology (Gollwitzer & Bargh, 1996; Higgins & Sorrentino, 1990; Kuhl, 2001). Research deals with how cognitive concepts such as attitudes, expectancies, values, intentions, goals and the like guide behavior (e.g., Ajzen, 1985; Bandura, 1986; Carver & Scheier, 1990; Dweck, 1999; Fishbein & Ajzen, 1975; Gollwitzer, 1999). In the present chapter we focus on a different aspect of the cognition-action interface and elaborate on a model of goal striving (action phase model, Gollwitzer, 1990; Gollwitzer & Bayer, 1999; Heckhausen & Gollwitzer, 1987) which offers a specific view on the interplay between cognition and action. More specifically, we analyze the way cognitive orientations (mindsets) associated with specific action phases affect goal-directed behavior. First, we present the core assumptions of the action phase model that guided our research. Second, we report on a series of experimental studies that lend support to our reasoning that action phase-dependent mindsets affect the setting of time goals as well as goal directed persistence. Finally, we discuss the implications of our findings for issues of action regulation.

The action phase model

The action phase model (Gollwitzer, 1990; Heckhausen & Gollwitzer, 1987) postulates that the predecisional phase (deliberation) and postdecisional phase (implementation) of goal pursuit are accompanied by distinct cognitive orientations (mindsets) that are thought to be functional for the specific task to be solved – deliberating on potential action goals versus implementing a chosen goal. In the predecisional phase, the appraisal of expected pros and cons of competing action goals and the consideration of the feasibility of these goals predominate. Accordingly, the corresponding cognitive orientation (*deliberative mindset*) is expected to be associated with an open-minded, relatively even-handed and accurate appraisal of evidence. In the postdecisional phase, the person is geared toward implementing the chosen goal. The *implemental mindset* should facilitate effective processing of implementational issues (i.e., when, where and how to act on one's goal). In addition, a comparatively closed-minded focus on those aspects speaking in favor of the chosen goal is thought to assist goal achievement since negative thoughts concerning its desirability and feasibility and a high distractibility would undermine the level of determination needed to adhere to one's goal.

A number of studies have confirmed the distinct cognitive characteristics of the two postulated mindsets. With regard to the *implemental mindset*, an overestimation of the desirability of the chosen goal has been demonstrated (Beckmann & Gollwitzer, 1987; Taylor & Gollwitzer, 1995, Study 3), as well as an illusory, positive perception of the goal's feasibility (Gollwitzer & Kinney, 1989; Taylor & Gollwitzer, 1995, Studies 1 and 2) and unduly optimistic predictions about the future (Gagné & Lydon, 2001). Moreover, cognitive tuning has been observed toward information that relates to the implementation of the chosen goal (Gollwitzer, Heckhausen, & Steller, 1990; Heckhausen & Gollwitzer, 1987, Study 1; Schmalt, 1990) as well as a reduced receptiveness toward incoming information (Gollwitzer & Heckhausen, 1987, Study 1; Heckhausen & Gollwitzer, 1987, Study 2).

By contrast, people who are in the *deliberative mindset* are found to display an impartial and objective analysis of information about the feasibility and desirability of competing action goals (Beckmann & Gollwitzer, 1987; Gollwitzer & Heckhausen, 1987, Study 2; Gollwitzer & Kinney, 1989; Taylor & Gollwitzer, 1995, Study 3) which is, furthermore, processed effectively (Gollwitzer et al., 1990; Heckhausen & Gollwitzer, 1987, Study 1; Schmalt, 1990). Finally, the deliberative mindset is characterized by open-mindedness toward all kinds of available information (Gollwitzer & Heckhausen, 1987).

To date, researchers have concentrated on differences between mindsets with regard to the cognitive characteristics reported above (for a summary, see Gollwitzer & Bayer, 1999). Although theory and data suggest a major role of mindsets in behavior regulation, this issue has been largely neglected so far. Consequently, the major aim of our research was to fill this void by investigating the effect of mindsets on variables related to behavior. More specifically, we sought to determine the two mindsets' role in *goal-setting* and *goal-directed persistence*.

Goal-setting and persistence are two of the most important phenomena of goal striving a motivational analysis focuses on (Heckhausen, 1991; Heckhausen & Heckhausen, 2005). On the one hand, by setting goals, the individual orients his or her behavior towards specific end-states and precludes other action alternatives. On the other hand, the difficulty of the goal determines the individual's performance, challenging goals leading to better performance than undemanding goals (Bandura, 1986; Locke & Latham, 1990). Moreover, many endeavors people pursue are not "one-shot" affairs that can be accomplished with a single set of actions (e.g., writing a postcard, buying a textbook) but longer lasting projects that require repeated and sustained effort (e.g., writing a book, studying a foreign language). Persistence is required not only when a goal pursuit is taken up again after it has rested for a while due to another project temporarily gaining priority or suitable opportunities for action having had to be awaited. It is also called for in the case of challenging goals, where one might encounter unforeseen difficulties and experience repeated failure (Heckhausen, 1991). Thus, setting demanding goals and persistently acting on them are important prerequisites for successful goal striving.

Following the theory advanced by the action phase model, one might speculate that the positively biased outlook on a goal's feasibility and desirability characteristic of the implemental mindset will motivate an individual to set challenging goals as well as to act persistently towards them. We tested this theoretical notion in a series of five experiments. However, before turning to these empirical studies, some remarks regarding the induction of mindsets as well-moderating conditions for mindset effects should be made.

The induction of mindsets and moderating conditions for mindset effects

Mindsets are usually induced through either one or the other of two different experimental procedures. In the first procedure, participants are asked to deliberate on an unresolved personal decision problem (e.g., "Should I spend a semester abroad?") or to plan the implementation of a chosen personal goal project (e.g., "I intend to spend the next semester abroad!"). In doing so, deliberative mindset participants fill out a pre-structured questionnaire asking for pros and cons of the goal in question as well as for potential difficulties arising in the course of the action. Implemental mindset participants also work on a questionnaire but are asked to list action steps necessary for the implementation of the respective goal, and to commit themselves to when and where they intend to execute the respective actions (e.g., Gollwitzer et al., 1990). In the second procedure used to induce mindsets, participants listen to a tape-recorded individual, who either thinks aloud about an unresolved personal decision problem, weighing pros and cons of the goal, or about concrete action steps planned to realize the chosen goal project (Frank, Brandstätter, Veit, & Blau, 2004).

The effects of the experimentally induced mindsets are measured by using a task that is completely independent from the mindset induction procedure (e.g., having participants judge the probability of certain risks, setting time goals), allowing the observed effects to be attributed to the induced mindsets and excluding potential alternative explanations (e.g., the effect of specific task sets; see Gollwitzer, 1990; Gollwitzer & Bayer, 1999).

The induction of deliberative and implemental mindsets consists of a kind of procedural priming (Smith, Branscombe, & Borman, 1988; see also Gollwitzer, 1990) which activates specific cognitive procedures involved in deliberating decisions or implementing a chosen goal, respectively. These specific cognitive orientations display a certain stability over time, tune the processing of goal-relevant information accordingly, and are carried over to different contexts (cf. Galinsky, Moskowitz, & Skurnik, 2000).

Gollwitzer and Bayer (1999) compared the activation of mindsets with the activation of knowledge structures (semantic priming) and reasoned that the transfer of mindset effects, like semantic priming effects, should only be observable under certain conditions. A large volume of literature in social psychology shows that an activated knowledge structure exerts an influence on the interpretation of a subsequent event only to the extent that the judgment task is ambiguous (e.g., Galinsky et al., 2000), that is, when competing interpretations exist for the given evidence. In such a situation, the primed semantic concept governs the judgment by favoring an interpretation of the evidence in line with the activated concept.

Accordingly, one might speculate that mindsets unfold their effect on behavior especially in ambiguous situations where no clear cues are available as to which kind of behavior is appropriate (i.e., behavioral conflict situations; for example, when it is at issue whether setting a specific goal is worthwhile or not, or whether one should continue or stop goal-striving). In such a case, the respective activated mindset should focus the person on mindset-specific aspects (e.g., for the implemental mindset, a positive appraisal of the goal) and structure behavior accordingly. In unambiguous situations not implying a behavioral conflict, situational characteristics should predominate in the regulation of behavior, overriding any mindset effect.

Goal setting and goal-directed persistence in implemental and deliberative mindsets

In the present research we set out to test the hypothesis that the implemental mindset in comparison to the deliberative mindset leads to the setting of more challenging goals and to higher task persistence only in ambiguous situations. In order to test this hypothesis, it is necessary to induce an implemental mindset or a deliberative mindset in participants and observe their behavior (goal-setting and persistence, respectively) in subjectively conflictual vs. nonconflictual situations. Behavioral conflict situations are viewed as situations in which combinations of a goal's characteristics (e.g., high feasibility and low desirability) instigate opposing forces (e.g., to act or not to act in pursuit of the goal).

In five experiments, an implemental mindset condition was contrasted with a deliberative mindset condition with regard to setting time goals (Studies 1, 2, and 3), persistence in solving an intricate geometrical puzzle (Study 4) or accomplishing a figure-estimating task presented on a computer (Study 5). For Studies 1, 2, and 3, we formulated the hypothesis that implemental mindset should be accompanied by shorter prediction times for completion of a task and with the setting of tighter time goals compared with the deliberative mindset when a behavioral conflict situation was given. For Studies 4 and 5, we expected the implemental as opposed to the deliberative mindset to lead to higher persistence when a behavioral conflict was present.

Predicting task accomplishment times and setting time goals

Many aspects of our life depend on predicting how long it will take us to achieve some long-term goal, such as obtaining a university degree or preparing for a sports contest, but also short-term activities like assembling a newly bought piece of furniture or preparing an opulent dinner. Prediction of task completion times also play a major role in business life – for example, forecasting how long it will take to finish a certain project or task and to calculate the respective financial resources accordingly (e.g., Buehler, Griffin, & Ross, 1994). Prediction of task completion times are inherently connected to the setting of time goals, that is, a person's commitment to finishing a project by a certain time.

Drawing on the different characteristics of the implemental vs. deliberative mindsets, one would assume that the implemental mindset with its closed-mindedness and its optimistic outlook may particularly blind people to risks and impediments involved in task completion, leading to optimistic predictions. In contrast, the deliberative mindset's careful and accurate appraisal should prevent people from making overly optimistic predictions. Therefore, we formulated the hypothesis that in ambiguous situations the implemental mindset should lead to *shorter prediction times* for completion of a task compared to the deliberative mindset.

Study 1: Writing a report in time

Frank et al. (2004) invited 82 students to participate in two allegedly independent studies on (a) personal goal striving (mindset manipulation) and (b) time management that asked participants to write a report and hand it in within a certain time period. Participants were randomly assigned to one of four experimental conditions (conflictual/deliberative, conflictual/implemental, nonconflictual/deliberative, nonconflictual/implemental). Deliberative versus implemental mindsets were induced by having participants listen to a tape that presented a male speaker either deliberating on a personal decision problem or planning the realization of a personal project. Behavioral conflict in this study was varied by information given to the participants that either unambiguously spoke in favor of fast enactment of the writing task (i.e., positive incentives for fast enactment and high probability of fast enactment) or neither favored fast nor slow accomplishment. All participants were told that they would receive a book token in return for sending back the report within two weeks. In the *low behavioral conflict situation*, participants were informed that the earlier they sent back their report, the higher the value of the book token would be (€ 10 on the first day, € 0.50 on the last day of the 14-day period); in addition, participants were informed that in a previous study, the percentage of report returns was highest within the first three days. In the *high behavioral conflict situation*, the value of the book token was kept constant at € 2.50 for returning the report within the two-week period, no matter on which day participants sent back the report.

In order to assess time goal setting, participants had to indicate "as accurately as possible" on a calendar sheet the day on which they would e-mail back the report. In order to make completing the report a not too easy task, participants received a list with a variety of questions which took at least 45 minutes to complete. Report return dates were recorded within the weeks following the experiment.

In order to test our hypothesis concerning time goal setting, predicted day of report submission was submitted to a 2 × 2 (Mindset × Behavioral Conflict) ANOVA. As can be seen in Figure 1, predicted task completion times did not differ between mindsets for the low behavioral conflict situation. There, deliberative as well as implemental mindset participants indicated that they would send their report back rather quickly. However, in the high behavioral conflict situation, the predicted time to report submission was higher for both mindsets, but implemental mindset participants were affected to a lesser extent by the increase in situational ambiguity regarding the promotion of fast enactment. Actually, the ANOVA yielded the expected significant effect for the interaction between mindsets and situation, $F(1, 75) = 4.3, p < .05$. The main effect for mindsets was not significant. In summary, these results support our hypothesis that the implemental mindset leads to a more optimistic prediction compared with the deliberative mindset when the situation involves a behavioral conflict.

Figure 1. Predicted task completion (in days) in Study 1.

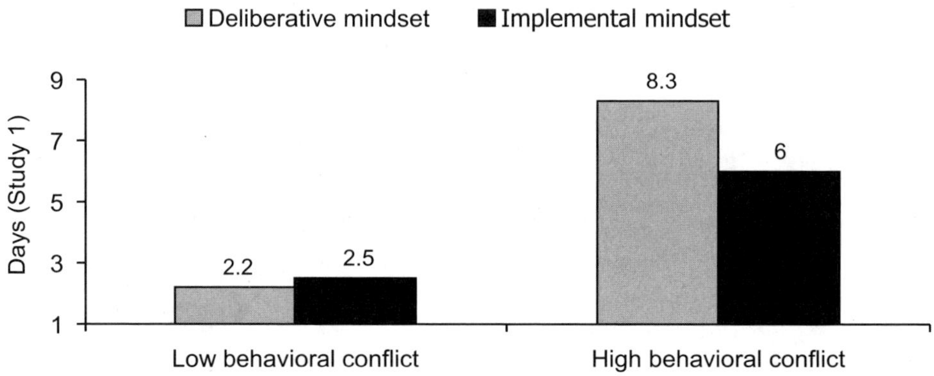

Forty-five participants (55% of our original sample) returned the report during the two-week period. The percentage of returns was only affected by the manipulation of the situation: Whereas in the low behavioral conflict situation 68% returned the report, only 39% did so in the high behavioral conflict situation; χ^2 (1, N = 81) = 6.36, $p < .02$. Although the percentage of returns was higher in the implemental mindset condition (62%) than in the deliberative mindset condition (48%), this difference was not significant; χ^2 (1, N = 81) = 1.58, $p > .21$.

For participants returning the report, *actual completion time* within the fixed two-week period paralleled the results for predicted completion times. An ANOVA with mindsets and behavioral conflict as independent variables revealed the expected Mindset × Behavioral Conflict interaction effect, $F(1, 41) = 8.3, p < .01$. Thus, in the high behavioral conflict situation, implemental mindset participants not only set shorter time goals but also returned the report more quickly (i.e., after a mean of 3.9 days) than deliberative mindset participants who handed in their report after a mean of 7.3 days. These results could be interpreted from a goal-setting perspective (Locke & Latham, 1990), with shorter prediction times reflecting more difficult goals which in turn have been shown to be associated with better performance.

In line with our hypotheses, implemental mindset participants gave shorter time predictions for task completion than deliberative mindset participants when the situation involved a high behavioral conflict with regard to the concomitant circumstances of task accomplishment. In addition, implemental mindset participants needed less time later on to actually complete the task. Obviously, participants in the high behavioral conflict situation, not knowing exactly when to act, heavily profited from an implemental mindset as

Gollwitzer and Bayer (1999) stated: "Situations in which swift initiation is hindered should benefit greatly from an implemental mindset" (p. 417).

In the second and third study, we sought to replicate the above findings with different types of time prediction tasks (i.e., in Study 2, estimating the time needed to prepare for an exam; in Study 3, estimating the time needed to finish several personal projects) and with different operationalizations of behavioral conflict (i.e., ambiguous versus unambiguous constellations of the value and expectancy of the respective goal).

Study 2: Studying for an exam

One hundred and seven students participated in the study. After reading a text either about a male student who deliberated on a personal decision problem (induction of the deliberative mindset) or about a male student who planned the action steps necessary to realize a personal project (induction of the implemental mindset), participants were asked to set a time goal in respect of how long they intended to study for an upcoming exam. Additionally, participants indicated how important it was for them, and how confident they were about passing the exam, how much test anxiety they experienced, and how regularly they attended the lectures. The constellations of low importance and high confidence or high importance and low confidence were interpreted as situations of high behavioral conflict. The constellations of low importance and low confidence or high importance and high confidence were interpreted as situations of low behavioral conflict.

The number of days participants intended to study for the upcoming exam was submitted to a 2 × 2 (Mindset × Behavioral Conflict) ANCOVA controlling for test anxiety and the degree of regularity with which students attended lectures. The two-way interaction turned out to be significant; $F\ (1,\ 106) = 3.83$, $p < .05$. As predicted, in the high behavioral conflict situation, implemental mindset participants intended to study fewer days ($M = 16.5$) than deliberative mindset participants ($M = 21.2$). In the low behavioral conflict condition, an unexpected result was obtained: Implemental mindset participants planned more days ($M = 24.0$) to prepare for the exam than deliberative mindset participants ($M = 18.5$).

Study 3: Completing personal assignments

In a third study on the effect of mindsets on setting time goals, we asked 99 participants to list personal assignments that they intended to complete in the near future and to indicate how long it would take them to finish these assignments. Additionally, participants rated how important the respective assignment was to them and how confident they were of completing it within the planned time period. Participants named assignments such as finishing a paper, preparing for an exam, and the like. Again, predicted time for completion of assignments was submitted to a 2 × 2 (Mindset × Behavioral Conflict) ANOVA. As predicted, the interaction was significant, $F(1,\ 94) = 4.3$, $p < .05$. Closer inspection of the data revealed that in the high behavioral conflict situation, implemental mindset participants on average estimated less time (in hours) needed to complete their tasks ($M = 5.2$) than deliberative participants ($M = 17.1$). In the low behavioral conflict situation, implemental and deliberative mindset participants' time predictions did not differ significantly ($M_i = 7.6$ vs. $M_d = 6.1$).

Persistence in pursuing a goal

Besides predicting task accomplishment times and setting time goals, another important aspect of successful goal striving is persistence in pursuing one's goals. Persistence is required not only when a goal pursuit is taken up again after it has rested for a while due to another project temporarily gaining priority or suitable opportunities for action having had to be awaited. It is also called for in the case of challenging goals where one might encounter unforeseen difficulties and experience repeated failure (Heckhausen, 1991). As Gollwitzer and Moskowitz (1996) point out, "all of the ... features of the implemental mindset should facilitate goal achievement as they allow the individual to effectively cope with classic problems of goal implementation" (p. 369) such as persistence in the face of difficulties. Accordingly, we (Brandstätter & Frank, 2002) hypothesized that an implemental as opposed to a deliberative mindset would increase persistence when a behavioral conflict situation is given. In order to test this hypothesis, we conducted two studies where we induced a deliberative or an implemental mindset in participants and observed their behavior in subjectively conflictual vs. nonconflictual situations while working on an intricate task.

Study 4: Solving an intricate puzzle

One hundred and thirty-nine participants (mean age 23 years) were invited to participate in two allegedly independent studies (i.e., a game study and a training program to enhance action efficiency). The so-called game study required participants to assemble seven pieces of wood to produce a given pattern (which was in fact not solvable), and was used to obtain the persistence measure. In the so-called training program the two mindsets were induced.

After participants had familiarized themselves with the puzzle, they rated the feasibility and desirability of solving the puzzle and were assigned to one of three experimental conditions, that is, an implemental mindset condition, a deliberative mindset condition, and a control condition with no mindset induced.

Participants in the *deliberative* mindset condition had to work on one of their own unresolved personal decision problems in the form of "Should I do X or not?" and deliberate on the pros and cons of the goal in question. By contrast, *implemental* mindset participants had to name an intended project and plan the action steps necessary for implementing it by specifying when, where, and how the action steps had to be performed.

When participants had finished the mindset induction phase of the experiment, they were asked to continue with the game until they had either solved the puzzle or were not enjoying it any longer. It was emphasized that it was entirely up to them when to stop. When participants resumed the game, the experimenter started a stopwatch to measure the time for which participants persisted to work on the puzzle. The end of the game was either determined by the participants themselves or by the experimenter if a participant's persistence exceeded a predefined maximum of 38 minutes.

Figure 2. Mean time (in minutes) devoted to solving the puzzle in Study 4.

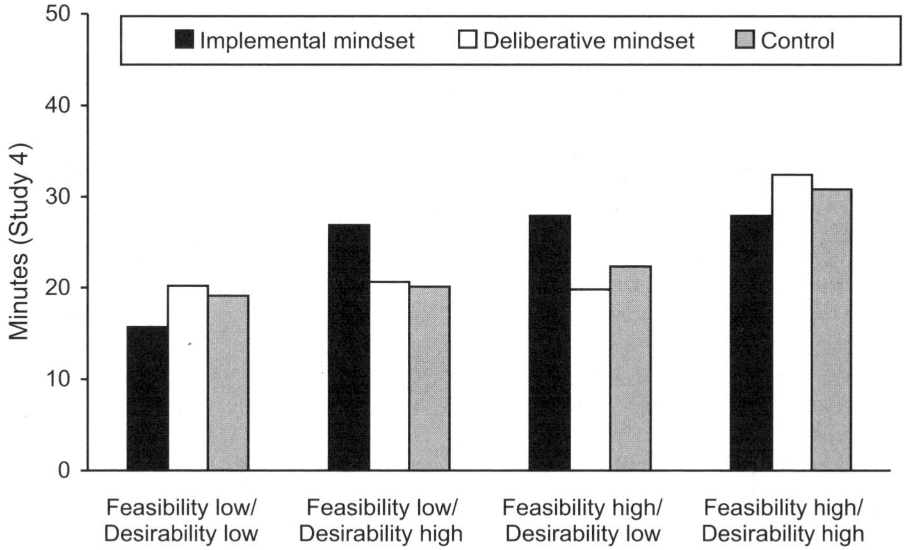

In order to create a variable of subjective behavioral conflict, desirability judgments were regressed on feasibility judgments, thus creating desirability scores independent of feasibility. The desirability scores (in terms of residuals) as well as participants' feasibility judgments were submitted to a median split leading to low/high desirability and low/high feasibility conditions, respectively.

The number of minutes spent on trying to solve the puzzle was submitted to a 2 × 2 × 2 (Mindset × Feasibility × Desirability) ANOVA. The analysis yielded significant main effects for feasibility and residualized desirability. High feasibility judgments led to higher persistence than low feasibility judgments. Similarly, participants who had indicated high desirability persisted longer than those who had indicated a low desirability. Neither the main effect for mindsets nor any two-way interactions reached statistical significance. More importantly, the predicted three-way interaction emerged, $F(1,61) = 5.50$, $p < .05$ (see Figure 2).

As expected, the mean time spent on trying to solve the puzzle did not differ between low feasibility/high desirability and high feasibility/low desirability within either the implemental or the deliberative mindset. Implemental mindset participants persisted significantly longer under behavioral conflict conditions than deliberative mindset participants. Furthermore, although it appears that implemental mindset participants displayed lower persistence than deliberative mindset participants in both the low/low and high/high conditions, neither of these planned contrasts were significant.

The results of this study confirm our hypothesis. In behavioral conflict situations, implemental mindset participants were more persistent in trying to solve a puzzle than deliberative mindset participants. In situations without behavioral conflict, no significant mindset effects could be observed. Furthermore, the means of the control group (see Figure 2) suggest that the effects of the mindset manipulation are due to greater persistence on the part of implemental mindset participants and not due to diminished persistence on the part of deliberative mindset participants.

Study 5: Estimating figure sizes

This study represents a conceptual replication of Study 4, however, it extends it in several important aspects. First, we sought to create an experimental task which had more of the characteristics of persistence towards an everyday goal, in which the pursuit of a goal makes successful goal achievement possible but is at the same time associated with costs. Following this line of reasoning, we used a game in which participants could allegedly reach a valuable goal but in which they had to pay for approaching it.

Second, the way we measured persistence in Study 4 was somewhat ambiguous as it encompassed two distinct aspects of the participants' occupation with their task: Activity aimed at solving the task, *and* dwelling on thoughts irrelevant to the task. In accordance with the action phase model, however, we were interested in persistence as an indicator of strong goal orientation (Gollwitzer, 1990). Another indicator of goal orientation is high action readiness (Brandstätter, Lengfelder, & Gollwitzer, 2001). Thus, in Study 5, we assessed persistence by recording the number of attempts to reach the goal in question and additionally measured the time participants needed to decide whether to continue or stop striving for the goal.

Third, we also collected information about possible mediating mechanisms. There is substantial evidence that mindsets affect the judgment of goal-related feasibility and desirability (e.g., Beckmann & Gollwitzer, 1987; Gollwitzer & Kinney, 1989), which in turn determines the level of persistence (e.g., Feather, 1962). Therefore, following the mindset manipulation we measured feasibility and desirability and analyzed its mediating role for persistence.

We hypothesized that in goal conditions involving a behavioral conflict, implemental mindset participants should not only show a higher degree of goal-directed persistence compared to deliberative mindset participants, but also a higher degree of action readiness. Moreover, feasibility and desirability estimates assessed after the mindset manipulation were expected to mediate the differential effect of mindsets on persistence. No differences between mindsets were expected with regard to goal conditions not involving a behavioral conflict.

The 99 participants in the study received • 7.50 (approximately US $7.50 at the time) for their participation. As in the other studies, they were told that they were to participate in two allegedly independent studies, that is, a study on action efficiency (mindset manipulation) and a computer game in which they could ostensibly win a jackpot of € 10 (approximately US $10). The participants' task was to estimate how much of the computer screen was covered by a geometrical figure (e.g., rhomb, triangle, ellipse, circle). For each correct answer, they would be awarded one point, which would be recorded by the computer. To win the jackpot, they had to amass a certain number of points (somewhere between 1 and 20) randomly selected by the computer which, however, actually never occurred. For each attempt, participants had to pay € 0.10. Participants were not to be given any feedback about the correctness of their estimates during the game. They were free to leave the game at any time even if they had not yet won the jackpot.

Having performed several practice trials, participants in the *high feasibility* condition were given positive feedback on their performance, whereas in the *low feasibility* condition participants were told that their performance was far below average. The subjective desirability of the game was assessed with questions. Once during the game, participants were asked to report on the game's feasibility and desirability.

After each trial, participants had to enter their estimate regarding the surface of the geometrical figure and indicate whether they wanted to continue the game or not by entering either "y" (yes, continue) or "n" (no, stop). The number of trials attempted and the time needed to decide whether to continue or stop were recorded by the computer.

A three-way ANOVA, including mindsets, feasibility, and desirability, yielded the expected, significant main effects for feasibility and desirability. Participants in the high feasibility condition attempted more trials than participants in the low feasibility condition. Similarly, participants who had indicated a high desirability at the beginning played for longer than those who had indicated low desirability. Neither the main effect for mindsets nor any two-way interactions reached conventional statistical significance. More importantly, the predicted three-way interaction effect emerged, $F(1, 88) = 4.2, p < .05$.

The three-way interaction is attributable to a distinct pattern of results in the two mindset conditions (see Figure 3). Neither within the implemental nor within the deliberative mindset did the mean number of trials differ between low feasibility/high desirability and high feasibility/low desirability. Furthermore, comparing the two mindsets with regard to these behavioral conflict goal conditions supports our hypotheses, since implemental mindset participants persisted significantly longer than deliberative mindset participants, $t(11.85) = 2.22, p < .05$. Additionally, as with Study 1, none of the comparisons for the combinations not involving a behavioral conflict approached statistical significance. Both implemental and deliberative mindset participants attempted comparably few trials when pursuing a goal with low feasibility and low desirability, but many trials when pursuing a goal with high feasibility and high desirability. The results regarding the degree of persistence fully replicate those of Study 4.

Figure 3. Mean number of trials attempted in Study 5.

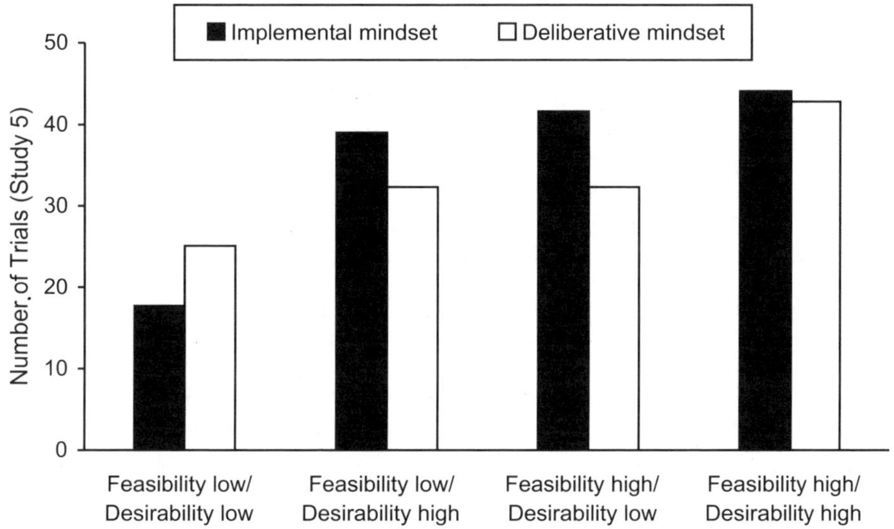

In order to test the mediating role of the Time 2 feasibility and desirability ratings on persistence, we computed a respective index by multiplying Time 2 Feasibility × Time 2 Desirability. The correlation between this Feasibility × Desirability index and the number of trials attempted was highly significant, $r(86) = .55$, $p < .001$. The Feasibility × Desirability index was used as a covariate in a Mindset × Feasibility at Time 1 × Desirability at Time 1 analysis of covariance (ANCOVA) on the number of trials attempted. When the index was introduced, the Mindset × Feasibility × Desirability interaction was no longer significant ($F < 1$). With this analysis, Study 5 also expands upon Study 4 in showing a mediating mechanism of the persistence-promoting effect of the implemental mindset.

Another indicator of goal orientation is high action readiness, which we predicted to be higher in implemental mindset participants than in deliberative mindset participants when a behavioral conflict was present. To test this hypothesis, we performed a three-way ANOVA including mindset, feasibility, and desirability on the logarithm of decision times. As predicted, the three-way interaction effect emerged, $F(1, 88) = 5.32$, $p < .05$. Decision times to a large extent mirrored the pattern of results regarding the number of trials attempted (see Table 1), which is also expressed by a highly significant negative correlation between these two variables, $r = -.62$, $p < .001$. As the planned comparison reveals, there was a general trend for implemental mindset participants to react faster than deliberative mindset participants under these behavioral conflict goal conditions, $t(88) = 1.55$, $p < .13$.

To sum up, the pattern of results for the mean decision times whether to continue the game or not was comparable to the pattern for the number of trials attempted. As predicted, the decision times of implemental mindset participants tended to be shorter than those of deliberative mindset participants only in the behavioral conflict goal conditions, that is, they hesitated less, which speaks for their high readiness for action. Thus, the heightened persistence of implemental mindset participants observed in *both* Study 4 and Study 5 is a case of vigorous persistence and not just dawdling.

Readers may remember that in the unfavorable goal condition (i.e., low feasibility/low desirability), implemental mindset participants persisted less than deliberative mindset participants, a nonsignificant trend which had already been observed for the unfavorable

Table 1. Means and standard deviations of decision times (log) whether to continue or stop (Study 5)

	Implemental mindset		Deliberative mindset	
	Feasibility		Feasibility	
Desirability	Low	High	Low	High
Low				
M	3.62	3.32	3.49	3.41
SD	.22	.21	.14	.33
High				
M	3.39	3.38	3.51	3.31
SD	.18	.22	.26	.10

goal condition in Study 4. Moreover, implemental mindset participants slowed down their decision times as compared to deliberative mindset participants when both goal characteristics were perceived as being unfavorable. Taken together, one might speculate whether under certain circumstances the implemental mindset prevents an individual from being unproductively persistent and prepares the individual for disengaging from the goal sooner than the deliberative mindset. This idea is supported by research by Aspinwall and Richter (1999) who showed that people with a high level of optimism disengage more easily from tasks where persistence obviously does not pay off, compared with people who have low optimism.

General discussion

Our work focuses on the interface between cognition and action, analyzing how the cognitive orientation associated with the post-decisional action phase (i.e., the implemental mindset) affects goal-directed behavior. The studies presented here significantly extend the theoretical and empirical implications of the action phase model (Gollwitzer, 1990; Heckhausen & Gollwitzer, 1987) regarding the regulation of goal-directed behavior. More specifically, we have been able to show that under certain conditions the implemental mindset affects setting time goals and persisting at a task – two important facets of successful goal striving (Buehler et al., 1994; Heckhausen, 1991). Finally, our work points to moderating conditions of the mindset effects that have not been investigated before.

In Studies 1, 2, and 3, implemental mindset participants predicted that they would need less time to accomplish a certain task than deliberative mindset participants if the situation allowed for the implemental mindset to unfold its effects (i.e., a situation where a behavioral conflict existed). One important strength of these studies is their ideographic-nomothetic approach (Emmons, 1989). That is, respondents were not just given a standardized experimental task to predict completion but every participant set time goals for his/her own project or problem. Thus, despite the heterogeneity of participants' projects we were able to observe the implemental mindset's effect on time predictions.

In Studies 4 and 5, the implemental mindset promoted persistence in an experimental task in comparison to the deliberative mindset only when the characteristics of that task implied a behavioral conflict between persistence and disengagement. Most notably, the pattern of the behavioral data in the fourth and fifth experiment were almost identical despite the fact that we used two completely different experimental tasks, both associated with specific measures of persistence. Mediational analyses in Study 5 lend some support to the postulated mediating role of feasibility and desirability judgments in the mindset effects on observed persistence.

We did *not* induce simple task sets by getting people to either weigh the pros and cons or to plan the execution of a task for which later on predictions and actual performance would be assessed. Such mental simulations have been shown to facilitate actual performance (e.g., Taylor, Pham, Rivkin, & Armor, 1998). More specifically, Taylor et al. (1998) found that a so-called process simulation of accomplishing a task leads to a higher percentage of respondents completing their task in a timely manner. Instead, we used two different mindset induction procedures, both working independently from the prediction/performance task, in order to demonstrate effects of inducing real mindsets (see also Gollwitzer, 1990). It is remarkable that such subtle induction procedures as the ones we used still resulted in mindset effects on prediction and even on performance of a totally unrelated second task.

Even more importantly, we were able to identify moderating conditions for the postulated mindset effects to occur, supplementing evidence that the implemental mindset does not unfold its effect universally (e.g., Gollwitzer & Kinney, 1989). Mindset effects were most pronounced when a behavioral conflict situation was given, that is, when the situation was ambiguous regarding whether to act or to refrain from acting. In that, our results parallel evidence from social cognition research (e.g., Galinsky et al., 2000; Higgins, 1996) that shows that primed semantic contents exert an influence on the interpretation of a subsequent event only to the extent that the judgment task is ambiguous (e.g., Galinsky et al., 2000), that is, when competing interpretations exist for the given evidence. In such a situation, the primed semantic concept governs social perception by promoting an interpretation of the evidence in line with the activated concept. Analogously, the implemental mindset governed behavior especially in situations which lacked clear clues as to whether to act immediately or later, to invest heavily or only a little in a project, to continue or stop an endeavor.

In our experiments, we were able to replicate the typical effects of motivational variables on goal-directed behavior put forward by expectancy valence theory (e.g., desirability, feasibility; Feather, 1962) and intrinsic motivation research (e.g., intrinsically motivating features of task, perceived competence; Deci & Ryan, 2000). More importantly, however, as our results demonstrate, mindsets contribute to the explanation of goal setting and persistence over and above these motivational variables. With this, our work points to the interplay of classic motivational concepts (i.e., feasibility and desirability) and self-regulative, so-called volitional, mechanisms of goal striving (i.e., the implemental mindset) that have up to now been treated independently of each other (Gollwitzer, 1999; Kuhl & Beckmann, 1994).

References

Ajzen, I. (1985). From intentions to actions: A theory of planned behaviour. In J. Kuhl & J. Beckmann (Ed.), *Action control: From cognition to behaviour* (pp. 11–39). Heidelberg: Springer-Verlag.

Aspinwall, L. G., & Richter, L. (1999). Optimism and self-mastery predict more rapid disengagement from unsolvable tasks in the presence of alternatives. *Motivation and Emotion, 23,* 221–245.

Bandura, A. (1986). *Social foundations of thought and action.* Englewood Cliffs, NJ: Prentice-Hall.

Beckmann, J., & Gollwitzer, P. M. (1987). Deliberative vs. implemental states of mind: The issue of impartiality in pre- and postdecisional information processing. *Social Cognition, 5,* 259–279.

Brandstätter, V., & Frank, E. (2002). Effects of deliberative and implemental mindsets on persistence in goal-directed behavior. *Personality and Social Psychology Bulletin, 28,* 1366–1378.

Brandstätter, V., Lengfelder, A., & Gollwitzer, P. M. (2001). Implementation intentions and efficient action initiation. *Journal of Personality and Social Psychology, 81,* 946–960.

Buehler, R., Griffin, D., & Ross, M. (1994). Exploring the "planning fallacy": Why people underestimate their task completion times. *Journal of Personality and Social Psychology, 67,* 366–382.
Carver, C. S., & Scheier, M. F. (1990). *On the self-regulation of behavior*. New York: Cambridge University Press.
Deci, E. L., & Ryan, R. M. (2000). The "what" and "why" of goal pursuits: Human needs and the self-determination of behavior. *Psychological Inquiry, 11,* 227–268.
Dweck, C. S. (1999). *Implicit personality theories*. New York: Psychology Press.
Emmons, R. A. (1989). The personal striving approach to personality. In L. A. Pervin (Ed.), *Goal concepts in personality and social psychology* (pp. 87–126). Hillsdale, NJ: Erlbaum.
Feather, N. T. (1962). The study of persistence. *Psychological Bulletin, 59,* 94–115.
Fishbein, M., & Ajzen, I. (1975). *Belief, attitude, intention, and behavior: An introduction to theory and research*. Reading, MA: Addison-Wesley.
Frank, E., Brandstätter, V., Veit, S., & Blau, M. (2004). *The role of deliberative vs. implemental mind-sets in prediction and performance.* Unpublished manuscript. University of Munich.
Gagné, F. M., & Lydon, J. E. (2001). Mind-set and close relationships: When bias leads to (in)accurate predictions. *Journal of Personality and Social Psychology, 81,* 85–96.
Galinsky, A. D., Moskowitz, G. B., & Skurnik, I. (2000). Counterfactuals as self-generated primes: Priming the simulation heuristic and the consideration of alternatives. *Social Cognition, 18,* 252–280.
Gollwitzer, P. M. (1990). Action phases and mind-sets. In E. T. Higgins & R. M. Sorrentino (Eds.), *Handbook of motivation and cognition* (Vol. 2, pp. 53–92). New York: Guilford.
Gollwitzer, P. M. (1999). Implementation intentions: Strong effects of simple plans. *American Psychologist, 54,* 493–503.
Gollwitzer, P. M., & Bargh, J. A. (Eds.) (1996). *The psychology of action: Linking cognition and motivation to behavior*. New York: Guilford.
Gollwitzer, P. M., & Bayer, U. (1999). Deliberative vs. implemental mindsets in the control of action. In S. Chaiken & Y. Trope (Eds.), *Dual-process theories in social psychology* (pp. 403–422). New York: Guilford.
Gollwitzer, P. M., & Heckhausen, H. (1987). *Breadth of attention and the counterplea heuristic: Further evidence on the motivational and volitional mind-set distinction.* Unpublished manuscript, Max-Planck-Institute for Psychological Research, Munich.
Gollwitzer, P. M., Heckhausen, H., & Steller, B. (1990). Deliberative and implemental mind-sets: Cognitive tuning toward congruous thoughts and information. *Journal of Personality and Social Psychology, 59,* 1119–1127.
Gollwitzer, P. M., & Kinney, R. F. (1989). Effects of deliberative and implemental mind-sets on illusion of control. *Journal of Personality and Social Psychology, 56,* 531–542.
Gollwitzer, P. M., & Moskowitz, G. B. (1996). Goal effects on action and cognition. In E. T. Higgins & A. W. Kruglanski (Eds.), *Social psychology. Handbook of basic principles* (pp. 361–399). New York: Guilford.
Heckhausen, H. (1991). *Motivation and action*. New York: Springer-Verlag.
Heckhausen, H., & Gollwitzer, P. M. (1987). Thought contents and cognitive functioning in motivational versus volitional states of mind. *Motivation and Emotion, 11,* 101–120.
Heckhausen, J., & Heckhausen, H. (2005). *Motivation und Handeln* [Motivation and action] (3rd edition). Berlin: Springer-Verlag.

Higgins, E. T. (1996). Knowledge activation: Accessibility, applicability, and salience. In E. T. Higgins & A. W. Kruglanski (Eds.), *Social Psychology: Handbook of basic principles* (pp. 133–168). New York: Guilford.

Higgins, E. T., & Sorrentino, R. M. (Eds.) (1990), *Handbook of motivation and cognition: Foundations of social behavior*. New York: Guilford.

Kuhl, J. (2001). *Motivation und Persönlichkeit* [Motivation and personality]. Göttingen: Hogrefe.

Kuhl, J., & Beckmann, J. (Eds.) (1994). *Volition and personality: Action versus state orientation*. Göttingen: Hogrefe.

Locke, E. A., & Latham, G. P. (1990). Work motivation and satisfaction: Light at the end of the tunnel. *Psychological Science, 1,* 240–246.

Schmalt, H.-D. (1990). Zustands- und dispositionsabhängige Unterschiede in der Informationsverarbeitung [State and trait dependent differences in information processing]. *Zeitschrift für Experimentelle und Angewandte Psychologie, 37,* 486–504.

Smith, E. R., Branscombe, N. R., & Bormann, C. (1988). Generality of the effects of practice on social judgment tasks. *Journal of Personality and Social Psychology, 54,* 385–395.

Taylor, S. E., & Gollwitzer, P. M. (1995). Effects of mindsets on positive illusions. *Journal of Personality and Social Psychology, 69,* 213–226.

Taylor, S. E., Pham, L. B., Rivkin, I. D., & Armor, D. A. (1998). Harnessing the imagination. Mental simulation, self-regulation, and coping. *American Psychologist, 53,* 429–439.

Biased Information Seeking After Decisions

Cognitive and Motivational Bases

Eva Jonas, Stefan Schulz-Hardt, Peter Fischer, & Dieter Frey

Research from different areas in social psychology shows that information search processes are often biased in favor of the information seeker's previously held beliefs, expectations, or desired conclusions. This has been shown, for example, in the field of social stereotypes (Johnston, 1996), attitudes (Lundgren & Prislin, 1998), expectations in negotiations (Pinkley, Griffith, & Northcraft, 1995), and self-serving conclusions (Frey, 1981b; Holton & Pyszczynski, 1989).

An information search that is clearly biased in favor of a preferred alternative leads to the preservation of the information seeker's position although this position may not be justified on the basis of all available information (Johnston, 1996; Pinkley et al., 1995). Furthermore, if people fail to correct a wrong decision because they have overlooked potential risks and warning signals there may be serious negative consequences (Janis, 1982; Nemeth & Rogers, 1996). To find an adequate decision alternative, an intensive and open-minded search, along with critical examination of the available information, is important. This seems especially true if new information crops up after making an initial decision, and so by correcting a wrong decision as early as possible one can avoid loss escalations (cf. Brockner & Rubin, 1985). Although biased information seeking also has functional aspects such as preventing people from remaining indecisive and providing the capacity to act (cf. Beckmann & Kuhl, 1984; Wicklund & Frey, 1981), in cases where a faulty decision has significant costs and where such consequences can be detected in advance, a strong bias in favor of the preferred or chosen alternative may increase the likelihood of bad outcomes (cf. Kray & Galinsky, 2003; Schulz-Hardt, 1997; von Haeften, 1999).

Because distortions in information search can be dangerous, the question arises of how people could be encouraged to undertake a balanced search for conflicting and supporting information. Furthermore, to what extent it is possible to identify conditions that enhance or counteract distortions in the search for information? In this chapter we give an overview of a large body of experiments regarding biased information seeking in decision-making. Additionally, we suggest a framework of motivational and cognitive bases for biased information seeking that helps to understand how and why different situational conditions lead to certain patterns in information search. After that we will discuss practical implications for decision-making and information seeking situations.

Dissonance theory research on selective exposure

An important theory addressing biased information seeking in decision-making is the theory of cognitive dissonance (Festinger, 1957, 1964), which proposes that, once committed to an alternative, people prefer information supporting this alternative (called *consonant* information) compared to information conflicting with the preferred decision alternative (called *dissonant* information). Dissonance theory posits that people experience aversive post-decisional conflicts because the commitment to one decision alternative implies relinquishing the positive aspects of the other alternatives and the acceptance of the negative aspects of the chosen alternative. Thus, in order to reduce post-decisional conflicts, people engage in a biased search for new information, preferring information that supports their decision and avoiding conflicting information. This phenomenon has also been called a "confirmation bias[1]."

In the experiments on information seeking after decisions, participants typically receive a questionnaire that starts with a description of a (sometimes hypothetical, sometimes real) decision problem – for example, whether the contract of a manager should be extended or whether alternative-healing methods should be covered by health insurance. Participants make a definite or tentative decision regarding this problem and then have the opportunity to search for additional information concerning the decision at hand. This additional information consists of 10, 12, or 16 experts' statements or articles, each summarized with a main thesis. Participants see the main theses and are asked to select those pieces of information they want to read in further detail. The main theses contain either decidedly positive or negative arguments for one of the (typically two) decision alternatives. Thus, after reading a particular main thesis, participants know whether the corresponding article will support or conflict with the (preliminary) decision. The dependent variable in these experiments is the confirmation bias, which is the difference value between the supporting pieces of information the participants mark minus the conflicting ones. (Supporting pieces are those in favor of the chosen or against the rejected alternative and vice versa for conflicting pieces of information.)

A large body of empirical studies (for overviews see Frey, 1986; Frey, Schulz-Hardt, & Stahlberg, 1996) has shown that there are many situations in which people reveal a preference for supporting information after having made a decision. Recent studies suggested that such a confirmation bias is not restricted to final decisions, but also arises after preliminary decisions (preference judgments) (Jonas, Schulz-Hardt, Frey, & Thelen,

1 In this context, the term "confirmation bias" has a slightly different meaning than in the context of hypothesis testing, where it is also often used (e.g., Snyder & White, 1981). In the latter, "confirmatory hypothesis testing" or "confirmation bias" respectively mean asking questions that are consistent with the hypothesis that is being tested. However, this way of asking questions does not imply that the person will confirm his or her hypothesis. In the research on decision making to which we are referring "confirmation bias" means requesting information that supports a pre-selected alternative – thus the decision maker using this strategy *knows* that he or she will get the confirmation sought.

2001; Schulz-Hardt, 1997). Moreover, biased information seeking can also be observed in group decision making (Schulz-Hardt, Frey, Lüthgens, & Moscovici, 2000; Schulz-Hardt, Jochims, & Frey, 2002).

Although all these results illustrate that biased information seeking is a widespread phenomenon in decision making, cognitive dissonance, which traces this behavior back to one single motive, namely the motivation to maintain consistency and to avoid threats to a position to which one feels committed (Frey, 1986), is not necessarily the only source to which biased information seeking can be traced back. Self-presentational concerns (Jonas, Schulz-Hardt, & Frey, 2005) or attempts to be particularly accurate (Schulz-Hardt, Fischer, & Frey, 2006) can also lead to distortions in information search. Among recent theoretical models that propose that more than just one motive may be involved when people deal with information (e.g., Kruglanski, 1989; Kunda, 1990), the multiple-motive heuristic systematic model (HSM, cf. Chaiken, Liberman, & Eagly, 1989; Chen & Chaiken, 1999) seems particularly useful to us.

Information search in the context of the multiple-motive heuristic systematic model (HSM)

Although originally conceptualized for explaining information processing in the area of attitude formation and change, the HSM can be applied to "a diverse range of judgmental domains" (Chen & Chaiken, 1999, p. 73). The HSM proposes that, on the one hand, the level or amount of people's motivation and ability will influence whether information is processed more systematically or more heuristically. On the other hand, the model differentiates between different types of motives that people may have and that may affect information processing in different ways. We suggest that the differentiation of the HSM into *defense*, *accuracy* and *impression* motivation can serve as an integrative framework for explaining and predicting biased information search.

Defense motivation refers to the desire to maintain the stability of the cognitive system. It can be seen as similar to the motivation to reduce cognitive dissonance because both concepts propose that people will strive to defend positions to which they feel committed with, for example, confirmatory biases in information processing and information search. Whereas in the case of defense motivation, the driving force leading to biases is an *intra*personal goal, *impression motivation* is concerned with *inter*personal goals. The information search and processing of impression-motivated people is led by the attempt to achieve desired interpersonal consequences. For example, in situations where the information seeker knows the opinion of significant social targets but has not revealed his or her beliefs to these social targets, a bias in the direction of these targets' position occurs (Lundgren & Prislin, 1998; Nemeth & Rogers, 1996). However, if the information seeker is bound by prior public commitments, a confirmation bias emerges that helps justify this opinion to others (Tetlock, 1992). The third motive, *accuracy motivation*, refers to the desire to hold beliefs that are objectively valid, to have an accurate representation of the world and to make good decisions. As a consequence, accuracy motivation can counteract a motivational tendency for self-confirmation and lead a decision maker to critically scrutinize his or her opinion by actively searching for supporting *and* conflicting information (Lundgren & Prislin, 1998). However, depending on people's prior knowledge of arguments in favor of a specific decision alternative, accuracy motivation can also enhance distortions in dealing with information (Chen & Chaiken, 1999).

In this article, we want to apply the multiple-motive approach of the HSM to the study of information seeking after preliminary and final decisions. We show that cognitive dissonance is only one reason that leads to biased information seeking, and that impression and accuracy motivation can also induce distortions in information search. We suggest that this approach is a useful framework for understanding people's behavior when searching for information in the context of decisions. However, knowledge about which motive is at work is itself not sufficient to predict people's information search because "motivation increases effort, which may increase or decrease bias" (Baumeister & Newman, 1994, p.3). Therefore it is also necessary to know people's cognitions about the benefits of decision supporting and conflicting information in order to know how they will satisfy the specific motive. As we will show, depending on those cognitions, all three motives can lead to a biased search in support of one's position, a balanced information search, or even an information search in conflict with one's position (disconfirmatory information search).

Studies on defense motivation

The concept of defense motivation proposes that people strive to maintain consistency and to defend positions to which they feel committed. More specifically, it refers to "the desire to hold attitudes and beliefs that are congruent with existing self-definitional attitudes and beliefs," which "leads to a directional bias that is consistently in line with existing self-beliefs" (Chaiken, Giner-Sorolla, & Chen, 1996, p.557). Therefore, people selectively process information so as to best preserve their self-concept and associated world views (Giner-Sorolla & Chaiken, 1997). However, what kind of information search satisfies defense concerns best? As suggested by Frey (1986), the specific kind of information search depends on cognitions about whether the addition of supporting information or the refutation of conflicting information more effectively helps to reach desired conclusions. More specifically, defense-motivated people search for supporting information when their cognitive system is not sufficiently stable and, by adding supporting information, further stabilization can be achieved. On the other hand, a search for conflicting information occurs when the cognitive system already is stable enough to refute the conflicting information or when the cognitive system is so weak that a revision of the decision is considered (Frey, 1986).

Defense motivation and the preference for supporting information

Research from various domains suggests that the higher the need to defend a desired conclusion, the stronger is the tendency for people to choose information supporting desirable rather than undesirable conclusions (for an overview, see Trope & Liberman, 1996). For example, Holton and Pyszczynski (1989) found that participants who had a greater desire to positively or negatively evaluate another person (because of previous praise or criticism by that person) revealed more selectivity in searching for information consistent with such an evaluation than those participants who just witnessed another person's praise or criticism. In a study by Boiney, Kennedy, and Nye (1997), decision-makers were confronted with the problem of whether a new product should be introduced into the market or not. Those participants with a strong motivation to introduce the product biased their judgment to support that desired conclusion more than neutral participants. A third example may be taken from research on biased information search processes within one's own memory. Sanitioso, Kunda, and Fong (1990) told undergraduate participants that either extroverts or introverts were more likely to have success. Subsequently, students who believed that introversion was related to success retrieved more instances of past shy behavior from their autobiographical memory, whereas those students who believed that extroversion predicted success listed more instances of outgoing behavior.

Studies on commitment influencing information search

One classical variable that increases people's defense motivation is enhancing their commitment to a position they are holding. The more people feel committed to a position, the more they are inclined to defend this position against criticism. In the literature on selective exposure to information there are several findings that support the notion that commitment increases the confirmation bias in information search. Brock and Balloun (1967) found in a "de-jamming" paradigm that committed churchgoers clarified audiotaped messages that were "mixed" with white noise more when it was consistent with their value system than when it was inconsistent. They also found a stronger tendency for smokers to clarify a communication that argued against the existence of a relation between smoking and lung cancer. In a political context, Sweeney and Gruber (1984) found that Nixon supporters reported less interest in and paid less attention to Watergate-related matters than undecided persons and McGovern supporters did. In a similar vein, Jonas, Graupmann, Fischer, Greitemeyer, and Frey (2003) investigated selective information search and evaluation processes in the context of the 1999 political party donation scandal of the Christian Democratic Union (CDU) in Germany. According to dissonance theory, the donation scandal should have increased cognitive dissonance especially among voters of the CDU (and its sister party Christian Social Union, CSU). In accordance with this assumption, CDU/CSU voters compared to voters of the Social Democratic Party (SPD) showed a stronger preference for supporting as opposed to conflicting information and evaluated the former as more important and interesting than the latter. Finally, Schwarz, Frey, and Kumpf (1980) manipulated commitment experimentally and found that participants who wrote an attitude-consistent essay (high commitment) were less interested in reading conflicting information than participants who wrote an irrelevant essay (low commitment).

Studies on the decision's salience influencing information search

Defense motivation should also be increased if one's own beliefs or decisions are made particularly salient. Jonas, Frey, and Greenberg (2005) suggest that salience of a decision should increase the salience of cognitive inconsistencies, increasing accessibility of cognitive discrepancies, and thereby increasing the discomfort resulting from decision-conflicting cognitions. This in turn should enhance defense motivation. As a consequence, enhanced defensive behavior should be observed, as for example, in an increased confirmation bias in information search. However, if the decision is less salient, for example because people are distracted from their decision, feelings of dissonance should be decreased, and thus confirmation bias in information seeking should also be reduced. This idea is supported by different areas of cognitive dissonance research showing that salience of dissonance increases the intensity of reactions to reduce dissonance, whereas distraction from dissonance reduces dissonance reduction reactions (see for example Zanna, Lepper, & Abelson, 1973 for the forbidden toy paradigm; Stone, Aronson, Crain, Winslow, & Fried, 1994 for the hypocrisy phenomenon; Newby-Clark, McGregor, & Zanna, 2002 for value ambivalence; Brock, 1962 for counter-attitudinal behavior).

We now report experiments in which we manipulated defense motivation by inducing participants to focus on their preliminary decision, thereby increasing the salience of decisions.

Studies on sequential vs. simultaneous information seeking

One circumstance that affects a decision's salience is the presentation mode of the available pieces of information during information search (Jonas, Schulz-Hardt, Frey et al., 2001; Jonas, Schulz-Hardt, & Frey, 2001). In a series of experiments, we presented the available pieces of information either sequentially or simultaneously after the preliminary decision. Simultaneous information presentation means that participants have an overview of all available pieces of information when choosing what to read in more detail (this kind of information presentation was typically used in selective exposure studies, for overviews see Frey, 1986). Sequential information presentation, on the other hand, means that participants get one or two pieces of information at a time and do not have an overview of all available pieces of information when deciding what to read in more detail.

We suggested that the presentation mode influences how much participants focus on their prior decision and that sequential presentation induces a focus on the decision, whereas simultaneous presentation leads to a focus on the information. As research from cognitive psychology has proposed, sequentially presenting items implies that each single item is compared with the person's prior belief, whereas under simultaneous presentation the different items are first compared with each other and then (if possible) integrated (Hogarth & Einhorn, 1992). Thus, sequential information presentation makes one's prior decision very salient because each new information title is compared with this decision (Hogarth & Einhorn, 1992). As a consequence, such an induced decision focus ought to increase the confirmation bias in information seeking. On the other hand, simultaneous information presentation leads participants to concentrate on comparing, evaluating, and integrating the new pieces of information, and only after that process do participants access the implications for the prior decision (Hogarth & Einhorn, 1992). As a consequence, such an induced information focus ought to lead to a lower confirmation bias compared to that induced by the sequential presentation mode.

Jonas, Schulz-Hardt, Frey et al. (2001) conducted a series of experiments in order to test this notion. In Experiment 1, after making a preliminary decision regarding a medical decision case (which was whether or not alternative medicine should be covered by health insurance), participants in the simultaneous information search condition were given all (16) available information titles at a time and were asked to mark those articles they wanted to read. Then they received the requested articles. In the sequential information search condition, participants received two main theses per sequence, one supporting and one conflicting with their prior preliminary decision. The information-seeking phase contained eight of these sequences and the participants were informed of this beforehand. In each sequence participants could choose one, both, or none of the presented articles. Once participants had made their choice, the experimenter handed out the chosen article(s). When the participants had read the article(s), the next sequence followed.

The results showed – as predicted – that a stronger preference for supporting information arose when information was presented and processed sequentially instead of simultaneously. In a second experiment, Jonas, Schulz-Hardt, Frey et al. (2001) demonstrated that this stronger confirmation bias was due to sequential *presentation* and not to sequential *processing* of information. Furthermore, in Experiments 3 and 4 the authors provided evidence that the increase in confirmation bias under sequential presentation was caused by increased focusing on the decision. No increased confirmation bias was observed in participants with a sequential information presentation if participants were distracted from their decision because they evaluated each article (on the basis of the information titles) with regard to how credible the article was expected to be, how competent the author seemed to be, and how persuasive the main argument was expected to be. In addition, it was shown that focusing on the decision increased participants' commitment to their decision, which partially mediated the effects.

Jonas, Schulz-Hardt, and Frey (2001) finally report an experiment that ruled out an alternative explanation for the increased confirmation bias in sequential information seeking. The alternative was that repeatedly being confronted with pieces of information to select from could induce the participants to search for more information altogether, and because less effort is required to process supporting information, they might just add the latter to their set. However, this alternative was not supported because when the number of information requests was fixed, participants still revealed a stronger confirmation bias with the information presented sequentially as compared to simultaneously.

To conclude, we suggest that sequential information presentation increases defense motivation by making the prior decision very salient. This salient decision should in turn increase the salience of the cognitive dissonance and, as a consequence, lead to a stronger confirmation bias compared to simultaneous information presentation. However, because the sequential information presentation results only provided indirect evidence for the decision focus hypothesis, we decided to test this hypothesis more directly by asking participants to think of their decision when searching for information (see below).

Studies on decision vs. information focus

Jonas, Frey et al. (2003, Experiment 5) compared participants who either focused on their decision while searching for information or who focused on the available information. The experimental procedure was similar to the one described above for testing sequential information seeking. Again, we used the medical decision case. The experimental manipulations took place in the following way. In each sequence, after reading the second information title, participants in the "decision focus" condition were asked to think again about their decision. On the other hand, participants in the information focus condition were instructed to concentrate on the information while choosing what to read in more detail. Again, the information focus manipulation took place by asking them to compare and evaluate the different pieces of information with regard to how credible this article was expected to be, how competent the author seemed to be, and how persuasive the main argument was expected to be. In this way we wanted to distract participants from focusing on their prior decision. In a third condition, the control group, no focus at all was introduced. Participants just selected the information they wanted to read without any manipulation. In accordance with the decision focus hypothesis, thinking of the decision increased commitment to the decision, whereas focusing on the information and thereby distracting participants from thinking about their decision prevented an increase in commitment. Although a confirmation bias emerged in all conditions, the decision focus resulted in a stronger bias as compared to the control group, and the information focus weakened it significantly.

The results of this experiment suggest that just repeatedly thinking about the preliminary decision leads to a stronger preference for supporting as opposed to conflicting information when searching for information on a decision problem. However, if a person's attention is distracted from the decision, this preference decreases and participants show a more balanced search for supporting and conflicting information.

There are many conditions that can induce a decision vs. information focus. For example, asking participants to give reasons why they have made a certain choice increases the salience of this choice and thus leads to an increased confirmation bias in dealing with information on the decision problem. In combining perspectives from social and educational psychology, Jonas, Frey et al. (2001) examined in their experiment how the explanation of choices made within a learning situation influenced the search for information and its evaluation. Students worked on a communication problem in which they had to choose one of five possible statements in three consecutive sequences. Participants had to explain their choice or not – a variable which constitutes an important aspect of learning environments within educational psychology (cf. e.g., Henninger, Mandl, & Law, 2001). Because the verbalization and explanation of a choice enhances the salience of the chosen alternative, an increased confirmation bias in information search was expected. The results were in accordance with this assumption, revealing a stronger preference for supportive information in participants who had given reasons for their choice, whereas participants who did not explain their choice revealed a balanced preference for supporting and conflicting information. In addition, participants who had to explain their choices also performed more poorly – in terms of fewer correct answers – than those who did not explain.

Further experiments by Jonas, Frey, et al. (2005) provided additional evidence for the decision vs. information focus hypothesis. In Experiment 3, the authors found that, whereas there was a confirmation bias in information seeking when participants were confronted with a real decision (whether they wanted to watch one movie or the other), this confirmation bias disappeared when participants had to pay money for the information search and thus had to focus on the available pieces of information. Experiment 2 conceptually replicated this finding. Participants who had to invest cognitive effort in order to search for information also revealed an almost balanced information search, whereas participants for whom the information was freely available showed a significant confirmation bias. We suggest that both results can be explained by assuming that costs for the information search, such as money or cognitive effort, lead participants to focus and concentrate on the available information. In line with this rationale, Experiment 4 by Jonas, Frey et al. (2003) illustrated that another form of information focus – asking participants to give reasons for their information search – also decreased the confirmation bias.

On the other hand, Experiments 1 and 2 by Jonas, Frey et al. (2005) suggested that promising participants a monetary reward if they found the correct decision alternative increased the confirmation bias. Assuming that the monetary reward increased participants' attention to their preliminary decision, this result can be interpreted in the context of the finding that repeatedly thinking about the decision while searching for information (Experiment 5 by Jonas, Frey et al., 2005 already outlined above) as well as giving reasons for a decision (Jonas, Frey et al., 2001) enhanced the confirmation bias. The results of Experiments 1 and 3 then hint at the idea that promising a reward for a decision might activate a decision focus, thereby increasing the decision's salience and in turn increasing confirmation bias. However, in the section on accuracy motivation we will see that this result could be also interpreted differently (see Schulz-Hardt et al., 2006, Experiment 4).

Mortality salience as a manipulation to increase people's need for defending worldview-relevant decisions

Jonas, Greenberg, and Frey (2003) employed a different manipulation of defense motivation that was derived from terror management theory (TMT, Greenberg, Solomon, & Pyszczynski, 1997). TMT posits that the pairing of the instinctive desire for self-preservation with the awareness of the inevitability of death creates the potential for paralyzing existential terror. According to TMT, this terror is managed by a cultural anxiety buffer. As a consequence, reminders of mortality intensify the desire to maintain faith in one's own cultural worldview and to defend it against threats. Jonas, Greenberg, and Frey (2003) investigated whether the increased defense motivation caused by mortality salience would increase the preference for supporting versus conflicting information after decisions.

The results showed that following mortality salience, people indeed showed an increased preference for information that supported their decision compared to information conflicting with it. However, this only occurred with regard to a worldview-relevant decision case involving a health policy that was being discussed at the time in the German media. Mortality salience did not affect information seeking in a fictitious decision scenario that involved extending or canceling the contract of a fictitious manager of a fashion store named Mr. Miller.

Defense motivation and the preference for conflicting information

The literature review thus far clearly indicates that seeking additional supporting information is an effective strategy for meeting defense needs. However, if a person holds the expectation that she or he will be able to refute conflicting information, the search and subsequent refutation of this kind of information is another effective strategy for defending one's own position. Frey (1986) suggested that the search and subsequent successful refutation of conflicting information – if possible – is preferred to simply avoiding conflicting information and searching for supporting information because this strategy more effectively serves long-term dissonance reduction. The expectation of being able to refute information can come from a person's cognitive system that is stable enough to refute the conflicting information, or can come from the belief that the conflicting information is weak and easy to refute.

This notion is supported by several experiments (for an overview see Frey, 1986). For example, when confronting participants with supporting and conflicting information, Lowin (1967) orthogonally manipulated the strength of the supporting and conflicting arguments. He found that weak conflicting information was preferred to the same extent as was strong supporting information. However, when compared to strong conflicting information, strong supporting information was clearly favored. Thus, the results suggest that people search for conflicting information if – because of the weakness of the arguments – they expect to be able to argue against these conflicting arguments. Another example comes from research by Kleinhesselink and Edwards (1975) who used a "de-jamming" paradigm. These authors also found that for weak and therefore easily refutable arguments, participants clarified the conflicting information more than the supporting. However, for difficult-to-refute arguments, supporting ones were clarified more often than conflicting ones were.

Instead of being able to refute arguments because they are weak, people are also able to argue against conflicting information if they have a stable cognitive system. After asking participants to make a decision, Frey (1981a, Experiment 3) presented either supporting or conflicting information to participants, thereby strengthening or destabilizing their cognitive system, respectively. Participants who received supporting information subsequently revealed a preference for conflicting over supporting information during information search (see also Schwarz et al., 1980).

Studies on impression motivation

Impression motivation refers to the desire to hold beliefs that are rewarded by a person's social environment. Thus, the processing of information depends on the interpersonal consequences of expressing particular positions. Impression-motivated perceivers take into account "the views of others who are actually present in the immediate social setting, as well as those of imagined others" (Chaiken et al., 1996, p. 563). For example, when the views of others are known and an individual strives to obtain a positive evaluation by supporting those views, people show information distortions that favor those views. On the other hand, impression-motivated individuals who think that a positive social evaluation is achieved by appearing especially knowledgeable and well informed in an upcoming discussion may exhibit a balanced search for information, carefully scrutinize all available information, and also prepare to counter-argue information that opposes the evaluator's opinions (Chaiken et al., 1996). Thus, the pattern of information search for impression-motivated individuals depends on cognitions about how to achieve positive evaluations by others.

An example that illustrates how people adapt their information search fairly flexibly to what seems appropriate in specific social contexts is a study by Freedman (1965). In this study, the usefulness of the different kinds of information was varied over three levels. In the "supporting more useful" condition, participants anticipated having to justify their decision by writing an essay; in the "conflicting more useful" condition, they expected to be confronted with a number of opposing arguments that they would have to refute; and in the "supporting and conflicting useful" condition the participants only had to give their opinion of decisions made by others. Freedman's results supported the prediction that information preferences would vary with the usefulness of the two types of information. Similar results were obtained by Canon (1964).

We will now report on different studies that illustrate more specifically how impression motivation can increase the preference for supporting as well as for conflicting information and how each pattern of information search can be understood when considering what is most useful in a specific situation to appear to others in a positive light.

Impression motivation and the preference for supporting information

In many social situations it is useful to be able to defend one's own standpoint with many arguments in favor of one's own beliefs. Levine and Russo (1995) conducted an experiment that illustrates that people search for information that best helps to defend their position in a social context and that this tendency is stronger the more this defense is needed. In this study, participants within majority and minority factions were asked to anticipate an interaction with others in which they would discuss a controversial issue. In order to prepare for the discussion, participants had the opportunity to search for information supporting and conflicting with their position. The results showed that within both minority and majority factions, the stronger the size of the anticipated opposing faction was (and the weaker the anticipated size of their own faction was), the more they were motivated to read information that would strengthen the defense of their position, thus leading to a stronger preference for supporting information. However, the goal for the minority participants with regard to the upcoming interaction might have been simply to avoid capitulation to the majority, whereas the goal for majority participants might have been to prevail in the discussion.

Not only people in a minority position in a discussion may feel the need to defend their positions to others, but also people who are accountable to others. In order to be able to best justify one's own position, people who are accountable to others might also reveal a confirmation bias in information search. We tested this hypothesis by examining information search among participants who were in the role of advisors interacting with participants in the role of clients.

Studies on accountability for the decision outcomes

Conducting an experiment with real interactions and real consequences for the participants (Jonas, Schulz-Hardt et al., 2005, Experiment 2), we asked participants who were in the role of advisors to either give a recommendation to a client or to make a binding decision on behalf of their client. As a second factor, we varied whether or not participants would have to justify their recommendation or their decision to their client (accountability).

Participants were first confronted with a client's decision problem. Then they had to make a preliminary decision about what they later wanted to recommend to the client. After that, participants had the opportunity to search for additional information regarding the client's decision problem. We predicted that accountability would increase impression motivation and thereby increase the participants' confirmation bias in information search. However, this was only expected to occur among participants who had to make a binding decision on behalf of their client because, if the decision of the advisor did not correspond to the client's preference, the advisor had to justify his or her choice and possibly react to complaints by the client. Since people tend to blame others less for their behavior if they can list several reasonable arguments (Tetlock, 1992), it would be helpful for the advisors to know as many advantages of the chosen alternative as possible and as many disadvantages as possible of the alternative not chosen, in order to best justify their decision. In contrast, such considerations were not necessary for advisors who gave a recommendation. If the alternative they selected did not correspond to the client's preference, the client could nevertheless choose his or her preferred alternative. Therefore, accountability for the recommendation should not induce a need to stock up on arguments justifying an advisor's choice.

The results of our experiment were in accordance with these predictions. For advisors making a binding decision on behalf of their client, accountability induced a strong preference for information supporting the advisor's preliminary choice. For advisors giving a non-binding recommendation, accountability had no significant effect on information search.

Impression motivation and the preference for conflicting information

If participants think that a balanced or self-critical information search is appropriate in a specific social context, this should counteract a tendency to prefer picking supporting information. In accordance with this rationale, Johnston (1996) found that, in the context of stereotypes, participants searched for less stereotypical information when they anticipated having to justify their opinion to a group that did not share the stereotype. This can be explained by the participants' desire to be seen in a positive light by the group and the expectation that this goal could not be achieved if they maintained the stereotype. However, participants revealed an information search that led to stereotype preservation when they anticipated having to justify their opinion to a group that shared the stereotype.

In an experiment by Lundgren and Prislin (1998, Experiment 1), students expected to participate in a discussion on whether tuition should be increased by 30%. Defense motivation was induced by framing the experiment as a survey of students' opinions about a tuition increase proposed for the next semester that would help the board of regents decide the issue. Impression motivation was induced by telling them that the purpose of the experiment was to examine agreeableness and other skills of rapport in a discussion about whether tuition should be increased in the distant future. Lundgren and Prislin then measured the total number of arguments read, the total time spent reading, the time spent reading pro-increase arguments, anti-increase arguments, and neutral arguments. Whereas defense-motivated participants spent more time reading anti-increase arguments than pro-increase arguments, impression-motivated participants spent about the same time reading pro-increase as well as anti-increase arguments. In other words, compared to defense motivation, impression motivation made participants pay relatively more attention to conflicting information. However, impression-motivated participants did not continue to think objectively about the tuition increase. Their thought valences index indicated that they processed more arguments in support of their partner's position than those conflicting with it.

Although we did not conduct experiments in our lab in which participants anticipated justifying their information search to a social target that would reward a self-critical information search, we did discover that people seem to consider a balanced information search as desirable when making decisions in a variety of different contexts (Jonas & Frey, 2003; Jonas, 2006). This is in accordance with the idea that people try to keep an "illusion of objectivity" (Pyszczynski & Greenberg, 1987) when making judgments and dealing with information. Because obvious information distortions can make it psychologically difficult to justify the decision process to oneself or others, people try to derive conclusions from available evidence as logically as possible. Inferences that do not appear to be in accordance with the available data produce discomfort for the individual (e.g., Baumeister & Newman, 1994; Chaiken et al., 1989; Kruglanski, 1989; Kunda, 1990; Pyszczynski & Greenberg, 1987). In support of this notion, Boiney et al. (1997) found that decision makers engage in information distortions very instrumentally and try to avoid them as much as possible. We think that, on the one hand, this strategy prevents defense-motivated people from exhibiting a confirmation bias that is so strong they could not justify it to themselves. On the other hand, the desire to be able to justify one's own behavior to others – and thus manage the impressions one makes – might also lead people to avoid distortions in information search that they would otherwise (i.e., without or with lower impression motivation) reveal. Two pieces of evidence that are in line with this reasoning can be derived from our studies already mentioned in the defense motivation section.

In the study involving the Christian Democratic Union (CDU) scandal in Germany, Jonas, Graupmann et al. (2003) found that, although voters of the party involved in the scandal (CDU/CSU) revealed a stronger confirmation bias than voters of the Social Democratic Party (SPD) when they were not aware that they had to indicate their party preference, they were significantly less biased in their information search when they had to indicate their party preference at the outset of the experiment. Thereby participants did not dispense with supporting pieces of information but instead added conflicting evidence – although they still considered the conflicting information to be less important than the supporting information. We suggest that this finding can be explained by assuming that people strive to not appear too biased (to themselves as well as to others) – a tendency that might occur particularly in situations such as the party donation scandal in which ignoring conflicting information would have meant denying quite overwhelming evidence.

Finally, as Jonas, Frey et al. (2005, Experiment 4) have shown, the pressure to justify one's information requests decreases the confirmation bias. On the one hand, the authors suggested that this induces participants to focus on the available pieces of information and thereby distracts them from focusing on the decision, which in turn reduces the salience of the cognitive dissonance resulting from the decision. However, when people focus on the information search because they have to give reasons of what pieces of information they want to read in more detail, they might not only become distracted from their decision but might also direct their attention to a different goal. In the context of justification this might mean that they concentrate on conducting an information search that can be justified compellingly – and that means conducting a balanced information search (Jonas & Frey, 2003).

Studies on Accuracy Motivation

Accuracy motivation refers to the desire to hold beliefs that are objectively valid and to have an accurate representation of the world (Chen & Chaiken, 1999). Accuracy motivation is assumed to be the main driving force that leads people to avoid bias and conduct a balanced, open-minded information search (Chaiken et al., 1989; Johnston, 1996; Lundgren & Prislin, 1998). For example Chen and Chaiken (1999, p. 77) presume that accuracy motivation leads to an "open-minded and evenhanded treatment of judgment-relevant information." However, Chen and Chaiken (p. 93) also admit that, "although the goal of accuracy-motivated individuals by definition is to seek the truth, this does not imply that their processing is necessarily unbiased. Cognitive factors, such as bias in one's knowledge base, may color the evaluative nature of processing. For instance, a person's greater knowledge of arguments on one side of an issue may result in stronger counter-arguing information supporting the other side of the issue."

We now want to outline our suggestion about how these at first glance contradictory statements can be combined. As we will explain below, striving for accuracy can lead to both an unbiased as well as a biased search for new information. As in the case of defense and impression motivation, whether this motivation leads to more or less bias in one's information search depends on the specific type of cognitions involved. More specifically, we will argue that in cases when the information seeker believes that a self-critical information search is useful to achieve accurate judgments and decisions, accuracy motivation leads to an *intention* to be unbiased in one's information search. However, accuracy-motivated persons may still *unintentionally* (but systematically) develop a confirmation bias in cases when they (a) try to pick the best pieces of information, (b) have at least some idea of the direction and content of the arguments given in the available pieces of information (e.g., an idea of how the different experts argue), and (c) due to principles of cognitive economy, test preference-inconsistent arguments more critically than preference-consistent ones, thereby gaining the impression that the consistent pieces of information will be of higher quality.

Accuracy motivation and the preference for conflicting information

Although there is inconsistent evidence concerning the effects of inducing accuracy motivation (for overview see Kunda, 1990), many researchers suggested that accuracy motivation has a de-biasing effect in information processing. For example, Baumeister and Newman (1994) assumed that accuracy-motivated people (in their terminology, "intuitive scientists") are especially thorough in their information search and consider the opposite when searching new evidence to reach an accurate decision. Johnston (1996) presented data suggesting that although perceivers normally were particularly susceptible to stereotypical thinking, accuracy-motivated participants (who were instructed to try to be as accurate as possible in their perception) revealed a balanced search for the same amount of stereotypic supporting as well as conflicting information. If, in contrast, no accuracy motivation was induced, stereotypes led to information distortions that supported maintenance of the (positive or negative) stereotype.

The notion that accuracy motivation indeed directs people's attention to conflicting information finds support in the study by Lundgren and Prislin (1998, Experiment 1) already mentioned in the section about impression motivation. As outlined, students expected to participate in a discussion on whether tuition should be increased by 30%. Accuracy motivation was induced by telling participants that the purpose of the experiment was to examine their logic and reasoning abilities in a discussion about a 30%

tuition increase in the distant future. In contrast to defense-motivated participants (as described before), accuracy-motivated participants spent about the same time reading pro and contra arguments. In addition, counter to impression-motivated participants, their thought-valence indices showed that they continued to think about the issue in a balanced way. Lundgren and Prislin (p.720) describe the information search of accuracy-motivated participants as follows: "Participants concerned with arriving at accurate attitudes engaged in exploratory processing based on the principle of objectivity. Similar to a scientist who seeks the solution to a controversy by impartially examining relevant evidence, our accuracy seekers thoroughly examined all of the available information, engaged in extensive and equally balanced thinking whereby they elaborated external information, and also generated novel arguments about the tuition increase." Thus, if people think their logic and reasoning abilities are examined they reveal a more balanced information search – a behavior that they consider as desirable when making a decision (Jonas & Frey, 2003).

Given these considerations, one should expect accuracy motivation to increase if the decision is particularly important or if the danger of making a faulty decision is made salient. We will now briefly report three studies addressing these aspects.

Studies examining the influence of experienced failure on information search

The danger of making a faulty decision should be particularly salient if a person has experienced failure in a preceding task. In two experiments, Jonas and Frey (2006) gave participants false feedback prior to the information search. In both experiments, the participants were told that they would participate in two separate studies. In the "first study," they worked on an intelligence task. When they finished, they were asked to estimate their performance on a scale from 1 to 100. Next, the "second study" engaged participants in a decision problem. After the participants had made a preliminary decision, they were told that the results of the intelligence test were ready and the administration of (false) positive or negative feedback took place. Participants received a sheet of paper on which their performance was indicated as either being much better or much worse than they had expected before. The participants in the control group did not receive any feedback. Then the participants returned to the decision problem and had the opportunity to seek additional related information. The information either supported or conflicted with their preliminary decision. The question was whether people who had just experienced failure would show a lower tendency for distortions in their information search than people who had just experienced success.

In Experiment 1, in which the decision problem and information search was about a time management problem of an insurance employer, the results revealed that only in the control and the positive feedback conditions was there a preference for supporting as compared to conflicting information. In the negative feedback condition, a tendency to prefer conflicting over supporting information was found. In Experiment 2, the medical decision case was used. We replicated the effect that negative feedback decreased the preference for supporting information as compared to the control group and the positive feedback group. In addition, we found that those participants who got positive feedback revealed an even stronger confirmation bias than the control group. Thus, Experiment 2 hints that positive feedback might even increase self-confirmation because people probably think that their strategy is somehow "safe." These findings supplement research by

Kray and Galinsky (2003) who made the possibility of a wrong decision salient by inducing – in an ostensibly unrelated study – a counterfactual mindset. This manipulation increased the search for conflicting information and, in addition, also led to better performance compared to a control group.

Study on increasing the decision's importance

As mentioned in the section about impression motivation, Jonas, Schulz-Hardt et al. (2005, Experiment 2) put participants in the role of a person who had to give advice to a client, varying what kind of decision the advisors had to make. Advisors either gave a recommendation and the client made the final decision themselves (low importance) or the advisor made a decision on the client's behalf and the client had to accept the advisor's decision (high importance). Jonas, Schulz-Hardt et al. (2005) suggested that in the conditions without accountability (i.e., no impression motivation manipulation), the awareness of making a decision on behalf of their client should increase the advisor's accuracy motivation. In support of this notion, Kunda (1990) also argues that accuracy motivation is heightened if a judgment has consequences for another person and McAllister, Mitchell, and Beach (1979) showed that accuracy motivation is lower if participants make a decision that will be checked by another person compared to a situation in which a person makes a decision without this check. As it has been suggested by Payne, Bettman, and Johnson (1993) that the greater the consequences of a choice, the more willing people usually are to invest effort in the decision process ("effort-accuracy trade-off"), we hypothesized that advisors who made a binding decision for a client were more self-critical in their information search than advisors giving a recommendation. This is exactly what we found. Whereas advisors giving a non-binding recommendation had a slight preference for supporting information, those participants who made a binding decision on behalf of their client strongly preferred conflicting information and thus critically scrutinized their initial preference. Again, it has to be emphasized that this was only true (and was only predicted) for advisors without accountability. As shown in the impression motivation section, in the case of advisors who had to justify their choice to the client (accountability), the same decision importance manipulation induced a strong confirmation bias – a bias that is instrumental in dealing with being accountable.

Accuracy motivation and the preference for supporting information

Given the outlined theoretical considerations and empirical studies on the effects of accuracy motivation, one might wonder how accuracy motivation can *in*crease (rather than *de*crease) a confirmation bias in information search. As we have just outlined, in cases when the information seeker believes that a self-critical information search is useful to achieve accurate judgments and decisions, accuracy motivation leads to an *intention* to be unbiased in one's information search. However, we suggest that there are also *unintentional* processes that lead people to develop a confirmation bias – and these processes are the stronger the higher people's accuracy motivation.

In contrast to intentional information seeking, Freedman and Sears (1965) discuss the idea that people might selectively expose themselves to supporting information without intending to do so. Among various examples, they mentioned financiers' preference for the *Wall Street Journal* over the *New York Post* simply because the former contains more information relevant to them than the latter. Given that financiers, in general, are relatively conservative, and that the *Wall Street Journal* can be seen as expressing more conservative views than the *New York Post*, the consequence of this preference is a de facto confirmation bias for the majority of the financiers. This example illustrates how information selection can be based on completely different attributes than the supportiveness of a particular piece of information, with a systematic confirmation bias occurring nevertheless.

However, Freedman and Sears' approach cannot explain why people – without intending to do so – should exhibit a confirmatory information search *irrespective of their particular opinion*, e.g., why progressive financiers should prefer the *New York Post* over the *Wall Street Journal*. To further develop Freedman and Sears' idea of de facto selectivity without an intention to exhibit this preference, Schulz-Hardt et al. (2006) recently presented a new approach to understanding unintended confirmatory information search based on a preference-consistent evaluation of expected information quality.

Asymmetric evaluation of expected information quality as a mediator for biased information search

A characteristic feature of the general research paradigm used in most studies on selective exposure to information is that, prior to selecting the information, the participants have at least some idea of the content of the available pieces of information. In particular, they not only know whether a particular piece of information will support or conflict with their own opinion, but they also get to know a specific argument of the particular piece of information. It should be emphasized that this is not an artificial characteristic of the classical research paradigm, but rather a feature that is present in many real life information seeking situations. If, for example, a political committee has to decide which experts should be invited to give their advice concerning a current topic, the members of the committee often know about the general opinion of these experts. As a consequence, people could use this knowledge in order to detect the best pieces of information. If people are aware that they cannot expose themselves to all available information, and if they expect that selecting the best information will help them to make a good judgment or decision, then people should select those pieces of information with the highest expected quality. According to Hastie, Penrod, and Pennington (1983), the quality of a piece of information depends on its credibility (i.e., whether it can be trusted) as well as the strength of its decisional implication (i.e., whether it captures an important decision-relevant attribute and clearly speaks for or against one of the alternatives). Thus, according to Schulz-Hardt et al. (2006), if people try to make an accurate decision, they should try to figure out which are the strongest, most relevant, and most credible pieces of information. As a means of detecting these, they should evaluate the main theses that are known to them.

At this critical point, bias is introduced. As a multitude of studies from the social information processing literature (e.g., research on "motivated reasoning," Ditto & Lopez, 1992; Ditto, Scepansky, Munro, Apanovitch, & Lockhart, 1998; the "prior belief effect," Edwards & Smith, 1996; Lord, Ross, & Lepper, 1979; or preference-consistent information processing during decisions, Russo, Medvec, & Meloy, 1996; Svenson, 1992), attest, the evaluation of arguments is systematically biased towards one's prior opinion:

Supporting arguments are judged to be stronger, more important, and more credible than conflicting arguments (e.g., Edwards & Smith, 1996; Greitemeyer & Schulz-Hardt, 2003; Koehler, 1993). Thus, if people base their information selection on their evaluation of expected information quality, they should exhibit a systematic confirmation bias without intending to do so.

It should be emphasized that this approach works without any intentional bias. Asymmetrical evaluation of arguments does not occur as a consequence of people actively and intentionally derogating the preference-inconsistent arguments; rather, it stems from people automatically directing more attention to arguments that are inconsistent with their preference than to preference-consistent arguments (Ditto et al., 1998; Edwards & Smith, 1996). Whereas the latter are accepted at face value, the former are tested critically and systematically. This systematic testing raises the likelihood of detecting weaknesses in the argument. As a consequence, the preference-inconsistent arguments seem to be of lower quality than the consistent ones.

The source of this attentional process can be motivational as well as cognitive in nature. People direct more attention to an argument and test it more critically if the argument conflicts with their desired conclusions (motivational process, cf. Ditto & Lopez, 1992; Ditto et al., 1998). In addition, people also pay more attention and exhibit more systematic testing if an argument is inconsistent with their prior knowledge or prior beliefs (cognitive process, cf. Edwards & Smith, 1996). In the case of the latter process, we should also expect people to hold more arguments consistent with their belief or their decisional preference than arguments that are inconsistent with this preference. As a consequence, more counterarguments exist against new arguments that are inconsistent with the person's opinion than against new arguments consistent with this opinion. This further intensifies the differential evaluation of arguments (Nisbett & Ross, 1980).

In sum, participants in the classic information search paradigm may exhibit a systematic confirmation bias simply because they try to pick the best pieces of information and in doing so over-represent consistent information in the group of subjectively "high-quality" pieces of information. These predictions have been confirmed in a series of experiments by Schulz-Hardt et al. (2006). For example, in their first experiment, the authors extended the "classic" information search procedure from dissonance theory research with an information evaluation measurement. After making a preliminary or final decision on a decision case and after receiving the overview sheet with the main theses of 12 expert statements available to them, the participants were asked to evaluate the expected quality of each statement with regard to credibility, importance, and strength. Subsequently, they selected those statements they wanted to read. As predicted, supporting statements were expected to be stronger, more important, and more credible than conflicting ones. Furthermore, the strength of this evaluation bias was systematically correlated with the strength of the subsequent confirmation bias in information search. When controlling for the evaluation bias, no confirmation bias occurred. These results held for reversible as well as for irreversible decisions.

In two other experiments (Schulz-Hardt et al., 2006, Experiments 2 and 5), the mediating role of differential argument evaluation was tested even more directly. In Experiment 2, the arguments were removed from the main theses, that is, the main theses only contained information about whether the particular expert statement would support or conflict with the participant's prior decision. Under these conditions, no differential argument evaluation is possible and, as expected, no confirmation bias in information search appeared. In Experiment 5, differential argument evaluation was blocked by means of a cognitive load task (cf. Ditto et al., 1998, Experiment 2). In the experimental condition, the participants had to listen to strings of letters through headphones and count the number of vowels while conducting the information search. Whereas asymmetric evaluation of expected information quality as well as a confirmation bias in information search were observed in the control condition (no load), participants in the cognitive load condition were balanced in both their argument evaluation and their information search. In addition, the differences in argument evaluation were shown to mediate the differences in information search between the two conditions.

Effects of heightened accuracy motivation on unintended confirmatory information search

The asymmetric evaluation process leading to unintended confirmatory information search only occurs if people, at least to some extent, select information on the basis of expected information quality. Thus, some accuracy motivation is necessary to trigger the process. Furthermore, in a somehow ironic twist, the more people strive for accuracy, the more intensively they may elaborate on the expected quality of information, and the more biased their information search may be. This may be especially true if, as in the classic information search paradigm, they have some a priori knowledge about arguments from available pieces of information that they evaluate and base their selection on. In this situation, factors that enhance accuracy motivation should *in*crease rather than *de*crease the confirmation bias.

This prediction was directly tested in an experiment by Schulz-Hardt et al. (2003, Experiment 4). For half of the participants, accuracy motivation was heightened by informing them that they would receive two cinema tickets if they made the correct decision in the end. The information search followed a preliminary decision in a case about whether a student should go abroad or not. The other half of the participants were informed that the cinema tickets would be distributed among them by drawing lots, and thus, whether or not they received the incentive would not depend on whether or not they made the correct decision in the end. As predicted, participants in the accuracy condition revealed a strong confirmation bias in information search. In contrast, participants in the low accuracy condition only showed a slight and non-significant preference for supporting information. This underlines our suggestion that incentives for being accurate can, under certain conditions, be counterproductive and lead to an increase in confirmation bias instead of de-biasing the information search.

Although it is not a direct manipulation of accuracy motivation, a factor recently investigated by Fischer, Jonas, Frey, and Schulz-Hardt (2005) also adds to this line of reasoning. They suggested that, in real decision-making situations, people seldom have the time and capacity to search for all available information about the decision problem. At the same time, they often must search for at least some pieces of information. For example, if the editor of a journal is about to decide whether to accept or reject a particular manuscript, he or she cannot ask all colleagues that are knowledgeable about the manuscript topic for a review. However, they also cannot completely abstain from peer reviewing. In the extreme case, the number of pieces of information to be requested may be completely predetermined (e.g., three peer reviews). In contrast to that, most studies on biased information search in the selective exposure paradigm do not pose such constraints upon the participants.

In a series of four experiments, Fischer, Jonas et al. (2005) showed that limiting the number of available pieces of information or even fixing the amount of information that has to be selected (i.e., exactly half of the available articles) increases the confirmation bias. They also found (Experiment 3) that just giving participants a cue of information scarcity (without an objective restriction) leads to the same increase in confirmation bias as explicitly restricting participants' information search options. This has implications for the proposed asymmetric evaluation process as a mediator for biased information search. Recognizing that one can only select half of the available pieces of information could make people try to more accurately pick the best pieces of information. Thus, although this manipulation should not affect participants' accuracy motivation with regard to the final decision, it could well heighten their accuracy motivation with regard to information search. If this were the case, then the reason for the stronger confirmation bias under these conditions should be that the evaluation of expected information quality is conducted more intensively and, thus, the asymmetry in information evaluation increases. To test this hypothesis, Fischer, Jonas et al. (Experiment 4) crossed the restriction factor with the cognitive load manipulation already explained in the context of the studies by Schulz-Hardt et al. (2006). The rationale behind this manipulation was that the asymmetric evaluation of expected information quality leading to a confirmation bias should disappear if the participants had to work on an additional cognitive load task. The results were in line with this prediction. Whereas without cognitive load the restriction effect was replicated, this effect was completely eliminated in the cognitive load conditions.

Intentional constraints on unintended confirmation bias

It should be emphasized that in showing that people can exhibit a systematic preference for supporting information without intending to do so, the findings of Schulz-Hardt et al. (2006) do not contradict (but rather supplement) the idea that people can also intentionally exhibit a confirmation bias. More specifically, one should expect that intentional processes such as those outlined in earlier sections of this chapter can constrain or override unintentional confirmation bias in information search. As a final piece of evidence, we want to briefly sketch two recent papers illuminating this interplay.

One of these is a series of experiments by Fischer, Schulz-Hardt, and Frey (2006). They dealt with a remarkable inconsistency in the biased information search literature, namely between the studies of Freedman and Sears (for an overview, see Freedman and Sears, 1965), showing a strong preference for information conflicting with the participants' prior decision, and the rest of this large body of literature that, more or less, speaks to a preference for supporting information (e.g., Frey, 1986; Frey et al., 1996). A specific characteristic of the Freedman and Sears (1965) studies was that only two pieces of information were provided, and the participants had to select only one of them. All other studies in the literature have been conducted with larger amounts of information.

In a series of four experiments, Fischer, Schulz-Hardt et al. (2006) showed that if only two pieces of information were provided, the participants preferred the conflicting information, whereas when more than two pieces of information (namely four, six, or ten) were available, a preference for supporting information was observed (in both cases the participants had to select exactly one piece of information). To explain this finding, they suggested that "normally" (i.e., if more than just two pieces of information are available and if no specific other motivation is induced) people choose the piece of information that, in their subjective opinion, is best. However, if only two pieces of information are presented, the opinion-consistency of information becomes a very salient feature. As a consequence, the person intentionally chooses the conflicting information in order to critically examine their prior decision.

This idea was directly tested in Experiment 4 of the Fischer, Schulz-Hardt et al. (2006) studies. The participants were given either two or ten pieces of additional information from which to choose. This factor was crossed with a specific instruction about what criteria should guide the information search. According to the above-mentioned hypothesis, the authors assumed that people who are confronted with two statements should pay attention to the opinion-consistency of the information, whereas people confronted with more pieces of information should pay particular attention to the quality of the arguments given. Thus, the instructions emphasized either the one or the other criterion – participants were either instructed to choose the most important and credible piece of information or to make their selection based on whether they wanted confirmation or disconfirmation of their prior opinion. In the former condition (choose the best information), the participants preferred supporting information, irrespective of whether two or ten items were available. In the latter condition, the participants predominantly chose the conflicting information (i.e., decided that they preferred critical appraisal over confirmation of their opinion). In the control condition (no instruction), the original effect was replicated: The participants selected supporting information if ten items were available and conflicting information if two items were available. These findings underscore that an intention to critically test one's prior choice can override the unintended confirmation bias brought about by asymmetric argument evaluation.

Then again, an intention to actively defend one's position towards others can, of course, replace or exaggerate an unintentional confirmation bias. This is illustrated in a study by Greitemeyer, Schulz-Hardt, and Frey (2003), although the focus of their study was not information *search* but information *evaluation* and *transmission*. One of their main findings was that participants who anticipated a group discussion with two other persons wanted to ask for more information consistent rather than inconsistent with their preference (biased information search), and they also intended to communicate more information that supported their preference than information that conflicted with their preference (biased information transmission). The latter effect was partially mediated by how the participants evaluated the information available to them. Since preference-consistent information was judged to be more credible and more important than preference-inconsistent information (biased evaluation), the participants were more willing to communicate the consistent rather than the inconsistent information. In other words, people may often systematically communicate more information in favor of their own opinion than information conflicting with this opinion, but this bias need not necessarily stem from an intention to defend one's preferred alternative; it may also be the consequence of an attempt to communicate the most valuable pieces of information in which there is a direct parallel to the information search we have outlined.

However, whereas the above-mentioned mediation worked well for individuals who were asked to imagine a discussion with persons holding the same preference as they held, it was much weaker in those conditions where participants thought about a discussion with persons who disagreed with them. It is conceivable that in the latter situation a motivation to convince these other persons comes in, and successfully convincing other persons often requires intentionally withholding conflicting arguments even if (or just because) they are strong. Thus, defense or impression motivation can override any unintentional biases engendered by asymmetric argument evaluation, including, of course, those biases in information search.

Conclusion and Summary

The research reported in this article illustrates that decision making situations are complex settings in which – depending on specific situational conditions – different motives can be activated that lead to biased information seeking. In order to better understand why and in what direction situational conditions affect the search for new information, we think it is useful to expand the dissonance theory approach to include the multiple motive approach of the HSM. Whereas defense motivation is similar to the motive to reduce cognitive dissonance, accuracy and impression motivation emphasize aspects of decision making and information search situations that have been largely neglected in research on selective exposure to information (for exceptions, see Johnston, 1996; Lundgren & Prislin, 1998; Schulz-Hardt et al., 2000). Taken as a whole, the research we reviewed in this article suggests that not only cognitive dissonance or defense motivation can induce confirmation bias in information seeking but also impression and accuracy motivation.

The revised version of dissonance theory (Festinger, 1964) takes into account searching for conflicting information if this is useful for future decisions and thus helps to reduce future dissonance. However, one might ask whether it is fruitful to expand cognitive dissonance theory in this way if this immunizes the theory against the possibility of falsification (any lack of information distortions could be interpreted as an attempt to avoid even greater dissonance in the future). For this reason we think it is more productive to unequivocally understand the motivation to reduce cognitive dissonance as a motive to defend positions to which one feels committed. In other situations, for example when people try to seek the truth, find the best decision alternative, or get rewards from their social environment, we suggest that qualitatively different motives like accuracy or impression motivation are at work.

However, knowing what motive is activated in a specific situation itself is not sufficient to predict information search because all motives can lead to a preference for supporting as well as conflicting information. Therefore, we additionally need to know people's cognitions regarding how they think they can best satisfy the activated motive.

Table 1 provides an overview of the conditions that activate defense, accuracy, or impression motivation and, given that this activation has occurred, lead to a preference for supporting or conflicting information. When defense-motivated people are committed to their decision, when they focus on the decision (instead of the available pieces of information), or when they want to regain faith in their cultural worldview, they should search for supporting information in order to achieve stabilization of the cognitive system. However, in situations in which defense-motivated people think they can refute conflicting information because their cognitive system is already very stable or because the conflicting evidence is very weak, a search for conflicting information can be observed.

Impression-motivated information search depends on expectations about what kind of behavior leads to social rewards. An increased confirmation bias can be observed when people have to defend their own standpoint to others or when they are accountable

Table 1. Summary of situational conditions that affect the preference for supporting and conflicting information dependent on different underlying motivations

	Preference for supporting information	Preference for conflicting information
Defense motivation	• Commitment to the decision • Salience of the decision (because of focusing on the decision as opposed to on the available pieces of information) • Desire to regain faith in one's own cultural worldview	• Low credibility of information • High stability of cognitive system
Impression motivation	• Justifying one's own standpoint to others • Accountability for decision result	• Getting along with others who have an opposite opinion • Attempt to appear unbiased • Justifying the information search
Accuracy motivation	• Focusing on the "best" information (because of, e.g., restricted information search or large amount of information)	• Evaluation of logic and reasoning abilities • Attempt to be as accurate as possible • Desire to prevent a wrong decision (because failure is salient or because of importance of decision)

for the decision result. A decrease in confirmation bias can be observed when people attempt to appear unbiased, when dealing with people who have an opposite opinion, or when justifying the information search.

In situations in which the information seeker wants to prevent a wrong decision and believes a self-critical information search useful to achieve this goal, accuracy motivation will de-bias information search. Telling participants that their logic and reasoning abilities are being examined, instructing them to be as accurate as possible in their judgment, increasing the salience of failure, or enhancing the decision's importance are situational conditions that can induce this intention to be accurate. Then again, if people do not focus on whether a piece of information confirms or disconfirms their opinion, but rather evaluate the quality of arguments in order to pick the best pieces of information, accuracy motivation introduces an unintended but nevertheless systematic confirmation bias in information search.

In the introductory section we pointed out the risks of biased information seeking and asked how we might suggest interventions for practical decision making. We think the situational framework we presented along with the knowledge about people's underlying motives and cognitions can be used to derive interventions for biased decision making.

As the framework illustrates, the specific intervention one chooses should depend on the motives and cognitions underlying information distortions. Otherwise, if people have wrong assumptions, the intervention might be ineffective. For example, if an employee has to justify to a supervisor why they hired a specific person and is therefore impression-motivated, the employee will probably search for information supporting their decision. As an intervention, it would be useful to ask the employee to justify the information search and thus concentrate on the decision process instead of concentrating on the decision result. However, if the supervisor thinks the employee lacks accuracy motivation and therefore emphasizes the negative consequences of future failures, this might even increase the employee's impression motivation and in turn information distortions.

When talking about interventions it is, in any case, important to have in mind that a confirmation bias can have both costs and benefits. As we have outlined in the introduction, on the one hand, a confirmation bias in information search can be seen as dysfunctional for a decision maker because it increases the likelihood of major risks of the preferred alternative being ignored (Janis, 1982, 1989; Nemeth & Rogers, 1996; Schulz-Hardt, 1997); thus, if the decision maker prefers a suboptimal alternative or even an alternative with obvious negative consequences, a confirmation bias makes it less likely that this faulty preference will be corrected (cf. Kray & Galinsky, 2003; von Haeften, 1999). On the other hand, the functional value of the confirmation bias is its impact on the decision maker's ability to act (Beckmann & Irle, 1985; Wicklund & Frey, 1981). The more the decision maker bolsters his/her preference, the less likely it is that they will remain indecisive and inactive, and the more emphatically the decision is implemented – and this insistence may itself be a major determinant of the decision's success (White, Dittrich, & Lang, 1980). Thus, from an action theory perspective (e.g., Gollwitzer & Bayer, 1999), a confirmation bias has costs during the evaluation of alternatives, but benefits during the implementation of a decision. This has to be considered when creating interventions for facilitating optimal decision making.

Acknowledgments

We are grateful to Mark Zanna and Andy Martens for helpful comments on an earlier draft of this chapter.

References

Baumeister, R. F. & Newman, L. S. (1994). Self-regulation of cognitive inference and decision processes. *Personality and Social Psychology Bulletin, 20,* 3–19.

Beckmann, J., & Kuhl, J. (1984). Altering information to gain action control: Functional aspects of human information processing in decision making. *Journal of Research in Personality, 18,* 224–237.

Beckmann, J., & Irle, M. (1985). Dissonance and action control. In J. Kuhl & J. Beckmann (Eds.), *Action control: From cognition to behavior* (pp. 129–150). Berlin: Springer.

Boiney, L. G., Kennedy, J. & Nye, P. (1997). Instrumental bias in motivated reasoning: More when more is needed. *Organizational Behavior and Human Decision Processes, 72,* 1–24.

Brock, T. C. (1962). Cognitive restructuring and attitude change. *Journal of Abnormal and Social Psychology, 64,* 264–271.
Brock, T. C. & Balloun, J. L. (1967). Behavioral receptivity to dissonant information. *Journal of Personality and Social Psychology, 6,* 413–428.
Brockner, J., & Rubin, J. Z. (1985). *Entrapment in escalating conflicts – a social psychological analysis.* New York: Springer.
Canon, L. K. (1964). *Self-confidence and selective exposure to information.* Stanford, Calif.: Stanford University Press.
Chaiken, S., Giner-Sorolla, R., & Chen, S. (1996). Beyond accuracy: Defense and impression motives in heuristic and systematic information processing. In P. M. Gollwitzer & J. A. Bargh (Eds.), *The psychology of action – Linking cognition and motivation to behavior* (pp. 553–578). New York, London: The Guilford Press.
Chaiken, S., Liberman, A., & Eagly, A. H. (1989). Heuristic and systematic information processing within and beyond the persuasion context. In J. S. Uhleman & J. A. Bargh (Eds.), *Unintended thought* (pp. 212–252). New York: Guilford Press.
Chen, S. & Chaiken, S. (1999). The heuristic-systematic model in its broader context. In S. Chaiken & Y. Trope (Eds.), *Dual process theories in social psychology.* New York: The Guilford Press.
Ditto, P. H., & Lopez, D. F. (1992). Motivated skepticism: Use of differential decision criteria for preferred and nonpreferred conclusions. *Journal of Personality and Social Psychology, 63,* 568–584.
Ditto, P. H., Scepansky, J. A., Munro, G. D., Apanovitch, A. M., & Lockhart, L. K. (1998). Motivated sensitivity to preference-inconsistent information. *Journal of Personality and Social Psychology, 75,* 53–69.
Edwards, K., & Smith, E. E. (1996). A disconfirmation bias in the evaluation of arguments. *Journal of Personality and Social Psychology, 71,* 5–24.
Festinger, L. (1957). *A theory of cognitive dissonance.* Stanford, CA: Stanford University Press.
Festinger, L. (1964). *Conflict, decision, and dissonance.* Stanford, CA: Stanford University Press.
Fischer, P., Jonas, E., Frey, D., & Schulz-Hardt, S. (2006). Selective exposure to information: The impact of information limits. *European Journal of Social Psychology, 35,* 469–492.
Fischer, P., Schulz-Hardt, S. & Frey, D. (2005). *Preference for supporting vs. conflicting information: Amount of information as a moderator for selective exposure.* Unpublished manuscript, University of Munich.
Freedman, J. L. (1965). Confidence, utility and selective exposure: A partial replication. *Journal of Personality and Social Psychology, 2,* 778–780.
Freedman, J. L., & Sears, D. O. (1965). Selective exposure. In L. Berkowitz (Ed.). *Advances in experimental social psychology* (Vol. 2, pp. 57–97). New York: Academic Press.
Frey, D. (1981a). Postdecisional preferences for decision-relevant information as a function of the competence of its source and the degree of familiarity with this information. *Journal of Experimental Social Psychology, 17,* 621–626.
Frey, D. (1981b). The effect of negative feedback about oneself and cost of information on preferences for information about the source of this feedback. *Journal of Experimental Social Psychology, 17,* 42–50.

Frey, D. (1986). Recent research on selective exposure to information. In L. Berkowitz (Ed.), *Advances in experimental social psychology* (Vol. 19, pp. 41–80). New York: Academic Press.

Frey, D., Schulz-Hardt, S., & Stahlberg, D. (1996). Information seeking among individuals and groups and possible consequences for decision-making in business and politics. In E. Witte & J. Davis (Eds.), *Understanding group behavior, Vol. II: Small group processes and interpersonal relations* (pp. 211–225). Mahwah, NJ: Erlbaum.

Giner-Sorolla, R., & Chaiken, S. (1997). Selective use of heuristic and systematic processing under defense motivation. *Personality and Social Psychology Bulletin, 23,* 84–97.

Gollwitzer, P., & Bayer, U. (1999). Deliberative versus implemental mindsets in the control of action. In S. Chaiken, & Y. Trope (Eds.), *Dual-process theories in social psychology* (pp. 403–422). New York: Guilford.

Greenberg, J., Solomon, S., & Pyszczynski, T. (1997). Terror management theory of self-esteem and cultural worldviews: Empirical assessments and conceptual refinements. In M. P. Zanna (Ed.), *Advances in experimental social psychology* (Vol. 29, pp. 61–139). San Diego: Academic Press.

Greitemeyer, T., & Schulz-Hardt, S. (2003). Preference-consistent evaluation of information in the hidden profile paradigm: Beyond group-level explanations for the dominance of shared information in group decisions. *Journal of Personality and Social Psychology, 84,* 322–339.

Greitemeyer, T., Schulz-Hardt, S., & Frey, D. (2003). Präferenzkonsistenz und Geteiltheit von Informationen als Einflussfaktoren auf Informationsbewertung und intendiertes Diskussionsverhalten bei Gruppenentscheidungen. *Zeitschrift für Sozialpsychologie, 34,* 9–23.

Hastie, R., Penrod, S. D., & Pennington, N. (1983). *Inside the jury.* Cambridge, MA: Harvard University Press.

Henninger, M., Mandl, H., & Law, L.-C. (2001). Training von Reflexion [Training of reflection]. In K. J. Klauer (Ed.), *Handbuch Kognitives Training* (pp. 236–260). Göttingen: Hogrefe.

Hogarth, R. M., & Einhorn, H. J. (1992). Order effects in belief updating: The belief-adjustment model. *Cognitive Psychology, 24*, 1–55.

Holton, B., & Pyszczynski, T. (1989). Biased information search in the interpersonal domain. *Personality and Social Psychology Bulletin, 15,* 42–51.

Janis, I. L. (1982). *Groupthink* (2nd, rev. ed.). Boston: Houghton Mifflin.

Janis, I. L. (1989). *Crucial decisions: Leadership in policymaking and crisis management.* New York: Free Press.

Johnston, L. (1996). Resisting change: Information-seeking and stereotype change. *European Journal of Social Psychology, 26,* 799–825.

Jonas, E. (2006). Unpublished data. University of Duisburg-Essen, Germany.

Jonas, E., & Frey, D. (2003). Information search and presentation in advisor-client interactions. *Organizational Behavior and Human Decision Processes, 91,* 154–168.

Jonas, E., & Frey, D. (2006). *The influence of previous failure experience on the preference for supporting vs. conflicting information.* Unpublished manuscript, University of Munich.

Jonas, E., Frey, D., & Greenberg, J. (2005). *Decision vs. information focus in information seeking: Factors that affect the preference for supporting and conflicting information after decisions.* Manuscript submitted for publication.

Jonas, E., Frey, D., Henninger, M., Pommer, M., Schulz-Hardt, S., Haeften, I. v., & Mandl, H. (2001). Erklärung des eigenen Handelns als Einflussfaktor auf Informationssuche und Informationsbewertung in einer sequentiellen Lernsituation. [Explaining one's own behavior as a factor influencing information search and information evaluation in a sequential learning situation.] *Zeitschrift für Entwicklungspsychologie und Pädagogische Psychologie, 33,* 242–252.

Jonas, E., Graupmann, V., Fischer, P., Greitemeyer, T., & Frey, D. (2003). Schwarze Kassen, weiße Westen? – Konfirmatorische Informationssuche und -bewertung im Kontext der Parteispendenaffäre der CDU. [Illegal accounts but clean slates? – Confirmatory information search and evaluation in the context of the political party donation scandal in Germany.] *Zeitschrift für Soziapsychologie, 34,* 47–61.

Jonas, E., Greenberg, J., & Frey, D. (2003). Connecting terror management and dissonance theory: Evidence that mortality salience increases the preference for supporting information after decisions. *Personality and Social Psychology Bulletin, 29,* 1181–1189.

Jonas, E., Schulz-Hardt, S., & Frey, D. (2001). Konfirmatorische Informationssuche bei simultaner vs. sequentieller Informationsvorgabe. *Zeitschrift für Experimentelle Psychologie, 48,* 239–247.

Jonas, E., Schulz-Hardt, S., & Frey, D. (2005). Giving advice or making decisions in someone else's place – The influence of impression, defense and accuracy motivation on the search of new information. *Personality and Social Psychology Bulletin, 31,* 977–990.

Jonas, E., Schulz-Hardt, S., Frey, D., & Thelen, N. (2001). Confirmation bias in sequential information search after preliminary decisions: An expansion of dissonance theoretical research on "selective exposure to information". *Journal of Personality and Social Psychology, 80,* 557–571.

Kleinhesselink, R. R., & Edwards, R. E. (1975). Seeking and avoiding belief- discrepant information as a function of its perceived refutability. *Journal of Personality and Social Psychology, 31*, 787–790.

Koehler, J. J. (1993). The influence of prior beliefs on scientific judgments of evidence quality. *Organizational Behavior and Human Decision Processes, 56,* 28–55.

Kray, L. J., & Galinsky, A. D. (2003). The debiasing effect of counterfactual mind-sets: Increasing the search for disconfirmatory information in group decisions. *Organizational Behavior and Human Decision Processes, 91,* 69–81.

Kruglanski, A. W. (1989). *Lay epistemics and human knowledge.* New York: Plenum Press.

Kunda, Z. (1990). The case for motivated reasoning. *Psychological Bulletin, 108,* 480–498.

Levine, J. M., & Russo, E. (1995). Impact of anticipated interaction on information acquisition. *Social Cognition, 13,* 293–317.

Lord, C. G., Ross, L., & Lepper, M. R. (1979). Biased assimilation and attitude polarization: The effects of prior theories on subsequently considered evidence. *Journal of Personality and Social Psychology, 37,* 2098–2109.

Lowin, A. (1967). Approach and avoidance: Alternative models of selective exposure to information. *Journal of Personality and Social Psychology, 6*, 1– 9.

Lundgren, S. R., & Prislin, R. (1998). Motivated cognitive processing and attitude change. *Personality and Social Psychology Bulletin, 24,* 715–726.

McAllister, D. W., Mitchell, T. R., & Beach, L. R. (1979). The contingency model for the selection of decision strategies: An empirical test of the effects of significance, accountability, and reversibility. *Organizational Behavior and Human Performance, 24,* 228–244.

Nemeth, C. J., & Rogers, J. (1996). Dissent and the search for information. *British Journal of Social Psychology, 35,* 67–76.

Newby-Clark, I., McGregor, I. R., & Zanna, M. P. (2002). Thinking and caring about cognitive inconsistency: When and for whom does attitudinal ambivalence feel uncomfortable? *Journal of Personality and Social Psychology, 82,* 157–166.

Nisbett, R. E., & Ross, L. (1980). *Human inference: Strategies and shortcomings of social judgement.* Englewood Cliffs: NJ: Prentice Hall.

Payne, J. W., Bettman, J. R., & Johnson, E. J. (1993). *The adaptive decision maker.* Cambridge: University Press.

Pinkley, R. L., Griffith, T. L., & Northcraft, G. B. (1995). "Fixed pie" a la mode: Information availability, information processing, and the negotiation of suboptimal agreements. *Organizational Behavior and Human Decision Processes, 62,* 101–112.

Pyszczynski, T., & Greenberg, J. (1987). Toward an integration of cognitive and motivational perspectives on social inferences: A biased hypothesis-testing model. In L. Berkowitz (Ed.), *Advances in experimental social psychology* (Vol. 20, pp. 297–340). New York: Academic Press.

Russo, J. E., Medvec, V. H., & Meloy, M. G. (1996). The distortion of information during decisions. *Organizational Behavior and Human Decision Processes, 66,* 102–110.

Sanitioso, R., Kunda, Z., & Fong, G. T. (1990). Motivated recruitment of autobiographical memory. *Journal of Personality and Social Psychology, 59,* 229–241.

Schulz-Hardt, S. (1997). *Realitätsflucht in Entscheidungsprozessen: Von Groupthink zum Entscheidungsautismus.* [Loosing reality in decision processes: From groupthink to autistic decision making]. Bern: Huber.

Schulz-Hardt, S., Fischer, P., & Frey, D. (2006). *Confirmation bias in accuracy-motivated decision-making: A cognitive explanation for biased information seeking.* Unpublished manuscript, University of Göttingen.

Schulz-Hardt, S., Frey, D., Lüthgens, C., & Moscovici, S. (2000). Biased information search in group decision making. *Journal of Personality and Social Psychology, 78,* 655–669.

Schulz-Hardt, S., Jochims, M., & Frey, D. (2002). Productive conflict in group decision making: Genuine and contrived dissent as strategies to counteract biased information seeking. *Organizational Behavior and Human Decision Processes, 88,* 563–586.

Svenson, O. (1992). Differentiation and consolidation theory of human decision making: A frame of reference for the study of pre- and post decision processes. *Acta Psychologica, 80,* 143–168.

Schwarz, N., Frey, D., & Kumpf, M. (1980). Interactive effects of writing and reading a persuasive essay on attitude change and selective exposure. *Journal of Experimental Social Psychology, 16,* 1–17.

Snyder, M., & White, P. (1981). Testing hypotheses about other people: Strategies of verification and falsification. *Personality and Social Psychology Bulletin, 7,* 39–43.

Stone, J., Aronson, E., Crain, A. L., Winslow, M. P., & Fried, C. B. (1994). Inducing hypocrisy as a means of encouraging young adults to use condoms. *Personality and Social Psychology Bulletin, 1,* 116–128.

Sweeney, P. D., & Gruber, K. L. (1984). Selective exposure: Voter information preferences and the Watergate affair. *Journal of Personality and Social Psychology, 46,* 1208–1221.

Tetlock, P. E. (1992). The impact of accountability on judgment and choice: Toward a social contingency model. *Advances in experimental social psychology, 25,* 331–376.

Trope, Y., & Liberman, A. (1996). Social hypothesis testing: Cognitive and motivational mechanisms. In E. T. Higgins & A. W. Kruglanski (Eds). *Social psychology – handbook of basic principles* (pp. 239–270). New York: Guilford.

von Haeften, I. D. (1999). *Das Golden Casket Paradigma: Der Zusammenhang zwischen Informationssuche und Fehlentscheidungen bei unvollständigem Informationsraum.* [The golden casket paradigm: the relationship between search for information and bad decisions under limited information] Aachen, Germany: Shaker.

White, S. E., Dittrich, J. E., & Lang, J. R. (1980). The effects of group decision-making procedures and problem-situation complexity on implementational attempts. *Administrative Science Quarterly, 25,* 428–440.

Wicklund, R. A., & Frey, D. (1981). Cognitive consistency: Motivational vs. nonmotivational perspectives. In J. Forgas (Ed.), *Social cognition: Perspectives on everyday understanding* (pp. 141–163). London: Academic Press.

Zanna, M. P., Lepper, M. R., & Abelson, R. P. (1973). Attentional mechanisms in children's devaluation of a forbidden activity in a forced-compliance situation. *Journal of Personality and Social Psychology, 28,* 355–359.

Fostering Reflection in the Training of Speech-Receptive Action

Michael Henninger & Heinz Mandl

Soft skills – fostering of speech-receptive action

The term "soft skills" is a label which includes those skills and qualifications exceeding the "hard skills" of a job. Whereas hard skills describe the qualifications directly related to the job, soft skills involve qualifications like teamwork, creativity, self-management, the ability to learn, flexibility, problem-solving, and, most importantly, communicative skills (Picot, Reichwald, & Wigand, 1996). This article focuses on the training of communicative behavior – i.e., the underlying cognitive actions – by fostering reflective processes. Most concepts designed to foster communicative behavior are realized in face-to-face settings. Interactive exercises, role plays, and group discussions are the dominant instructional techniques which are applied in the training of communicative behavior (Brons-Albert, 1995; Fittkau & Schulz von Thun, 1994; Günther & Sperber, 1995). The learner's performance in exercises and role plays is the focus of reflection and feedback. Yet, mostly it is only the observable part of performance which is addressed and discussed (Jaskolski, 1999). Communicative behavior, however, consists of two parts: speech-productive action (i.e., speaking), which is the more observable part of communicative behavior, and speech-receptive action (i.e., hearing and understanding utterances), which occurs more often and which is a more covert process inside the person (Herrmann, 1992; Rummer, 1996).

Speech-productive parts of communicative behavior are mostly focused by training concepts due to the fact that they are more observable than the speech-receptive parts (Brons-Albert, 1995). Speech-receptive action occurs more covertly inside the person and consists of individual cognitive skills, which are hardly accessible. Thus, conventional forms of communication training are not applicable for the fostering of speech-receptive skills because they depend on the observability and accessibility of speech-related action. In this article, we will show that software can help in reflecting and changing not directly accessible and visible parts of social skills. To illustrate what this kind of software might look like, we describe a computer-based learning environment which is designed to train the individual cognitive skills of speech-receptive behavior. By embedding the software into communication training, it is possible to foster both parts of communicative behavior – speech reception and speech production.

As mentioned above, the individual and not observable part of communication, the speech-receptive behavior is rarely targeted in communication training concepts. Training approaches dealing with speech-receptive action mainly aim at fostering active listening, which is in fact a hybrid between speech-receptive and speech-productive action. Active listening means listening to the other person carefully and then paraphrasing or asking questions with the intention of a deep understanding of what the other has meant to convey with his or her utterance (Frey, 2000; Hargie, Saunders, & Dickson, 1994; Schulz von Thun, 1994). Thus, it implies to give the other person feedback about what one has understood. This form of feedback is the topic of exercises and reflection in training concepts which aim at fostering active listening. Giving feedback, however, is a form of speech-productive action, even if it is based on speech-receptive action. Thus, it is again the more observable part of communicative behavior, which is at the center of those training approaches. The individual cognitive processes of understanding utterances again are more or less neglected.

The individual cognitive processes involved in speech-receptive action occur on different levels. According to psycholinguistic theories (Herrmann, 1992), the processes hereby involved range from the perception of acoustic elements via the semantic identification of words and syntactical identification of grammatical structures to the pragmatic interpretation of utterances. For the training of communicative behavior, higher-order skills of speech-receptive action like the pragmatic interpretation of utterances are more relevant. Looking at various psycholinguistic models, one can find that they all postulate different pragmatic aspects of meaning, which implies that an utterance can have several different connotations. These different aspects of meaning can be found in every single utterance and thus can be the basis of interpretations. Interpretations of utterances focusing on the different connotations, however, can often be the cause of misunderstandings. This may be illustrated by an example:

> In a car nearing a crossing, the following dialog takes place:
> *The husband says to his wife who is driving the car: "The traffic lights are red." As a reaction to this statement his wife explodes: "You always tell me how to drive. I'm able to drive without you constantly intervening. If you don't have confidence in the way I drive, you might as well walk home!"*

If we have a look at this scene, we see that the situation escalated rapidly. What seems to have happened is that the woman felt criticized by her husband's remark, and that this particular understanding of his utterance caused her to react rather aggressively. In order to avoid such aggressive reactions that might lead to a conflict, it seems necessary to develop a more differentiated understanding of utterances. This implies that the speech-receptive skill includes differentiating between the various aspects of meaning contained in an utterance into account. In order to develop such a differentiated and reflected understanding, the learners need to be able to analyze speech utterances according to different aspects of meaning. But which aspects of meaning should be differentiated? According to which criteria? There are several models which can be found in the literature. Among the most prominent approaches are the models of Bühler (1934), Watzlawick, Beavin, and Jackson (1967) and Schulz von Thun (1994).

Karl Bühler (1934) postulated three different aspects of speech in every utterance: what the speaker says about himself (expression), about what objects or facts the speaker informs the listener (representation), and what the speaker wants the listener to do or to think (appeal).

Watzlawick et al. (1967) made a distinction between two aspects of interpersonal communication by differentiating between the content of an utterance and what is said about the interpersonal relationship of the conversational partners.

The German psychologist Schulz von Thun (1994) combined the models of Bühler and Watzlawick and colleagues (1967) and postulated four different aspects of human language: the aspect of interpersonal relationship, the aspect of representation, the aspect of self-expression, and the aspect of appeal.

In our training approach for fostering a differentiated understanding of speech utterances (see below), the participants learn how to analyze speech utterances according to the model of Bühler (1934). An earlier version of the learning environment worked with the model of Schulz von Thun (1994) but the problem was that the four levels could not be clearly distinguished by the learners. The model of Watzlawik et al. (1967) exceeds individual cognitive processes, because it pays attention to the level of interpersonal relationship. This level involves the mutual background and history of the conversation partners, which is difficult to analyze for an outsider. Since our aim is to foster the individual cognitive processes of speech-receptive action, the theoretical framework of Bühler (1934) was chosen as a consequence: This model provides a comprehensive and rather practicable model of the different levels or functions of human language and it is based on individual cognitive processes.

In everyday life, communicative behavior occurs quickly and the individual rarely has to think about how to speak or how to understand utterances. This is due to the fact that the underlying communicative skills are highly automated (Antos, 1996; Herrmann, 1992; Leontiev, 1981). This way, the individual is able to understand utterances even in complicated and stressful situations like debates or controversies without having to think about how to do this. The automaticity of communicative behavior enables the use of language in complex situations, but also makes communicative behavior difficult to change. According to the literature (Antos, 1992; Leontiev, 1981; Schooler, Ohlsson, & Brooks, 1993), automated skills can be de-automated by bringing the steps of action into consciousness. The de-automated skills can subsequently be changed by reflecting the own action. In order to allow the learner to "function" in everyday life, the skills then have to be re-automated again. This can be achieved by repeatedly training and exercising the acquired or modified skills (Hacker, 1998; Leontiev, 1981). In short, due to the automaticity of communicative behavior the following steps are necessary for changing it:

- bringing the actual action into consciousness
- **reflecting one's own action**
- exercising and training the new forms of communicative behavior, i.e., speech receptive and speech productive action.

Since reflection is a central aspect in bringing knowledge into action, we will explicate this cognitive activity. After the following section on reflection, we will focus on our specific training concept of soft skills, where reflection plays an important role in changing communicative behavior.

Theoretical models of reflection

Questioning one's thinking and acting, reflecting thoughts and behavior can be considered important in coping with complex problems and tasks (e.g., constructing a house, negotiating). The self-reflexivity of thinking is often even emphasized as the characteristic that distinguishes humans from other creatures. Since reflection is regarded to be crucial for human cognitive functioning, it seems reasonable to wonder in how far it is possible to train reflection as a skill. In order to analyze this question in detail, we will first describe the theoretical approaches to reflection.

For Dewey (1925/1981, 1933/1986), reflection is a form of thinking triggered by the doubt and perplexity perceived in a situation, and results in problem solution in the light of previous experiences. According to Vygotsky's (1978; 1987/1998) definition, reflection is the transferal of argumentation from a social level to an internal one. Schön (1987) describes reflection as an internal dialogue of thinking and acting through which performance can be enhanced. The reasons for the differences in the definitions of reflection lie in the varying temporal dimensions of reflection, i.e., reflection can refer to present times but it can also be anticipative or retrospective in nature.

Reflection is a dynamical cognitive process that can link past, present, and future activities. Reflection enables planning before action, which makes it possible for the acting person to revise or regulate the prospective course of activity. This kind of proactive reflection can prepare the agent for a wide range of unforeseen contingencies. During action, reflection can optimize the course of activity and at the same time enable a progress of learning. After action, reflection provides a basis for evaluating the activities performed. Additionally, reflection can foster the transfer of insight and knowledge from previous experiences to future actions in different situations. Reflection can also facilitate knowledge transfer by supporting the de-contextualization of knowledge. Furthermore, the awareness of the characteristics of acquired cognitive strategies and their applicability in a novel situation can be increased by reflection. In sum, reflection plays a regulatory, adaptive, integrative, organizational, anticipatory as well as evaluative role in cognitive activities.

In this paper, the following elements are regarded as fundamental for reflection: consciousness of thought and action, contextualized problem-settings, problem-relevant experiences, and possibilities for action. With these components, an operational definition is formulated: Reflection is a process during which a person pays attention to a problem, evaluates this problem on the background of a previously set goal and of his/her past experiences, generates options for action, relates the expectable outcomes of these options to the present situation, and makes decisions for future actions with the aim of solving the problem.

The wide definition of the term reflection makes it difficult to choose and present the ideas of authors who have dealt with this subject. After all, the subject of reflection concerns all fields of psychology and extends to philosophy. The presentation below will therefore be restricted to three models that are closely linked to one another and roughly mirror the temporal development of the deliberations on reflection. The starting point will be Dewey's work "How we think" (1933/1986), which is considered to be the basis for the present research on thinking. Dewey's contemplations can be related to those of Vygotsky (1978), who considers the development of higher-level cognitive skills to be mediated by social interactions, i.e., through the use of speech and other cultural tools.

The latest and most comprehensive analysis of reflection has been provided by Schön (1983, 1987; Schön & Rein, 1994). All three social-constructivist theories share the assumption that knowledge and action are social in nature and situated in specific contexts with respect to their origin, organization, and application. While Dewey's theory is mostly philosophically oriented, Schön includes Vygotsky's considerations of the guided interaction of teachers and students in his work and thereby extends Dewey's model. Thus, practical approaches can be derived from the theoretical ideas.

Reflective inquiry: Dewey's pragmatic view of reflection

Dewey is considered a key figure with respect to the concept of reflection. Historically, his works root in the conjectures of famous philosophers like Socrates, Plato and Locke. For Dewey, reflection can be understood as a form of special thinking involving active chaining of evolving ideas and is caused by a "state of doubt, hesitation, perplexity, mental difficulty, in which thinking originates" (1933/1986, p. 121). With regard to the topic of this book, knowledge and action, the role of reflection can be described as a process of regulating the dialectic relationship between knowing and acting. Judging by its function, reflective thinking is a tool for problem-solving. It can be seen as a cycle of repeated inquiry about one's thinking and acting. This process of inquiry is a goal-oriented impulse in order to determine a course of actions in such a way that the instability perceived in a situation can be counteracted. According to Dewey, there exist two types of inquiry: perceptual and reflective. Perceptual inquiry means adapting to perceptive constraints of a situation and leads to situation-specific ad hoc actions. Reflective inquiry entails the manipulation of the person's inner symbolic representations and leads to reflected actions (Burke, 1994; Dewey, 1933/1986). However, this dichotomization of thinking into reflective and non-reflective thinking, the latter in the sense of idle and chaotic thinking, seems to be problematic. Reflection is probably not a bi-polar process, but ought to be conceived as a continuum (Kompf & Bond, 1995). It seems evident that non-reflective and reflective thinking are complementary rather than mutually exclusive (Korthagen, 1993). According to Dewey, reflective behavior is a consequence of sustained doubts about one's thinking or acting and integration of this reflection process into further inquiries. Dewey specified three attitudes required for reflection: The inquirer should be open-minded for new information, truly interested in the subject, and prepared to take the responsibility for his or her actions.

Dewey considers speech as a particularly important tool for reflection: "being the tool of tools, [it] is the cherishing mother of all significance" (Dewey, 1933/1986, p. 146). Reflective thinking is represented by linguistic expression. In correspondence with Dewey's pragmatic social behaviorism (Garrison, 1995), communication and action in a social setting can be regarded as external manifestations of reflective thinking. Dewey distinguishes reflective thinking, which leads to planned action, from non-reflective thinking, which results in impulsive action. Based on Dewey's original model (Baron, 1981), five phases of reflective thinking can be derived: (1) problem recognition; (2) specification of possibilities for new actions or beliefs; (3) evaluation of these possibilities by drawing on memory, questioning or experimenting; (4) revision of the possibilities; (5) decision-making of whether to continue to look for evidence or to carry out one of the found possibilities. These phases which can vary in their duration depending on the type of inquiry can overlap in time.

Dewey's deliberations about reflective thinking make it necessary to analyze the reciprocal relationship between the agent and the world. In particular, his conviction that the mind has a social origin bears important implications for the development of a cooperative learning paradigm. Dewey (1938/1986) considers reflection a tendency that can be influenced by values, expectations, and habits. This view implies that reflective inquiry ought to be included in the process of education and development as early as possible and should be supported throughout school and adult life. The attitudinal variables mentioned above (open-mindedness, interest, responsibility) as well as the skills concerning the phases of reflection (problem recognition, specification of options, evaluation, revision, decision) could be starting points for fostering reflection. To verbalize and explain thinking or action are particularly important tools for promoting reflection.

Self-regulated learning: Vygotsky's sociolinguistic perspective on reflection

Vygotsky's theory of development (1978, 1987/1998), as one of the pillars upon which constructivist learning theories are built, addresses the question of how psychological processes or metacognitive skills can be fostered. Thereby, particular emphasis is placed on the importance of self-regulation as a crucial educational goal. Vygotsky considers reflection as self-regulation, a skill that is developed as follows: First, the individual experiences a regulation by others, which occurs in the zone of proximal development. Learning is facilitated by adult guidance or collaboration with more capable peers. Vygotsky emphasizes that conscious awareness is an essential pre-condition for this kind of learning influenced by modeling. Through this special mode of social interaction in the zone of proximal development, the form and content of self-regulation are gradually transferred from the more competent partner and internalized by the learner. The Vygotskian view also stresses that sociolinguistic experience is indispensable for the development of metacognition and that intersubjectivity is a primary means for knowledge construction. This implies that reflection can strongly be facilitated by modeling and verbal communication. Vygotsky claims that reflection plays a mediating role by transforming meaningful experiences into abstracted knowledge. These developmental transformations are enabled by verbal communication, i.e., inner speech of the learner supports the internalization of socially mediated problem solutions by re-formulating or explaining the perceived problem solutions in own words. Reflection has a strong impact on self-regulative strategies like planning, self-monitoring, self-evaluation, and self-corrective behavior. By assuming a social origin of learning – in other words the co-construction of knowledge – Vygotsky answers the question how complex cognitive competencies emerge from less complex skills.

Like Dewey (1933/1986), Vygotsky regarded speech as the most potent cultural tool in achieving convergence of meaning and co-construction of knowledge during social interaction. The dialectic relationship and the reciprocal transformations between intra- and interpsychological processes are central ideas of Vygotsky's theory. According to this approach, high-level cognitive processes like reflection develop through continual, dynamic interactions between the agent and the world. Furthermore, Vygotsky assumes that not only the content but also the form of psychological processes changes dynamically in the course of the ontogenetic development.

Reflective practitioner: Schön's communicative view of reflection

In the contemporary domain of professional education, Schön's (1983, 1987) notion of the "reflective practitioner" has an impact on many fields, including teacher education (e.g., Grimmet & Erickson, 1988), social work education (e.g., Hallett, 1997), or managerial training (e.g., Daudelin, 1996). Schön claims that reflection *on* action and reflection *in* action should more strongly be considered as essential factors for the development of professional artistry. This professional artistry refers to the embodied expertise that practitioners demonstrate in problematic situations of practice. Reflection *on* action means thinking back on the action already accomplished or pausing in the midst of an action to "stop-and-think" (i.e., offline). Reflection *in* action, on the other hand, occurs while an action is being undertaken (i.e., online) and implies moment-by-moment "active experimentation." Generally, reflection *in* action is conceptually more complex, developmentally more mature, and functionally more significant than reflection *on* action (see Schön, 1983, 1987). According to Schön, an internship is a good example for a learning situation that enables reflection: The participation in an expert culture on a trial basis[1]. Yet, the effectiveness of an internship mainly depends on the social interactions between the students and experts. Particularly important are reciprocally reflective dialogues between the coaching expert and the student. This view of externally initiated self-reflection can also be found in the works of Dörner (1976, 1979, 1982) and Putz-Osterloh (1985). They both emphasize that self-reflection, i.e., reflecting one's own thoughts, actions, or the results of one's actions, can be encouraged by others. The learner is either asked to reflect on something at a specific time or another person interrupts his/her actions with questions and thus causes the reflection. Through this kind of communication, the involved persons can gradually bring their interpretations of the concepts concerned in line. According to Schön, the development of professional artistry can be depicted as three phases: technical rationality, reflection *on* action, and reflection *in* action. Each of these phases is characterized by certain verbal and behavioral performances. Schön writes for instance about the particularly important reflection *in* action: "... when practitioners reflect in action, they describe their own intuitive understanding" (Schön, 1983, p. 276). According to Schön, the reflection of one's actions includes the perception, the framing and the reframing of the problem with respect to the inquirer's repertoire of relevant knowledge and experiences, and eventually the generation of new possibilities for action. It needs to be mentioned that the skills which are decisive for successful reflection *on* action and reflection *in* action generally are very similar to the skills of thinking and problem-solving. There exists a range of approaches as to how these skills can be fostered (see Bransford, Sherwood, & Sturdevant, 1987; Lipman, 1987), but they will not be presented here.

Summary of the three theories on reflection

From the arguments of the three scholars certain general features of reflection can be extracted. First, reflection entails consciousness, experience, and action. Second, reflection is stimulated by a problem and the context in which it is embedded. Third, reflection is developmental in nature. It can be portrayed as Dewey's evolutionary view about per-

[1] There are relations to the concept of "legitimate peripheral participation" by Lave and Wenger (1991).

ceptual and reflective inquiry (Dewey, 1933/1986), or Vygotsky's transformation from social dialogue to inner speech. Schön (1987) describes three phases of the emergence of professional artistry from reflection (technical qualification, reflection *on* action, reflection *in* action). Fourth, reflection can be fostered: All three authors claim that reflective processes are supported by verbal activities, e.g., verbalizations or self-explanations, and by giving modeling cues related to action. Sixth, reflection is recursive or cyclical in nature. This feature of reflection becomes particularly evident in Dewey's five phases and in Schön's framing and reframing of the problem concerned.

The description of the three approaches makes clear that reflection is of high significance for cognitive problem-solving activities and for changing automated action. Therefore, the question as to how these theoretical ideas can be transferred into practice is not only relevant from a scientific but also from a pragmatic point of view. In the following sections, we will sketch instructional possibilities for fostering reflection and thereafter introduce a training concept for this goal of fostering reflection.

Instructional conditions for a training of reflection

The three theoretical models described above focus on the central role of social guidance and negotiation processes for fostering reflection. These "social processes" as well as the reflection itself are strongly influenced by speech. Yet, it remains unclear which consequences could be drawn for the support or training of reflection. Concrete instructional suggestions can be found in the approaches of situated learning since they also deal with reflection (see Henninger, Mandl, Pommer, & Linz, 1999). The basic assumption of situated learning is that cognition and context, knowledge and action, individual and sociocultural development cannot be separated. Situated learning can, for example, mean that a novice is introduced into a "community of practice" or that the acquisition of skills is supported by coaching, modeling, and reflected imitation of experts (Collins & Brown, 1988; see Vygotsky's concept of the zone of proximal development). The situated learning principles relevant for the support of reflection will be explained below. Subsequently, the method of modeling will be analyzed with respect to the training of reflection. And finally, the potentials of new media for this purpose will be dealt with.

Principles of situated learning approaches

Since the approaches of situated learning emphasize reflection as a main learning principle (e.g., Bransford, Franks, Vye, & Sherwood, 1989; Collins, 1996; Gerstenmaier & Mandl, 1999), it seems reasonable to investigate them in order to derive suggestions for the support of reflection. The following instructional approaches of situated learning concentrate on different aspects: According to Bransford's *anchored instruction approach* (Bransford et al., 1989; Cognition and Technology Group at Vanderbilt, 1992, 1993, 1994), a "narrative anchor" is particularly important for learning. The *cognitive flexibility theory* (Spiro, Feltovich, Jacobson, & Coulson, 1992) underlines the significance of multiple perspectives. The *cognitive apprenticeship approach* (Collins, Brown, & Newman, 1989) applies the principles that have long been successful within the training of craftsmen to the systematic teaching of cognitive skills.

From these situated approaches to learning, especially from the cognitive apprenticeship approach (Collins et al., 1989), principles for the design of learning environments can be extracted. They refer to content, sequencing, social embedding, and teaching methods. Here, we will concentrate on those methods that seem to be especially appropriate for fostering reflection: *modeling*, *coaching*, *articulation* and *exploration*.

For *modeling*, the expert needs to externalize the internal cognitive processes while carrying out a certain activity. This makes the individual steps of thinking and learning for the learner tangible and comprehensible. *Coaching* is a method that requires the expert to carry out several activities, for example, giving feedback, providing support (e.g., cues for the problem solution), and offering new problem settings. In this way, the learner is supported in gradually approaching the level of the expert's problem-solving skills. *Articulation* comprises all methods that aim at the learner's communication of his/her cognitive processes and knowledge with the purpose of refining them. *Exploration* is a method that induces the learner to tackle a problem by him- or herself and also to pursue own goal settings. In the end, the training of reflection will be successful only after the learner's successful completion of an exploration phase, i.e., if he or she succeeded in regulating their reflection processes and actions by themselves.

Role modeling as a method for fostering reflection

There is a big variety of cognitive strategies that can facilitate reflection. The effectiveness of these strategies not only depends on their features, but also on how skillful the user can apply these strategies. The modeling method for fostering reflection, which was already mentioned above in the context of situated learning environments, can involve problems. First, modeling does not guarantee that the learner really learns reflective thinking. If a big imbalance between the expert's and the learner's knowledge exists (Jarvis, 1987), this method might lead to cognitive overload on part of the learner (Sweller, 1988). The modeling does not lead to learning success either, when the learner pays attention to irrelevant aspects of the expert's actions or misinterprets them. Possible differences between the expert and the learner in the way of reflecting can also lead to difficulties. It was shown that an expert's reflection includes the profound structure of problem solutions, whereas the reflection of learners, who are less familiar with a domain, is based on rather superficial features (hierarchies of reflection: Hatton & Smith, 1995). Comprehension gaps of the learner can, on the one hand, be supportive in that they induce cognitive conflicts that motivate the creation or modification of knowledge. On the other hand, the gaps can be so immense that the learner is incapable of following the expert. In order to prevent or minimize comprehension problems and to help the learner represent and externalize his or her thoughts, it could be useful to guide the learner by individual support according to the cognitive apprenticeship approach (e.g., coaching, see Collins et al., 1989).

Use of new media for the training of reflection

Reflection as a complex cognitive activity seems predestined to be supported by new media. The increased access to information, the possibility to externalize cognitive activities, as well as the documentation of reflective thinking, all of which can, for example, be achieved with computer programs, can facilitate, deepen, and expand reflection. In the following, we will elaborate on the technological aspects of tutorial support of reflection, the question concerning the modality of the offered information, aspects of collaboration within the framework of new media, and the accessibility of information.

Tutorial support

An important field for the use of new media is tutoring. In correspondence with Vygotsky's concept of the zone of proximal development and Schön's "reflective internship" (1987; Schön & Rein, 1994), it is assumed that one tutor per learner presents the most effective means to foster reflection. This method is most costly, of course. In order to make use the advantages of this method, yet with less efforts and costs, so-called virtual tutors were developed. By now, this form of tutoring has been so much refined that it can compete with physically present tutors (see Anderson and the ACT* group, 1995). Fundamental for both forms of tutoring is that learners receive prompt feedback. The use of new media in this respect is mainly restricted to well-structured domains such as algebra, geometry, and programming (see Geyken, Mandl, & Reiter, 1995). Whether virtual tutors can also be implemented into less well-structured domains such as reading and writing still has to be investigated empirically.

Choice of modality of information offer

Through the use of new media the possibilities for information have strongly been increased, yet the choice of a modality of information (textual, auditory, visual, or multimodal) for a specific target group remains a challenge. A large part of the information is still presented in the textual modality (see Heflich, 1997; Henninger et al., 1999; Hoel & Gudmundsdóttir, 1996). If learners are supposed to externalize their reflections, those whose capability of expression is limited are discriminated against. An alternative in this respect is the auditory modality, i.e., the recording of the learners' verbal reflections. In the development of instructional designs, the interindividual variations in the use of the different modalities have been neglected so far. Consequently, disadvantageous effects can show in learning with multimedia if a learner is forced to use information in a representation system that is not apt for her or him (Mayer, 1997). Although visual forms of representation proved particularly suitable for the acquisition of abstract concepts because they induce profound reflection processes (see Collins & Brown, 1988; Stenning & Oberlander, 1995), their undifferentiated use can nevertheless cause a fixation of the learner on certain problem-solving strategies (see Greene & Petre, 1992). Furthermore, the advantages and disadvantages of synchronous and asynchronous communication have to be considered. Synchronous communication enables a constant flow of ideas and immediate feedback, whereas asynchronous communication leaves more time for organizing and reflecting the ideas. On the other hand, the latter form of communication could lead to misunderstandings and disruptions in comprehension because of the lack of immediate feedback.

Collaborative modality of reflection

Collaborative learning is well compatible with the approaches on the fostering of reflection. The articulation of one's reflection and the exchange with others support the creation and clarification of own thoughts. Particularly the use of video-mediated communication can promote the impression of co-presence (Dillenbourg, 1999; Finn, Sellen, & Wilbur, 1997), which is a main fundament for the negotiation process (Clark & Brennan, 1991). One of the advantages of discussion groups is that their members can draw on different knowledge backgrounds and take up different views, which can give impulses to reflection.

Increased accessibility of information

If a learning environment – as for example our web-based training tool CaiManOnline©[2] – offers connectivity to the Worldwide Web, learners have access to a tremendous wealth of information that can serve as a basis for reflection. Yet, a sensible use of such information requires a high reflective ability. Especially for novices, whose domain-specific knowledge often is still poor, it is difficult to make use of the potentials of new media. Therefore, it would be advantageous to provide the learners with additional tutorial and/or technological services so that they can find and use the relevant information (Roschelle & Pea, 1999).

Reflection as a tool for changing soft skills *with software*

An examination of the literature leads to the conclusion that the theoretical models and instructional approaches described above have had a strong influence on the design of trainings of reflection (see Brown & Palincsar, 1989; Francis, 1995; Friedman & Lipshitz, 1992; Heflich, 1997; Henninger, 1999; Henninger & Mandl, 2000; Hoel & Gudmundsdóttir, 1996; Lehtinen & Repo, 1996; Scardamalia & Bereiter, 1987; Schoenfeld, 1985; Zeichner & Liston, 1987). In the following paragraphs, we will present our approach for the support of reflection in the training of soft skills, which was mentioned in the sections above.

The learning environment CaiMan©[3] aims at fostering a differentiated analysis of conversational utterances on the basis of the model of Karl Bühler (1934). The learners should not only gain knowledge about the model of Bühler but learn to apply it as well. Yet, it is easier to gain knowledge about communicative behavior than to change the actual action in everyday situations (Henninger & Mandl, 2000). This means that the learner often knows which action might be effective and adequate in certain situations but is not able to perform this action and reverts to an older, rather dysfunctional action. One of the reasons for the described gap between the knowledge about action and the actual performance of this behavior can be the automaticity of communicative behavior (Antos, 1996; Herrmann, 1992; Leontiev, 1981). To change automated action you first have to bring aspects of this action into consciousness, for example, single processes or results of the automated action.

One possibility for bringing automated cognitive processes like speech receptive or productive action into consciousness is to verbalize them (Schooler et al., 1993). With respect to the de-automation of speech-receptive action this means that the learners should verbalize what they have understood. The reflection of these processes can be supported

2 For further information, see http://www.caimanonline.de
3 "CaiMan" stands for "computer-aided multimedia applications."

by supplying the learners with other solutions like those of an expert, for example. The learners can compare their own verbalized solutions with the expert's solutions and thus gain a basis for their reflection (Henninger & Mandl, 2000).

It seems difficult, however, to bring speech-receptive processes into consciousness, reflect them, and to take part in a conversation at the same time. All these processes together would cause too high a cognitive load for the learner (Rummer, 1996). To lower the cognitive load for the learner, it is necessary to reduce the cognitive tasks which the learner has to deal with while changing his or her action. In the case of speech-receptive action, these tasks are: remembering the utterance, explicating one's own analysis, revising and refining the analysis, and comparing it with an expert's solutions. Only the relevant tasks should be "in the mind" of the learner. Less relevant tasks, like remembering the utterances or the own analysis, could be taken over by using software.

For the fostering of de-automation and reflection, computer programs can serve as cognitive tools (Jonassen, 1992; Mandl, Gruber, & Renkl, 1995) by supporting cognitive processing and sharing "the cognitive burden of carrying out an intellectual task" (Salomon, 1993, p. 182). By storing the learner's solutions, for example, the computer can relieve the learner of this cognitive burden of having to remember his/her solution and the learner can thus focus on reflecting his or her solution. This reflection can be supported by supplying the learner with the opportunity to compare his/her own solution with the solution of an expert. By supporting the reflection of one's own action, computer-supported learning environments can help to de-automate this action.

Software can also be employed when it comes to re-automation. Re-automation can be achieved by training and exercising the acquired or changed skills, a task for which computer programs have been used since their early days (Kremer & Sloane, 1998; Mandl et al., 1995). Thus, computer programs can help the learner to carry out those activities which have been identified as central for changing communicative behavior.

Summarizing the points above, a computer-supported learning environment which is designed to foster speech-receptive action has to support the **de-automation** of the action by:

- supporting the learner in bringing his/her own action into consciousness,
- supporting the reflection of the learner's action,
- reducing the cognitive load caused by reflection.

The **re-automation** of communicative behavior can be supported by:

- providing the learner with the opportunity to repeatedly exercise the changed or newly acquired action processes.

In the following section we will take a closer look at the possibilities and limitations of software programs for the training of communicative behavior.

Software for the training of communicative behavior?

We have seen that instructional reasons suggest the use of software to help foster more differentiated analyses of speech utterances. As discussed above, computer-supported learning environments can support the de- and re-automation of communicative behavior. Yet, for many learners it does not seem natural to foster communicative behavior and other soft skills with the help of computers. Just as other soft skills, communicative behavior is social in nature and is a part of human interaction. According to a situated view of learning, skills should be taught in the setting they are embedded in in everyday life or at least in settings which come as close as possible to the respective real-life context (Collins et al., 1989; Greeno & The Middle School Mathematics Through Application Project Group, 1998; Law, 2000). Thus, communicative behavior – i.e., the underlying action processes – should be fostered in the setting it is applied in: human interaction.

According to Barron (1998) the shortcomings of multimedia products for the training of soft skills lie in their inability to depict the complexity of social interaction. He hopes that these shortcomings can be overcome by the progress in technical development, which enables more complex simulations of social interactions as well as more interactivity for the learner. This might be true to some extent but it seems doubtful if computer simulations will ever come close to the authenticity of real social settings in face-to-face training situations.

A different view regarding the use of software for the training of soft skills is the integration of the software into course settings. The advantages of both – classroom learning and computer-supported learning – can thus be combined. The trainer can focus on training social situations, face-to-face discussions, on exercises and on giving feedback on the contributions of the learners, whereas the software can be used to train the individual cognitive skills underlying the social competencies (Cohen & Rustad, 1998).

A growing number of authors state that the use of computer-supported learning environments makes most sense if these learning environments are integrated into curricula and combined with co-operative and other forms of learning (Glowalla & Häfele, 1997; Kerres, 2000). By carrying out time-consuming cognitive activities with the help of computer-supported learning environments, time can be gained for cooperative classroom activities (DeCorte, 1994, 1996). Kerres (2000) argues for the use of hybrid learning arrangements. This term "hybrid learning arrangements" stands for a combination of computer-supported learning environments and other forms of teaching and training. Another term used for this type of learning arrangements is "blended learning concepts" (Barbian, 2002). This combination should be designed on the basis of didactic concepts. According to his view, medial learning arrangements are meant to be part of didactic problem solutions. Reusser (1993) states that computer programs should be used in education "as supportive cognitive tools in the service of explicit pedagogical goals" (p. 145). The software should be designed on the basis of a cognitive analysis of curricular tasks and processes. Schofield (1999) also stresses the importance of explicit educational goals to determine where and how the use of computers is likely to be most effective. Her claim is that "we need to think more carefully about exactly how computer use can change instruction and when and where such changes are most likely to promote valued outcomes" (p. 174). This means that software should not be used in an unreflected way, but that it should be integrated as a tool in order to reach specific instructional goals.

To summarize, the authors quoted above demand that the integration of computer-supported learning environments into classroom settings and collaborative forms of learning should depend on an explicit cognitive analysis of the curricular tasks and instructional goals. This cognitive analysis includes a detailed description of the subject matter (van Merrienboer, 1997). The learning goals and, subsequently, the learning activities can be determined after classifying and describing the specific skills and types of knowledge relevant in the subject matter.

Looking at the domain communication (see above) two major aspects have to be taken into account: a) the division of communicative behavior in speech-receptive and speech-productive action. b) The high automation of the underlying cognitive processes. The first aspect makes it necessary to offer both individual and social forms of learning. The second point requires a learning scenario which allows de- and re-automation of communicative processes. We consider these aspects in our training concept, which integrates a multimedia learning environment into a face-to-face course setting. In the following section, we present the integration of our computer-supported learning environment CaiMan© into a face-to-face training of communicative behavior and describe it in closer detail.

Training speech-receptive action with the aid of the computer-supported learning environment CaiMan©

Integrating CaiMan© into a communication training

Communicative behavior does not only consist of speech-receptive processes, which are fostered with the help of the computer-supported learning environment CaiMan©, but also of speech-productive processes (Hermann, 1992). In order to profit from the fostered speech-receptive skills, the learners have to be able to employ these skills in social interactions – by reacting to the utterances they now are able to analyze in a more differentiated way. As shown above, the observable communicative behavior in social interactions is best trained in face-to-face settings. Due to this reason, the learning sessions with the computer-supported learning environment CaiMan© are framed by two face-to-face training modules, each with a duration of two days. The schedule of the training is depicted in Figure 1.

The first face-to-face group session aims at sensitizing the learners for communicative processes. With the help of various exercises, the learners consciously experience their own communicative behavior and reflect upon their performance. The last exercise of the first group session aims at demonstrating the difficulties and the problems that arise when analyzing and understanding the utterances of others, thus making the learning goal of the computer-supported learning environment CaiMan© apparent to the learners. After the first group session the learners attend six individual learning sessions with the learning environment CaiMan©. In the second group session, the students learn and

Figure 1. Schedule of the training.

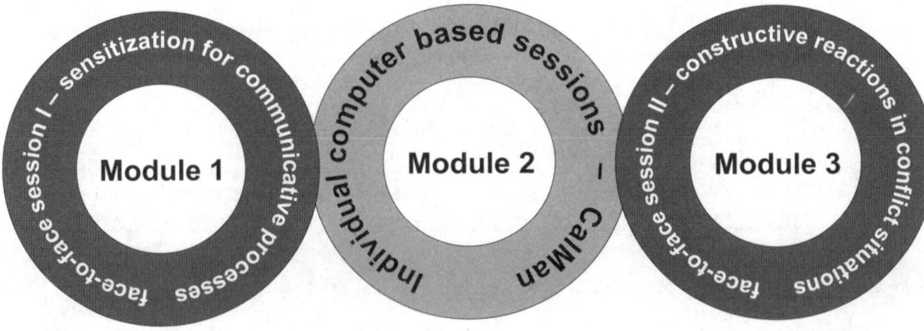

train how to react to the utterances of others in a constructive way. They learn how to react to utterances based on the differentiated analysis which they have learned with the help of the computer-supported learning environment CaiMan©. In the following paragraphs, this learning environment will be described regarding its design criteria.

The use of multimedia for de-automation

As shown above, changing and fostering speech-receptive action – like the analysis of conversational utterances – demands **de-automation** by bringing the individual's own action into consciousness and reflecting it and **re-automation** by repeatedly exercising the new forms of speech-related action processes. Because all of this cannot be done while the learner is in the midst of a conversation, a computer-supported learning environment was designed to foster the ability of analyzing conversational utterances. Computer-supported learning environments allow the repeated use of video sequences and can help to reduce cognitive load: By writing down and documenting the analyses the learners do not have to memorize them and can still use them as a basis for their reflection.

Structuring the analysis of utterances

The computer-supported learning environment CaiMan© was developed to foster the ability to analyze conversational utterances in a differentiated way. The learners are asked to no longer analyze utterances in an unreflected way but to differentiate the utterances according to the three functions of speech postulated by Karl Bühler (1934) – *appeal*, *expres-*

Figure 2. Screenshot of the computer-supported learning environment CaiMan©.

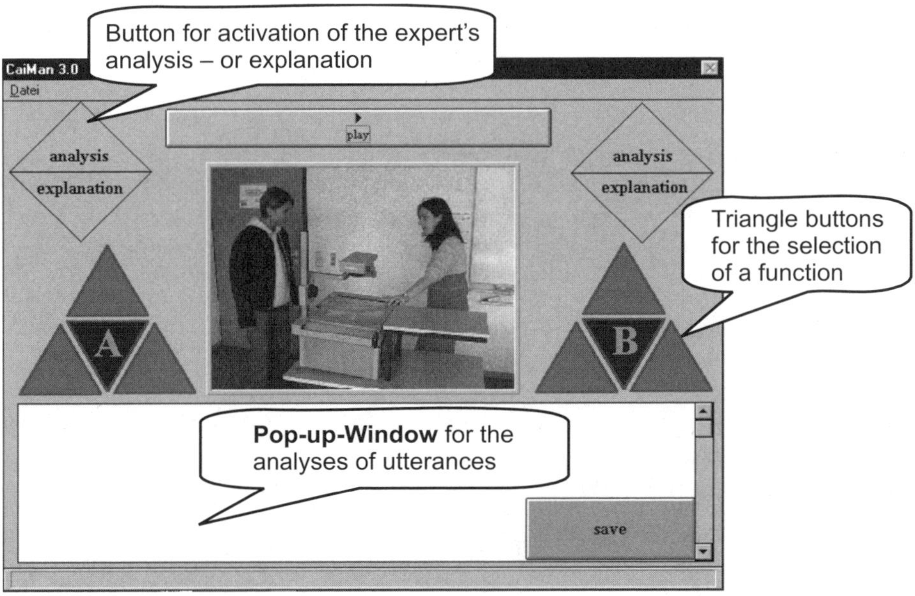

sion, and *representation*. In using this model, the subject asks himself/herself the following questions: "What does the speaker want the listener to do?" (appeal), "What does the speaker express about himself/herself?" (expression) and "About what objects or facts does the speaker inform the listener?" (representation). These three functions of speech can be found in every utterance. While learning with CaiMan©, the learners have to analyze utterances regarding each of the three functions (see Figure 2)

The use of video sequences

Conversational utterances are part of dialogs. In dialogs information is not only transmitted by verbal speech but also by intonation and nonverbal action (Argyle, 1988; Foppa, 1994). In order to analyze utterances in dialogs properly, the learner needs to process the information which is transmitted verbally, nonverbally, and by intonation. This information can be displayed with the help of video sequences. Another advantage of video sequences is that they can be displayed repeatedly. Watching a video sequence several times can help the learner to analyze the utterances.

Externalizing the analyses

The analyses need to be externalized and documented for them to be tangible for reflection. This can best be achieved by having the learners write down their analyses. Lammon, Secules, Petrosino, Hackett, Bransford, and Goldman (1996) describe the advantages of having the learners write down their ideas and solutions: "...articulating ideas in writing encourages students to formulate their theories explicitly, it clearly facilitates memory, and it supports reflection and revision" (p. 249). The computer-supported learning environment CaiMan© enables the externalization and documentation of analyses by providing the learners with the opportunity to enter their analyses for each function of speech and to recall these analyses later.

Explaining the analyses

Verbalizing the analyses is only the first step of the de-automation of speech-receptive action. The externalization of the analyses documents the final product but not the processes or the cues which were used to get to the analyses. The explanation of one's own action constitutes a central part of reflection (Henninger, Mandl, & Law, 2000; Law, Mandl, & Henninger, 1998). According to various authors, the explanation of one's action or solutions provides the learners with a powerful opportunity for learning (Chi, 2000; Dominowski, 1998; Ericsson & Simon, 1998). Our learning environment supports the reflection of the analyses by requesting the learners to enter explanations for each of their analyses.

Fostering reflection by providing an expert's analyses and explanations

In order to give the learners an orientation for the reflection of their analyses, they are provided with the analyses and explanations of an expert for each function of speech.

They can compare their own analyses with those of the expert. Thus, the expert provides a model of how conversational utterances can be analyzed (Bandura, 1971; Collins et al., 1989). By reflecting the expert's analyses and explanations, the learner creates a mental model of how analyses and explanations might be done. Therefore, by providing the learners with the opportunity to verbalize and reflect their analyses of conversational utterances, the computer-supported learning environment CaiMan© constitutes a suitable tool for the de-automation of speech-receptive action. Different ways for fostering reflection have been examined in experimental studies (see the section on searching for ways to foster reflection).

Re-Automation by repeated exercise

(Re-)Automation of skills is achieved by repeatedly exercising the skills (Hacker, 1998; Leontiev, 1981). This implies that the learning environment CaiMan© should provide the learners with the opportunity to repeatedly practice the analyses of conversational utterances. In each session with the learning environment the learners analyze two different video sequences depicting a dyadic conflict situation. In both sequences the learners have to analyze the utterances of both conversational partners. CaiMan© is applied during six sessions in each course. Thus, the learners undergo a number of learning cycles in which they practice the analysis of conversational utterances. This provides the learners with a basis for re-automating the analysis of conversational utterances.

Factors of success for the integration of software into the training of soft skills

The learning software CaiMan© has been integrated into concepts for the training of communicative behavior for several years now. During all this time, it has been subject to educational and psychological research. Instructional and motivational factors were also investigated in the studies dealing with CaiMan©. This research has shown that this learning software is successful in improving the differentiated analysis of conversational utterances and that it is highly accepted by the learners (Henninger, 1999; Henninger & Mandl, 1993, 2000; Henninger, Mandl, & Pommer, 1994; Henninger et al., 1999). Seven factors can be identified, which have been shown to be responsible for the success of the learning environment CaiMan©:

1) Description of the subject matter

The accurate description of the subject allows the definition of learning goals and the identification of the kind of knowledge and/or skills to be taught. The learning environment CaiMan© was designed on the basis of an explicit description of the subject matter. This description lead to the learning goal of a differentiated understanding. Furthermore, the instructional design is affected by the description of the subject matter. The subject matter of speech-reception requires the de- and re-automation of the skills which are to be fostered (Henninger, 1999; Henninger & Mandl, 2000).

2) Software as a tool

Software should not be used as an end in itself. Only the thoughtful integration of learning software into the service of instructional goals will lead to success (Kerres, 2000; Reusser, 1993; Schofield, 1999). The learners have to realize by themselves the necessity to use the software for learning. In our case, the learning gains of the software CaiMan© connect the two face-to-face training sessions and the learners can realize that it is necessary to work with CaiMan© in order to succeed in the second face-to-face group session (Henninger, 1999).

3) Integration of software into a course setting

The use of software makes most sense if it is integrated into conventional forms of learning and teaching (Kerres, 2000). This is especially the case with the training of soft skills because they consist of both individual cognitive skills and social interactive skills. The computer-supported learning environment CaiMan© is integrated into a face-to-face course setting. The fostering of speech-productive and of speech-receptive action thus can be related to each other. This is important because there is no conversational situation in everyday life which consists only of one of the two parts of communicative behavior.

4) Authentic learning scenarios

A basic assumption of situated learning approaches is the authenticity of the learning scenario (Collins et al., 1989; Greeno & The Middle School Mathematics Through Application Project Group, 1998; Law, 2000). The context of learning should be similar to the context in which the acquired knowledge and skills are used in everyday life. The computer-supported learning environment CaiMan© is embedded into an authentic learning scenario: The analysis of conversational utterances is conducted on the basis of realistic conversational situations. These scenarios are displayed in the form of video sequences. A high degree of authenticity of the integrated video sequences, however, did not have a positive impact on the learning results (Henninger et al., 1999).

5) Easy to use

The aim of learning software as a cognitive tool is to support the learner's reflection by reducing the cognitive load the learner is confronted with. This can only be the case if the use of the software itself is easy and comprehensible. The computer-supported learning environment CaiMan© is easy to use and does not offer more features than necessary.

6) Obligatory participation

The learner can only profit from software if he/she uses it. Thus, we do not consider it helpful if the use of learning environments is voluntary. Especially if the computer-supported learning environment is embedded into a course setting, it is necessary to establish the same or a similar level of knowledge in all the learners. Learning with CaiMan© is obligatory for the participants of the communication training. Several studies (Linz, 2003; Pommer, 2000) showed that the learning environment CaiMan© is successful in teaching a differentiated analysis of conversational utterances independent of the learners' motivation.

7) Adaptability of the software

No training is like another. In many cases, it is important to emphasize different contents and to adapt training concepts to the situation of the clients. Thus, it is necessary for a computer-supported learning environment, which is integrated into such a training, to be adaptable to the special situation of each training. The computer-supported learning environment CaiMan© can be adapted to the knowledge and interests of the learner: The instructor has the possibility to integrate different video sequences in the learning environment and to activate various instructional features – such as the request for the learner's explanations or the accessibility and content of the expert's analyses and explanations – as desired.

To sum up, although the use of computer-supported learning environments for the training of soft skills might appear paradoxical at first sight, we could show that the integration of such software can be successful. We could identify seven factors which are responsible for this success. The drawback most often voiced by the learners is that they miss direct support and the possibility to discuss their analyses. Consequently, the current CaiMan© version, so-called CaiMan© Online, provides online-coaching via internet.

Searching for ways to foster reflection: Two empirical studies

As mentioned above, reflection is an important process to modify one's own action. According to all three models of reflection, verbalization or explanations of action is one of the key elements of reflection. And – with regard to Schön – reflection *in* action (i.e., online) which implies moment-by-moment "active experimentation" is conceptually more complex, developmentally more mature, and functionally more significant than reflection *on* action (see Schön, 1983, 1987). Thus we used our learning tool CaiMan© to create a learning scenario which enables the learners to reflect in action, e.g., analyze utterances by using explanations or verbalizations of their action. In two studies we examined whether different operationalizations of fostering reflection have effects on learning results (speech-receptive action).

Study 1: Examination of reflection support by providing an extended possibility for reflection (additional explanation of an expert)

Goal

In this study, we investigated in how far the support of reflective processes with the help of an extension of the reflection possibilities leads to better learning gains. It is, for example, unclear which degree of information density the expert's modeling should have, and also which modality (textual, auditory, visual, or multimodal) should be used for the information transmission.

Theoretical background and research questions

Speech-receptive action, i.e., the analysis of communicative utterances, is largely automated. In order to be able to change this speech-receptive action, it therefore first needs to be de-automated. This de-automation can be achieved by bringing the speech-receptive action and its consequences into consciousness with the help of the multimedia learning environment CaiMan.© The learning environment provides the learners with possibilities to make them aware of their own speech-receptive action. It is the task of the learners to analyze communicative utterances according to the three functions of speech by Bühler (1934): appeal, expression, and representation. Reflection acts as a central learning principle; with its help, the learners become aware of their communicative behavior and its background. According to Collins and his colleagues (1989), reflection is the central principle for changing cognitive processes. Due to interlocked cognitive processes, reflection needs to be supported. Collins and Brown (1988) call a method which supports reflection "abstracted replay," i.e., the cognitive reflecting on one's own problem solution and its comparison to an expert's solution.

The research questions were the following: Is there a stronger increase in the quality of the speech-receptive action in the learning condition "high possibility for reflection" than in the learning condition "low possibility for reflection"?

Method

Participants

30 participants of the University of Munich participated in this training which was part of a communication training. They were randomly assigned to one of the two learning conditions.

Description of the learning environment

The learning environment is the multimedia learning environment CaiMan©. Video sequences of dyadic conflicts are implemented into the user interface. In each training session, the participants are given two conversation sequences (dialogue between person A and person B with one change of speaker per sequence). It is the task of the participants to analyze each communicative utterance for both speakers (Person A and Person B) according to the three functions of speech by Bühler (1934): representation (what information is contained in the utterance), expression (what the speaker expresses about himself), and appeal (what the speaker wants the hearer to do). The analyses are entered in the respective windows. Immediately after giving their analyses, the participants can view an expert's analysis (and explanation). The participant follows these steps for each sequence and for all three functions of speech and both communication partners in the video sequence.

Variation of learning conditions

The learning conditions differed in the following way: learners in the condition "extended possibility for reflection" could compare their analysis to an expert's analysis and explanation. In this explanation, the expert explains what aspects in the utterance made him reach his analysis. In the learning condition "non-extended possibility for reflection," the learners only had an expert's analysis to compare their analysis to.

Design

The training consisted of 6 individual sessions of which only the sessions 1–4 are considered in this study. The training sessions have an average duration of about one hour and are done with at least one day in between. In each session, the participants work on two sequences of a conversation with one change of speaker (A-B, A-B). They analyze these sequences for each person (A and B) according to the three functions of speech (representation, expression, appeal).

Studied variables

The quality of analysis of the three functions of speech formed the dependent measure. The independent variable was the variation in the learning conditions "extended possibility of reflection" and "non-extended possibility of reflection."

Instruments

The quality of analysis was determined through a comparison of the number of arguments in the analysis of the learner with those in the expert's analysis by two raters (interrater-reliability $r = 0.78$).

Description of a training session

The written instruction was read out by the experimenter (contains an explanation of the learning environment and the task) at the beginning of a session.

Beginning of the learning session
Task: Analysis of video sequence **1**

Comparison of learners analysis with expert's analysis (Learning condition "Limited opportunity for reflection")
or *Comparison of learners analysis with* <u>*expert's analysis*</u> <u>*and explanation*</u> *(Learning condition: "Extended opportunity for reflection")*

Analysis of video sequence **2** in an analogue fashion
End of the learning session

Results

Effects of the treatment variations on learning outcomes are detectable by looking at the interaction effect learning condition × changes in the quality of analysis. We could not find any effect of the treatment variation (see Table 1).

In addition, we conducted a *t* test to look at the learning effects in each condition. In contrast to further studies (see Henninger et al., 1999), we found only one significant change in the function "expression" in the learning condition "extended possibility for reflection." However, the decline of the mean indicates not an improvement but a decline in the performance. The same effect – but only on a 10% level of significance – could be observed in the learning condition "non-extended possibility for reflection" (see Table 2).

Table 1. Analysis of variance: Influence of the variation of the learning conditions on changes in the quality of analysis

		Function of speech					
		Representation		Expression		Appeal	
Source	*df*	*F*	*p*	*F*	*p*	*F*	*p*
Learning condition x Changes in the quality of analysis	1,28	0.19	n.s.	0.18	n.s.	0.84	n.s.

Note: $N = 30$.

Table 2. Comparison of means of the quality of analysis for the learning conditions (pre/post)

		Function of speech		
Learning condition		Representation	Expression	Appeal
Extended possibility for reflection	**t1**	0.61	0.49	0.31
	t4	0.70	0.33	0.49
t test		n.s.	*	*
Non-extended possibility for reflection	**t1**	0.57	0.43	0.36
	t4	0.71	0.31	0.42
t test		n.s.	+	n.s.

Note: $n_{\text{extended possibility for reflection}} = 16$; $n_{\text{non-extended possibility for reflection}} = 14$; $+p < .10$; $*p < .05$.

Discussion

Considering the theories on reflection, we expected positive effects of giving additional possibilities for reflection because the learners would thus be able to reflect on their own action in a more differentiated way. Our expectation that the learning condition with an "extended possibility for reflection" would lead to more changes in the quality of analysis of speech-receptive action than the learning condition with "non-extended possibility for reflection" was not confirmed.

We have two possible explanations. The first is that the additional explanations given by an expert are too differentiated and too complex. Thus the learners – novices in describing and explaining speech-receptive action – could not draw relations between their and the expert's explanation. A deeper look into the logfiles shows that the expert's reflection includes the profound structure of problem solutions, whereas the reflection of learners who are less familiar with a domain is based on rather superficial features (hierarchies of reflection: Hatton & Smith, 1995). Comprehension gaps of the learner can, on the one hand, be supportive in that they induce cognitive conflicts that motivate the creation or modification of knowledge. On the other hand, the gaps can be so immense that the learner is incapable of following the expert. The latter could be responsible for the failure of the extended possibility for reflection.

The second explanation follows a closer examination of the operationalization. The learning environment offers this possibility for reflection but whether or not this "knowledge offer" is used by the participants is their own decision. Furthermore, the chosen instructional support is not directly connected to speech-receptive action. The participants have to analyze communicative utterances but do not have to explain these. Therefore, the knowledge offer does not have an equivalent on the level of action. Considering the results of this study, it remains open whether an instructional support of reflection cannot still lead to an enhanced performance. The problem of the lack of correspondence between the instructional support on the knowledge and the action level described above leaves room for interpretations. In order to close this gap, another study was conducted in which the participants were given the possibility to explain their analysis as well. This study is described in the following section.

Study 2: Self-explanation as a method to support reflection

Goal

In this study, we wanted to answer the question of whether the reflection support "self-explanations" would lead to better learning gains.

Theoretical background and research question

Nearly all studies on self-explanations show a positive influence of self-explanations on knowledge acquisition, performance, or transfer. However, these studies were mostly conducted in complex, well-structured and static domains, such as mathematics, physics, or biology. A higher degree of self-explanations seems to have a positive effect, as long as this does not lead to a reduced quality of the self-explanations. Self-explanations seem to be superior to "pure" verbalizations (thinking aloud). With respect to verbalizations (thinking aloud), it needs to be examined in how far these represent "spontaneous self-explanations" (Chi, Bassok, Lewis, Reimann, & Glaser, 1989). Instructional explanations seem to have a positive effect when they encourage the learners to give self-explanations; giving instructional explanations therefore does not replace learners' own activities.

But what about the domain of *changing skills*? First, the question needs to be answered whether the results gained from studies on knowledge acquisition or knowledge application (problem solving) can be transferred to this area of changing skills. One example from the pedagogical domain where changing skills takes place is that of communicative behavior – understanding as well as speaking. Communicative behavior is highly automated in adult native speakers, therefore, changes can only occur after de-automating the respective processes or action patterns (see above). The goal of knowledge acquisition or application often lies in enhancing or fostering behavior. Our learning situation, however, aims at changing the underlying cognitive processes of a certain behavior. The processes we are dealing with – processes of understanding – are highly automated. Therefore, changing this processes needs de-automation and reflection.

Studies have shown that verbalizations or self-explanations of automated action sequences can have negative effects on learners working on a task (see Schooler et al., 1993). This is explained by the fact that, in this case, self-explanations compete with the goal behavior itself. However, self-explanations can be helpful when de-automation and reflection of one's action are the goal – as is the case with changing behavior. For this behavior change in a cyclic and sequential learning environment, which includes repetitions within each learning phase and which comprises several sequential learning phases, it seems sensible to have the self-explanations after the goal behavior. Thus, two effects are achieved: first, a (direct) competition of self-explanations and goal behavior is avoided, and, second, self-explanations foster de-automation and reflection. This again has an effect on the behavior – or sequences of action – in the next learning phase (-cycle).

The research question was the following: Do self-explanations in addition to instructional explanations facilitate the changing of speech receptive action?

Method

Participants

Twenty students of the Technical University of Munich participated in this training, which was a part of a communication training course. The participants were randomly assigned to the learning conditions.

Description of the learning environment

The same learning environment was employed as in Study 1.

Variation of learning conditions

The learning conditions differed in the following way: learners in the condition "with self-explanation" had to give an explanation for their analysis in addition to the analysis itself. In the learning condition "without self-explanation," the learners only had to give an analysis but no explanation. Both conditions had access to an expert's analysis and explanation.

Design

The training consisted of 6 individual sessions of which only the sessions 1–4 are considered in this study. The training sessions have an average duration of about one hour and are done with at least one day in between. In each session, the participants work on two sequences of a conversation with one change of speaker (A-B, A-B). They analyze these sequences for each person (A and B) according to the three functions of speech (representation, expression, appeal). In the learning condition "with self-explanation," the participants had to give an additional explanation for their analyses of communicative utterances.

Studied variables

The quality of analyses of the three functions of speech formed the dependent measure. The independent variable was the variation in the learning conditions "with self-explanations" and "without self-explanations."

Instruments

The quality of analyses of the communicative utterances was assessed through two experts' ratings. The number of arguments contained in the participants' analyses are compared to the number of arguments contained in the expert's analysis (interrater-reliability: r = .78).

Description of a training session

The written instruction was read out by the experimenter (contains an explanation of the learning environment and the task) at the beginning of a session.

Beginning of the learning session
Task: Analysis of video sequence **1**

Comparison of learners analysis with an expert's analysis and explanation (Learning condition: "without self-explanations")
or *Comparison of learners analysis and explanation with an expert's analysis and explanation (learning condition: "with self-explanation")*

Analysis of video sequence **2** in an analogue fashion
End of the learning session

Results

In this study we found a significant interaction effect between treatment and learning gains (function: representation, see Table 3). But – comparable with Study 1 – the treatment with self-explanations did not lead to higher learning gains. For the function "representation," the condition without self-explanations leads to better learning gains as compared than the condition with self-explanations. For the function "expression," a significant decline in the quality of analysis could be observed in both treatments. No significant change in quality of analysis could be detected for function "appeal" (see Table 4).

Table 3. Analysis of variance: Effects of the variation in the learning conditions on changes in the quality of analysis

		Function of speech					
		Representation		Expression		Appeal	
Source	*df*	*F*	*p*	*F*	*p*	*F*	*p*
Learning condition x Changes in the quality of analysis	1,18	10.84	**	0.07	n.s.	0.02	n.s.

Note: $N = 20$; ** $p < .01$.

Table 4. Comparison of means of the quality of analysis for the learning conditions (pre/post)

		Function of speech		
Learning condition		Representation	Expression	Appeal
Extended possibility for reflection	**t1**	0.61	0.47	0.53
	t4	0.73	0.28	0.61
t test	+	*	n.s.	
Non-extended possibility for reflection	**t1**	0.41	0.51	0.43
	t4	0.83	0.30	0.49
t test	***	*	n.s.	

Note: $N_{\text{extended possibility for reflection}} = 9$; $N_{\text{Non-extended possibility for reflection}} = 11$; + $p < .10$; * $p < .05$; *** $p < .001$.

Discussion

Our expectation that higher learning gains can be achieved with a support of reflection in the form of self-explanations than without this form of support of reflection was not confirmed. There was even an advantage for the learning condition where the learners only had to give an analysis but had an expert's analysis and explanation, i.e., where the possibilities for action did not correspond.

The question remains why the participants were not able to profit from the possibility to compare their analysis with an expert's. One explanation might be that explaining their analysis claims more of the participants' cognitive resources, which might reduce the quality of their analyses. Such performance-reducing effects as the result of a complex learning situation where several behaviors are possible were also reported by Stark, Graf, Renkl, Mandl, and Gruber (1995). Therefore, it seems sensible to assess the influence of the task complexity in further studies.

Discussion of both studies

Considering the results, our assumption that reflection could be fostered by extending the possibilities for reflection – additional expert's analyses – or by creating direct links between information about action and the results of action, i.e., in the form of the analysis window and the explanation window, could not be confirmed. Thus it is not astonishing that an enhanced quality of analysis of speech-receptive action could not be observed in the extended reflection conditions.

What does this mean? Is reflection a cognitive activity that cannot be fostered? According to the leading theories in this field, which were described in the section on the theoretical models of reflection, there have to be ways to foster reflection. And, in fact, it seems very unrealistic to assume that changing such a complex cognitive behavior as communication could be successful without a related cognitive activity, like thinking about one's own action. In the light of previous studies in which substantial learning gains could be reported (see Henninger, 1999), it seems plausible to argue that, for example, the five phases of reflective thinking based on Dewey are supported by the learning environment CaiMan©:

(1) Problem recognition: the participants can find deficits in their analyses by comparing their solutions to those of an expert
(2) Specification of possibilities for new actions or beliefs: by comparing one's own solutions with those of an expert, participants are requested to specify alternatives of speech-receptive actions
(3) Evaluation of these possibilities by drawing on memory
(4) Revision of the possibilities by questioning or experimenting: the participants can check and revise their solutions by comparing them with the expert's
(5) Decision-making of whether to continue to look for evidence or to carry out one of the found possibilities, which may result in the change of communicative behavior: the participants are free to look more or less intensively at the explanations of the expert – the evidence for his or her analysis

The fact that the participants in all learning conditions were able to enhance their quality of analysis leads to the conclusion that they were able to profit from the comparison of their own behavior or action outcome with those of an expert, independent of the different learning conditions. This means that the methods chosen were not able to significantly enhance this process of comparison (points 3 to 5 in Dewey's model). Therefore, the question remains whether a more suitable application of the design principle "reflection" can be achieved by a more direct support of this process of comparison. Or whether we are trapped in a ceiling effect: The participants might profit from the general support of reflection – writing down their own analyses and thinking about them by comparing them with the expert's – offered by CaiMan©. It may be possible that more reflection in the short period of time in the learning sessions cannot be realized by the participants.

Considering our results and Schön's model, we favor searching for ways to foster reflection *in* action more than our "old" approach of looking for a way to foster reflection *on* action in the future. Reflection *on* action – pausing in the midst of an action to "stop-and-think" (i.e., offline) – is a first step in enhancing communicative behavior. But for a lasting and a stronger effect, it seems more fruitful to develop tools that foster reflection *in* action, i.e., reflection when an action is being undertaken (i.e., online), and which implies moment-by-moment "active experimentation."

Final remarks

In this article we have shown that communication skills can be trained with software but there are several aspects which need to be paid attention to when designing a communication training concept. As demonstrated, a blended approach seems to be the best solution, combining the advantages of traditional face-to-face training and the possibilities offered by software and new technologies. With the help of didactically designed software, traditional concepts can be optimized. However, it must not be forgotten that it has largely a supportive function. Face-to-face training cannot be replaced by it. A tool like CaiMan© cannot stand alone but has to be integrated into a training concept.

One of the most important functions of software-based training tools is the support of reflection. A multimedia learning environment like CaiMan© should serve as a tool for learners by offering them possibilities to think about their actions. One of the central aspects in changing automated action is being aware of the results and – if possible – of the underlying cognitive processes of the targeted action. Applying this to communicative action, this means that a person should be aware of the results and processes of speech-receptive action, i.e., the understanding of utterances, and speech-productive action, i.e., using communication techniques. According to Schön (1983), training software should offer possibilities to break ongoing processes and fix the result so that a person can reflect on the own action and modify it.

Our research shows that it is very difficult to enhance reflection beyond the level which can be reached by realizing the five points named by Dewey (see the discussion section of both studies); at least if the experimental evidence should be delivered by short-time intervention studies. With regard to the domain communication with highly over-learned action processes, and keeping in mind the deliberations on reflection, we suggest that it can be very fruitful to develop and examine reflection-based learning scenarios in long-term studies. These learning scenarios should try to realize reflection *in* action, for example, in the form of software tools that allow participants to reflect their action in everyday settings and with ongoing support by trainers. Future research has to show whether there are ways to foster communication skills using software more than it can be done by short-time intervention programs as we have shown it with our tool CaiMan©.

References

Anderson, J. R., & the ACT* group. (1995). *The advanced computer tutoring project.* Available at: http://act.psy.cmu.edu/ACT/tutor/ (retrieved 10.08.2001).

Antos, G. (1992). Demosthenes oder: Über die Verbesserung von Kommunikation [Demosthenes or on the "improvement of communication"]. In R. Fiehler & W. Sucharowski (Eds.), *Kommunikationsberatung und Kommunikationstrainings, Anwendungsfelder der Diskursforschung* (pp. 52–66). Opladen, Germany: Westdeutscher Verlag.

Antos, G. (1996). *Laien-Linguistik. Studien zu Sprach- und Kommunikationsproblemen im Alltag. Am Beispiel von Sprachratgebern und Kommunikationstrainings* [Lay linguistics. Studies on language and communication problems in everyday life. Exemplified by communication guides and communication trainings]. Tübingen, Germany: Niemeyer.

Argyle, M. (1988). *Bodily communication*. London: Methuen & Co. Ltd.

Bandura, A. (1971). Analysis of modeling processes. In A. Bandura (Ed.), *Psychological Modeling* (pp. 1–62). Chicago, IL: Aldine.

Barbian, J. (2002). *Blended works. Online Learning*. July 1. Available at: http://www.onlinelearningmag.com/training/search/search_display.jsp?vnu_content_id=1526767 (retrieved 06.09.2002).

Baron, J. (1981). Reflective thinking as a goal of education. *Intelligence, 5,* 291–309.

Barron, T. (1998). The hard facts about soft-skills software. *Training and Development, 52*(6), 48–51.

Bransford, J. D., Franks, J. J., Vye, N. J., & Sherwood, R. D. (1989). New approaches to learning and instruction: Because wisdom can't be told. In S. Vosniadou & A. Ortony (Eds.), *Similarity and analogical reasoning* (pp. 470–497). Cambridge, MA: Cambridge University Press.

Bransford, J. D., Sherwood, R. D., & Sturdevant, T. (1987). Teaching thinking and problem solving. In J. B. Baron, & R. J. Sternberg (Eds.), *Teaching thinking skills: Theory and practice* (pp. 162–181). New York: Freeman.

Brons-Albert, R. (1995). *Auswirkungen von Kommunikationstraining auf das Gesprächsverhalten* [Effects of communication training on communicative action]. Tübingen, Germany: Gunter Narr.

Brown, A. L., & Palincsar, A. S. (1989). Guided, cooperative learning and individual knowledge acquisition. In L. B. Resnick (Ed.), *Knowing, learning and instruction* (pp. 393–451). Hillsdale, NJ: Erlbaum.

Bühler, K. (1934). *Sprachtheorie: Die Darstellungsfunktion der Sprache* [Speech theory: the representational function of speech]. Jena, Germany: Fischer.

Burke, T. (1994). *Dewey's new logic*. Chicago, IL: University of Chicago Press.

Chi, M. T. H. (2000). Self-explaining expository texts: The dual processes of generating inferences and repairing mental models. In R. Glaser (Ed.), *Advances in Instructional Psychology* (pp. 161–238). Mahwah, NJ: Erlbaum.

Chi, M. T. H., Bassok, M., Lewis, M. W., Reimann, P., & Glaser, R. (1989). Self explanations: How students study and use examples in learning to solve problems. *Cognitive Science,* 13, 145–182.

Clark, H. H., & Brennan, S. E. (1991). Grounding in communication. In L. B. Resnick, J. M. Levine, & S. D.Teasley (Eds.), *Perspectives on socially shared cognition* (pp. 127–149). Washington: American Psychological Association.

Cognition and Technology Group at Vanderbilt. (1992). The Jasper Series as an example of anchored instruction: Theory, program description, and assessment data. *Educational Psychologist, 27,* 291–315.

Cognition and Technology Group at Vanderbilt. (1993). Designing learning environments that support thinking: The Jasper Series as a case study. In T. M. Duffy, J. Lowych, D. H. Jonassen, & T. M. Welsh (Eds.), *Designing environments for constructive learning* (pp. 9–36). Berlin, Germany: Springer.

Cognition and Technology Group at Vanderbilt. (1994). Multimedia environments for enhancing student learning in mathematics. In S. Vosniadou, E. de Corte, & H. Mandl (Eds.), *Technology-based learning environments. Psychological and educational foundations* (pp. 167–173). Berlin, Germany: Springer.

Cohen, S. L., & Rustad, J. M. (1998). High-Tech/High-Touch: High Time? *Training and Development, 52*(12), 30–37.

Collins, A. (1996). Design issues for learning environments. In S. Vosniadou, E. de Corte, R. Glaser, & H. Mandl (Eds.), *International perspectives on the design of technology-supported learning environments* (pp. 342–363). Mahwah, NJ: Erlbaum.

Collins, A., & Brown, J. S. (1988). The computer as a tool for learning through reflection. In H. Mandl & A. Lesgold (Eds.), *Learning issues for intelligent tutoring systems* (pp. 1–18). New York: Springer.

Collins, A., Brown J. S., & Newman, S. E. (1989). Cognitive apprenticeship: Teaching the craft of reading, writing and mathematics. In L. B. Resnick (Ed.), *Knowing, learning and instruction* (pp. 453–494). Hillsdale, NJ: Erlbaum.

Daudelin, M. W. (1996). Learning from experience through reflection. *Organizational Dynamics, 24*(3), 36-48.

DeCorte, E. (1994). Toward the integration of computers in powerful learning environments. In S. Vosniadou, E. DeCorte, & H. Mandl (Eds.), *Technology-Based Learning Environments* (pp. 19–25). Berlin, Germany: Springer.

DeCorte, E. (1996). Changing views of computer-supported learning environments for the acquisition of knowledge and thinking skills. In S. Vosniadou, E. DeCorte, R. Glaser, & H. Mandl (Eds.), *International perspectives on the design of technology-supported learning environments* (pp. 129–145). Mahwah, NJ: Erlbaum.

Dewey, J. (1925/1981). Experience and nature. In J. A. Boydston (Ed.), *John Dewey: The later works, 1925–1953* (Vol. 1, pp. 1–326). Carbondale, IL: Southern Illinois University Press.

Dewey, J. (1933/1986). How we think. In J. A. Boydston (Ed.), *John Dewey: The later works, 1925–1953* (Vol. 8, pp. 105–352). Carbondale, IL: Southern Illinois University Press.

Dewey, J. (1938/1986). Logic: The theory of inquiry. In J. A. Boydston (Ed.), *John Dewey: The later works, 1925–1953* (Vol. 12, pp. 1–527). Carbondale, IL: Southern Illinois University Press.

Dillenbourg, P. (Ed.). (1999). *Collaborative learning*. Pergamon: Elsevier Science.

Dominowski, R. L. (1998). Verbalization and problem solving. In D. J. Hacker, J. Dunlosky, & A. C. Graesser (Eds.), *Metacognition in education theory and practice* (pp. 25–45). Mahwah, NJ: Erlbaum.

Dörner, D. (1976). *Problemlösen als Informationsverarbeitung* [Problem-solving as information processing]. Stuttgart, Germany: Kohlhammer.

Dörner, D. (1979). Self-reflection and problem solving. In F. Klix (Ed.), *Human and artificial intelligence* (pp. 101–127). Amsterdam: North-Holland.

Dörner, D. (1982). Lernen des Wissens- und Kompetenzerwerbs [Learning to acquire knowledge and skills]. In B. Treiber & F. E. Weinert (Eds.), *Lehr-Lern-Forschung* (pp. 134–148). Munich, Germany: Urban & Schwarzenberg.

Ericsson, K. A., & Simon, H. A. (1998). How to study thinking in everyday life: Contrasting think-aloud protocols with descriptions and explanations of thinking. *Mind, Culture, and Activity, 5*(3), 178–186.

Finn, K. E., Sellen, A. J., & Wilbur, S. B. (Eds.). (1997). *Video-media communication*. Mahwah, NJ: Erlbaum.

Fittkau, B., & Schulz von Thun, F. (1994). Grundzüge unseres Kommunikations- und Verhaltenstrainings für Berufspraktiker [Basic characteristics of our communication and action training for professionals]. In B. Fittkau, H.-M. Müller-Wolf, & F. Schulz von Thun (Eds.), *Kommunizieren lernen (und umlernen)* (pp. 101–113). Aachen-Hahn, Germany: Hahner Verlagsgesellschaft.

Foppa, K. (1994). Wie muß man was wissen, um sprechen (und verstehen) zu können? [How does one have to know something in order to be able to speak (and understand)?]. In H.-J. Kornadt, J. Grabowski, & R. Mangold-Allwin (Eds.), *Sprache und Kognition: Perspektiven moderner Sprachpsychologie* (pp. 93–111). Berlin, Germany: Spektrum Akademischer Verlag.

Francis, D. (1995). The reflective journal. *Teaching & Teacher Education, 11*(3), 229–241.

Frey, D. (2000). Kommunikations- und Kooperationskultur aus sozialpsychologischer Sicht [Communication and cooperation culture from a social psychological perspective]. In H. Mandl & G. Reinmann-Rothmeier (Eds.), *Wissensmanagement* (pp. 73–92). Munich, Germany: Oldenbourg.

Friedman, V. J., & Lipshitz, R. (1992). Teaching people to shift cognitive gears. *Journal of Applied Actional Science, 28*(1), 118–136.

Garrison, J. (1995). Deweyan pragmatism and the epistemology of contemporary social constructivism. *American Educational Research Journal, 32*(4), 716–740.

Gerstenmaier, J., & Mandl, H. (1999). Konstruktivistische Ansätze in der Erwachsenenbildung und Weiterbildung [Constructivistic approaches in adult and further education]. In R. Tippelt (Ed.), *Handbuch Erwachsenenbildung/Weiterbildung*. Opladen, Germany: Leske & Budrich.

Geyken, A., Mandl, H., & Reiter, W. (1995). *Qualität in der Weiterbildung, selbstgesteuertes Lernen mit Tele–Tutoring* [Quality in further education: self-regulated learning with tele-tutoring]. Munich, Germany: Siemens AG.

Glowalla, U., & Häfele, G. (1997). Einsatz elektronischer Medien: Befunde, Probleme und Perspektiven [Employment of electronic media: Findings, problems and perspectives]. In L. J. Issing & P. Klimsa (Eds.), *Information und Lernen mit Multimedia* (pp. 415–434). Weinheim, Germany: Beltz.

Greene, T. R. G., & Petre, M. (1992). When visual programs are harder to read than textual programs. *Proceedings of the 6th European Conference on Cognitive Ergonomics* (ECCE-6), Hungary.

Greeno, J. G., & The Middle School Mathematics Through Applications Project Group. (1998). The situativity of knowing, learning, and research. *American Psychologist, 53,* 5–26.

Grimmett, P. P., & Erickson, G. L. (Eds.). (1988). *Reflection in teacher education*. New York: Teachers College Columbia University.

Günther, U., & Sperber, W. (1995). *Handbuch für Kommunikations- und Verhaltenstrainer* [Handbook for communication and action trainers]. Munich, Germany: Reinhardt.

Hacker, W. (1998). *Allgemeine Arbeitspsychologie* [General work psychology]. Göttingen, Germany: Huber.

Hallett, C. E. (1997). Learning through reflection in the community: The relevance of Schön's theories of coaching to nursing education. *International Journal of Nursing Studies, 34*(2), 103–110.

Hargie, O., Saunders, C., & Dickson, D. (1994). *Social skills in interpersonal communication*. London: Routledge.

Hatton, N., & Smith, D. (1995). Reflection in teacher education. *Teaching & Teacher Education, 11*(3), 33–49.

Heflich, D. A. (1997, March). *Online interviews: Research as a reflective dialogue*. Paper presented at the Annual Meeting of the American Educational Research Associations, Chicago, IL.

Henninger, M. (1999). *Die Förderung sprachlich-kommunikativen Handelns* [The Fostering of communicative action]. Unpublished professorial dissertation, Ludwig-Maximilians-Universität Munich, Germany.

Henninger, M., & Mandl, H. (1993). Konstruktivistisches Kommunikations- und Verhaltenstraining mit dem multimedialen Tool CaiMan© [Constructivistic communication and action training with the multimedia tool CaiMan©]. In Bundesinstitut für Berufsbildung (Ed.), *Multimediales Lernen in neuen Qualifizierungsstrategien: Entwicklungstendenzen und Lösungswege* (pp. 119–126). Nuremberg, Germany: BW Bildung und Wissen Verlag.

Henninger, M., & Mandl H. (2000). Vom Wissen zum Handeln – ein Ansatz zur Förderung kommunikativen Handelns [From knowledge to action – An approach for the fostering of communicative action]. In H. Mandl & J. Gerstenmaier (Eds.), *Die Kluft zwischen Wissen und Handeln* (pp. 197–219). Göttingen, Germany: Hogrefe.

Henninger, M., Mandl, H., & Law, L.-C. (2000). Training der Reflexion [Training of reflection]. In K. J. Klauer (Ed.), *Kognitives Training* (pp. 235–260). Göttingen, Germany: Hogrefe.

Henninger, M., Mandl, H., & Pommer, M. (1994). Ein multimediales Trainingstool zur Förderung der Differenzierungsfähigkeit von Gesprächsinhalten [A multimedia tool for the fostering of the ability to differentiatedly analyze communicative utterances]. *Zeitschrift für Unterrichtswissenschaft, 3,* 203–214.

Henninger, M., Mandl, H., Pommer, M., & Linz, M. (1999). Die Veränderung sprachrezeptiven Handelns: Einfluß des instruktionalen Gestaltungsprinzips Authentizität [Changing speech-receptive action: the influence of the instructional design principle of authenticity]. *Zeitschrift für Entwicklungspsychologie und Pädagogische Psychologie, 31*(1), 1–10.

Herrmann, T. (1992). Sprechen und Sprachverstehen [Speaking and understanding speech]. In H. Spada (Eds.) *Allgemeine Psychologie* (pp. 281–322). Bern, Switzerland: Huber.

Hoel, T. L., & Gudmundsdóttir, S. (1996). *The Reflect Project: Interactive pedagogy using information technology*. Lund, Sweden: Lund University.

Jarvis, P. (1987). Meaningful and meaningless experience. *Adult Education, 37*(3), 164–172.

Jaskolski, E. W. (1999). Kooperation – eine Haltung [Cooperation – An attitude]. In A. Mönnich & E. W. Jaskolski (Eds.), *Kooperation in der Kommunikation* (pp. 18–36). Munich, Germany: Reinhardt.

Jonassen, D. H. (1992). What are cognitive tools? In P. A. Kommers, D. H. Jonassen, & J. T. Mayes (Eds.), *Cognitive tools for learning* (pp. 1–6). Berlin, Germany: Springer.

Kerres, M. (2000). Computerunterstütztes Lernen als Element hybrider Lernarrangements [Computer-supported learning as an element of hybrid learning arrangements]. In R. Kammerl (Ed.), *Computerunterstütztes Lernen*. Munich, Germany: Oldenbourg.

Kompf, M., & Bond, W. R. (1995, April). *Through the looking glass: Some criticisms of reflection*. Paper presented at the Annual Meeting of the American Educational Research Association, San Francisco, CA.

Korthagen, F. A. (1993). Two modes of reflection. *Teacher and Teacher Education, 9*(3), 317–326.

Kremer, H. H., & Sloane, P. F. E. (1998). *The implied learner in multimedia arrangements* (MTW Heft 8) Munich, Germany: Ludwig-Maximilians-Universität, Institut für Wirtschafts- und Sozialpädagogik.

Lave, J., & Wenger, E. (1991). *Community of practice*. Cambridge, MA: MIT Press.

Lammon, M., Secules, T., Petrosino, A. J., Hackett, R., Bransford, J. D., & Goldman, S. R. (1996). Schools for thought: Overview of the project and lessons learned from one of the sites. In L. Schauble & R. Glaser (Eds.), *Innovations in learning. New environments for education* (pp. 243–288). Mahwah, NJ: Erlbaum.

Law, L. C. (2000). Die Überwindung der Kluft zwischen Wissen und Handeln aus situativer Sicht [Overcoming the gap between knowledge and action from a situated point of view]. In H. Mandl & J. Gerstenmaier (Eds.), *Die Kluft zwischen Wissen und Handeln* (pp. 253–288). Göttingen, Germany: Hogrefe.

Law, L.-C., Mandl, H., & Henninger, M. (1998). *Training of reflection: Its feasibility and boundary conditions* (Research report no. 89). Munich, Germany: Ludwig-

Maximilians-Universität, Lehrstuhl für Empirische Pädagogik und Pädagogische Psychologie.
Lehtinen, E., & Repo, S. (1996). Activity, social interaction, and reflective abstraction. In S. Vosniadou, E. de Corte, R. Glaser, & H. Mandl (Eds.), *International perspectives on the psychological foundations of technology-based learning environments* (pp.105–128). New York: Springer.
Leontiev, A. A. (1981). *Psychology and the language learning process*. New York: Pergamon Press.
Linz, M. (2003). *Erklärungskraft des Motivations-Prozess-Modells von Dweck & Leggett bei der Veränderung sprachrezeptiven Handelns* [Explanatory power of the motivation process model of von Dweck & Leggett in the change of speech-receptive negotiations]. Munich, Germany: München Akademischer Verlag.
Lipman, M. (1987). Some thoughts on the foundations of reflective education. In J. B. Baron, & R. J. Sternberg (Eds.), *Teaching thinking skills: Theory and practice* (pp. 151–161). New York: Freeman.
Mandl, H., Gruber, H., & Renkl, A. (1995). Situiertes Lernen in multimedialen Lernumgebungen [Situated learning in multimedia learning environments]. In L. J. Issing & P. Klimsa (Eds.), *Information und Lernen mit Multimedia. Ein Lehrbuch zur Multimedia-Didaktik und -Anwendung* (pp. 167–177). Weinheim, Germany: Beltz.
Mayer, R. E. (1997). Multimedia learning: Are we asking the right question? *Educational Psychologist, 32*(1), 1–19.
Merrienboer, J. G. van. (1997). *Training complex cognitive skills*. Englewood Cliffs, NJ: Educational Technology Publications.
Picot, A., Reichwald, R., & Wigand, R. T. (1996). *Die grenzenlose Unternehmung* [The limitless enterprise]. Wiesbaden, Germany: Gabler.
Pommer, M. (2003). *Die Förderung sprachrezeptiven Handelns durch informative Rückmeldung*. Münster: Waxmann.
Putz-Osterloh, W. (1985). Selbstreflexion, Testintelligenz und interindividuelle Unterschiede bei der Bewältigung komplexer Probleme [Self-reflection, test intelligence and differences in coping with complex problems]. *Sprache & Kognition, 4,* 203–216.
Reusser, K. (1993). Tutoring systems and pedagogical theory: Representational tools for understanding, planning and reflection in problem solving. In S. P. Lajoie & S. J. Derry (Eds.), *Computers as Cognitive Tools* (pp. 143–178). Hillsdale, NJ: Erlbaum.
Roschelle, J., & Pea, R. (1999). Trajectories from today's WWW to a powerful educational infrastructure. *Educational Researcher, 28*(5), 22–25.
Rummer, R. (1996). *Kognitive Beanspruchung beim Sprechen* [Cognitive load while speaking]. Weinheim, Germany: Beltz.
Salomon, G. (1993). On the nature of pedagogic computer tools: The case of the writing partner. In S. P. Lajoie & S. J. Derry (Eds.), *Computers as cognitive tools* (pp. 179–196). Hillsdale, NJ: Erlbaum.
Scardamalia, M., & Bereiter, C. (1987). Knowledge telling and knowledge transforming in written composition. In S. Rosenberg (Ed.), *Advances in applied psycholinguistics* (Volume 2, pp. 142–175). Cambridge, MA: Cambridge University Press.
Schön, D. A. (1983). *The reflective practitioner*. New York: Basic Books.
Schön, D. A. (1987). *Educating the reflective practitioner*. San Francisco: Jossey-Bass.
Schön, D., & Rein, M. (1994). *Frame reflection*. New York: Basic Books.

Schoenfeld, A. H. (1985). *Mathematical problem solving*. New York: Academic Press.
Schofield, J. W. (1999). Goals, computer use, and education: A sociocultural issue. *The Journal of the Learning Sciences, 8*(19), 171–175.
Schooler, J. W., Ohlsson, S., & Brooks, K. (1993). Thoughts beyond words: When language overshadows insight. *Journal of Experimental Psychology, 122*(2), 166–183.
Schulz von Thun, F. (1994). Psychologische Vorgänge in der zwischenmenschlichen Kommunikation [Psychological operations in interpersonal communication]. In B. Fittkau, H.-M. Müller-Wolf, & F. Schulz von Thun (Eds.), *Kommunizieren lernen (und umlernen)* (pp. 9–100). Aachen-Hahn, Germany: Hahner Verlagsgesellschaft.
Spiro R. J., Feltovich, P. J., Jacobson, M. J., & Coulson, R. L. (1992). Cognitive flexibility, constructivism, and hypertext: Random access instruction advanced knowledge acquisition in ill-structured domains. In T. M. Duffy, & D. H. Jonassen (Eds.), *Constructivism and the technology of instruction* (pp. 57–76). Hillsdale, NJ: Erlbaum.
Stark, R., Graf, M., Renkl, A., Mandl, H., & Gruber, H. (1995). Förderung von Handlungskompetenz durch geleitetes Problemlösen und multiple Lernkontexte [Fostering action competence by guided problem-solving and multiple learning contexts]. *Zeitschrift für Entwicklungspsychologie und Pädagogische Psychologie, 27,* 289–312.
Stenning, K., & Oberlander, J. (1995). A cognitive theory of graphical and linguistic reasoning: Logic and implementation. *Cognitive Science,* 19 (1), 97–140.
Sweller, J. (1988). Cognitive load during problem solving. *Cognitive Science, 12,* 257–285.
Vygotsky, L. S. (1978). *Mind in society: The development of higher psychological processes*. Cambridge, MA: Harvard University Press.
Vygotsky, L. S. (1987/1998). Child Psychology. In R. W. Rieber (Ed.), *The collected works of L. S. Vygotsky. Volume 5: Child psychology* (pp. 3–296). New York: Plenum.
Watzlawick, P., Beavin, J. & Jackson, D. (1967). *Pragmatics of human communication: A study of interactional patterns, pathologies & paradoxes*. New York: W. W. Norton.
Zeichner, K., & Liston, D. (1987). Teaching student teachers to reflect. *Harvard Educational Review, 57,* 23–48.

The Implications of Veridical Causal Knowledge for the Functionality of Reactions

Friedrich Försterling

Antecedents of causal attributions

Attribution theory assumes that the motivation to gain a realistic understanding of the causes of events is one of the central springs of action (Heider, 1958; Kelley, 1967; see for a summary, Försterling, 2001). In addition, attribution theorists assume that in order to gain such a causal understanding of events the "man on the street" uses mechanisms and tools which are in principle similar to those used by scientists. Heider (1958) and Kelley (1967) suggested that causal induction can be described with the covariation principle. This principle is central to the scientific testing of hypotheses and it assumes that "that condition will be held responsible for an effect that is present when the effect is present and absent when the effect is absent" (p. 152). For instance, we trace back success (effect) of a person (P) at a certain task (T) to the person's disposition (e.g., high ability) when the person always succeeds at this (high consistency) and at other tasks (low distinctiveness) and when other individuals fail at this task (low consensus). In this example, the effect covaries with the person (P) and not with the task (T) or with circumstances. However, if the person only succeeds consistently with one specific task (high consistency) at which other individuals also succeed (high consensus) and if he fails at other tasks (high distinctiveness of success), then we tend to attribute success to the entity (e.g., task difficulty). In this case, the effect covaries with the task and not with the person or circumstances.

Empirical examination of Kelley's covariation principle as well as of it's various refinements revealed that individuals' causal judgments reflect the available covariation information remarkably well (see Försterling, 1989, for a summary).

Emotional and behavioral consequences of causal attributions

In his attributional analysis of achievement-related behavior, Weiner has documented that causal attributions for success and failure determine emotional reactions following an outcome (see Weiner, 1986, for a summary). For instance, success attributed to the individual person gives rise to the emotion of pride, whereas internally attributed failure leads to shame. By contrast, such esteem-related affects will not accompany outcomes which are attributed to the ease or difficulty of the task (i.e., external causes). Causal attributions for success and failure also determine subsequent expectancies. Failure attributed to stable causes (such as lack of ability) reduce expectations to succeed at the respective task in the future more so than causal ascriptions to variable causes (e.g., chance or lack of effort).

The attributionally mediated affective reactions and expectancy changes guide reactions subsequent to an achievement outcome. Internal and stable attributions for failure and external and variable ones for success should have a debilitating influence on subsequent achievement behavior. They maximize negative and minimize positive affect and they lead to reduced expectancies. By contrast, external and variable attributions for failure and internal and stable ones for success lead to high expectations of success and they maximize positive and minimize negative affects in response to the outcome. Hence, this pattern of causal ascriptions should enhance achievement strivings. All these assumptions reflect the importance of hedonistic motivational mechanisms as achievement behavior is conceptualized as an attempt to maximize expected value (i.e., affect) and to minimize costs (i.e., negative emotions).

Abramson, Seligman & Teasdale (1978) make similar assumptions to those of Weiner's in their attributional analysis of depression and learned helplessness. They suggest that tracing back failure to internal, stable, and global causes can lead to depression and helplessness. By contrast, making internal, variable, and specific attributions for failure will protect the individual from becoming helpless following the non-attainment of a goal. Finally, Dweck and Legget (1988) assume that the implicit theory that one's intelligence is stable and not modifiable has a negative impact on achievement behavior, whereas the belief that one's intelligence can be modified and improved influences achievement behavior favorably.

The relation between attributional models of motivation and conceptions of the antecendents of causal inferences

The attributional models introduced by Abramson et al. (1978) und Weiner (1986) address exclusively the cognitive, emotional, and behavioral consequences (R = Reactions) of causal attributions (C = Cognition); and they are largely guided by hedonistic (expectancy × value) assumptions. They do not explicitly refer to or integrate the "rational" (non-hedonistic) models of the antecedents (S = Stimuli) of causal attributions (C) such as Kelley's (1967) covariation model. This fact applies in the same way to more recent motivational conceptions such as Dweck's model (see Dweck & Legget; 1988).

Similarly, and as already indicated, the models about attributional antecedents largely ignore the cognitve, emotional, and behavioral consequences of causal explanations.

(see Försterling, 1986, 1994; Schuster, Rudolph, & Försterling, 1998). The entire S–C–R sequence is not addressed by these models, and an integration of theoretical assumptions and empirical findings of these two branches of attribution theory is not provided.

The lack of integration between models of the antecedents and those of the consequences of causal attributions might be responsible for certain shortcomings and inconsistencies of attributional models of action. We have introduced such an integration of models of the antecedents and consequences of causal knowledge (see Försterling, 1986; 1994; Försterling & Bühner, 2003; Försterling & Rudolph, 1988). In the following, we describe this integrative model and report recent empirical tests of this conception.

Shortcomings of attributional models of behavior

Motivational conceptions based on attributions and self-concepts (e.g., Abramson et al., 1978; Dweck, Chiu, & Hong, 1995; Weiner, 1986) typically suggest that certain attributions or ways to view the self have desirable consequences, whereas others lead to undesirable consequences. This might be due to the fact these models did not take account of models of the antecedents of causal cognitions. For instance, Weiner's achievement motivation model suggests that attributions of failure to lack of ability have unfavorable consequences (reduced expectations of success, debilitating esteem-related emotions, lack of persistence, and performance deficits). By contrast, attributions of failure to chance lead to more desirable consequences (e.g., high expectations of success, lack of esteem-related emotions, persistence and high performance. Similarly, Abramson et al. (1978) maintain that tracing back negative events to internal, stable, and global causes leads to helplessness and depression. Attributions of negative events to external, stable, and specific causes, on the other hand, prevent individuals from such undesirable reactions. Finally, Dweck et al. (1995) suggest that the naive belief that one's intelligence is stable leads to negative consequences and the assumption that one's ability is changeable leads to positive consequences.

As reduced persistence, performance deficits, and depression are often conceived of as unproductive and disadvantageous, attributional models gave rise to training programs designed to ameliorate achievement deficits and helplessness (see Försterling, 1985, 1988, for a summary). In these programs, participants are taught to substitute the "disadvantageous" cognitions (e.g., lack of ability) with "advantageous" ones (e.g., lack of effort). As a consequence of this cognitive restructuring, more favorable behavioral and emotional reactions are expected, and are in fact achieved.

The underlying logic of these attributional retraining programs can be characterized as follows: (1) Certain non-desirable reactions are triggered by certain causal attributions. (2) comparatively more desirable reactions are caused by other attributions. (3) Hence, in order to reduce undesirable reactions and increase desirable ones, one needs to reduce the (causal) cognitions leading to undesirable reactions and to increase cognitions which lead to desirable behavioral consequences. This logic implies that the consequences of a cognition (e.g., whether it leads to persistence or not) are used to determine its appropriateness and change worthiness. A transfer of this logic to another example clearly reveals its shortcomings. (1) A person starts feeling depressed whenever s/he realizes that her/his wallet is empty. (2) She feels good as long as she believes s/he has 100 Euro in her/his wallet. (3) When this person feels depressed, one should "teach" her/him to believe that s/he has 100 Euro in her wallet.

Intuitively, however, it does not seem advisable to always assume to have 100 Euro – specifically when the wallet is, in fact, empty. In the same way, it might not be wise to always avoid attributions to lack of ability (Försterling, 1985, 1988). Under certain circumstances it might be quite reasonable (and helpful) to trace back failure to lack of ability (or to believe the wallet is empty). This might seem especially advisable when one in fact does not possess the respective abilities (or finances). An overestimation of one's abilities (or finances) may lead one to risk dangerous situations which one might not be able to master (or pay). It could also lead one to invest too much effort into goals which might objectively be unattainable (or to shop too much), or it could prevent one from searching for help (or from going to the bank). It is remarkable that none of the attributional and self-concept theories discussed thus far has specified conditions or circumstances in which it is functional to make internal, stable, and global attributions (e.g., to lack of ability). These theories judge the appropriateness of a cognition exclusively on the basis of its behavioral and emotional consequences, and not on the basis of the extent to which a cognition reflects the antecedent information or, in other words, "reality."

By contrast, theories about the antecedents of causal knowledge assume that individuals want to be realistically informed about their personal attributes and that a realistic knowledge of the causes of events is highly adaptive. Attributional models which were originally sparked by these theories about the antecedents do not fully take up this idea. With respect to self-perceived abilities or ability attributions, attribution models and attributional theories would arrive at different predictions. The assumption of rational attribution theories would be that, with regard to a certain task, about 50 per cent of the individuals working on it should perceive themselves to have over average and about 50 per cent should believe to possess under average ability with regard to this task. According to these theories, knowledge about where one's ability level is located should be adaptive, independent of whether one has high or low ability. However, according to theories about the motivational consequences of attributions, everybody who believes they possess high abilities should benefit from this belief; hence an imaginary attributional training program might be designed to teach everybody to possess high ability in order to assure goal attainment.

A relational motivational model

In order to take account of the ideas and criticisms outlined above, I have introduced an attributional motivational model which integrates basic assumptions and empirical findings of research on causal antecedents with models and findings of attributional consequences (Försterling, 1986, 1994). This model assumes that it does not make sense to determine a priori a certain behavioral reaction (e.g., lack of persistence) or a certain attribution (e.g., low ability) as change worthy and to define, in the meantime, a different reaction (e.g., persistence) or attribution (e.g., lack of effort) as desirable. It depends much more on the antecedent conditions (i.e., information about covariation) whether an attribution and the accompanying behaviors and emotions are worthy of change. The central assumption of the models is that *realistic attributions (or, more generally, realistic "naive" theories) are functional (i.e., lead to goal attainment).*

To determine whether a certain causal explanation is realistic or veridical, we use covariation conceptions as introduced above (see Försterling, 1989, 1992; Heider, 1958; Kelley, 1967). We consider an attribution to be realistic when it reflects the antecedent covariation information and/or when it is not falsified by contradicting covariation information. According to this definition, causal attributions are unrealistic when they are inferences which violate the normative covariation principle.

Empirical tests of the integrative model

Before summarizing research designed to test the integrative model, we will briefly summarize the central theoretical ideas elaborated thus far. Both the attributional analysis of achievement-oriented behavior (see Weiner, 1986) as well as the attributional reformulation of the theory of learned helplessness (Abramson et al., 1978) do not refer to antecedent attributional information (covariation information). These models define certain attributions as "maladaptive" because they lead to reactions which they define to be worthy of change. This logic seems inconsistent with the central assumptions of theories about the antecedents of attributions (Heider, 1958; Kelley, 1967), which assume and document that individuals are motivated to gain and are capable of gaining a realistic picture of the causal structure of events, and that such a realistic understanding has adaptive value. We have introduced a motivational model integrating the attributional perspective and the perspective on attribution antecedents. It assumes that it is functional to make realistic and dysfunctional to make unrealistic attributions.

Thus far, empirical studies investigating the relation between the veridicality of causal attributions (as defined above) and the functionality of causal attributions and subsequent behavioral and emotional reactions do not exist (see, for an exception, Försterling & Rudolph, 1988). Subsequently, we will report a series of recently conducted studies which were designed to test the integrative attributional model. The characteristic feature of these studies differs from studies testing models about the antecedents of attributions, which manipulate (covariation-) information as the independent variable and assess causal attributions as dependent variable (e.g., McArthur, 1972). And it also differs from studies manipulating causal attributions as independent variables and assessing behaviors and emotions as dependent variables (e.g., Weiner, Russell & Lerman, 1978). By contrast, the studies reported here simultaneously manipulate or assess antecedent attributionally relevant information *and* causal attributions; subsequently, behavioral indicators are assessed. These studies address the attributional analysis of achievement-oriented behavior and the attributional reformulation of learned helplessness theory.

Applications to achievement behavior

Försterling & Morgenstern (2002) applied the integrative attributional model to the analysis of achievement-related behavior. Thus far, studies investigating the role of attributions for achievement-oriented behavior induced achievement outcomes (e.g., failure) in (hypothetical or real) situations, manipulated causal attributions, and assessed, as dependent variables, various indicators of achievement motivation or behaviors (e.g., affective reactions, expectations of success and subsequent performance). Such studies consistently documented that people who attribute failure to internal and stable causes (i.e., lack of ability), report reduced success expectancies for renewed attempts, to work on the respective task, they persisted less at the task, and they showed reduced task performance when compared to individuals attributing failure to external variable causes such as chance (see Meyer, 1973).

However, the paradigm used in these studies might not be able to uncover the disadvantages of unrealistic attributions (e.g., to high ability) and the advantages of realistic causal ascriptions (e.g., to low ability). Many achievement tasks are characterized by the fact that performance is required at various different tasks within a limited amount of time. For instance, a college degree consists of credit points for various courses differing in content and the successful management of a business implies activities as diverse as bookkeeping, marketing, and motivating coworkers. These examples have in common that the allocation of time in one area (e.g., bookkeeping) implies that this time is not available for another area (e.g., marketing). In addition, investing time in areas in which one has little talent might be punished in such settings. And it seems plausible that individuals with a realistic self-assessment of their weaknesses might be less prone to such misallocations of investment of time into areas for which one possesses only little competence. Hence, people who know where their strengths and weaknesses lie might be more successful in the overall tasks than those who do not possess such a realistic knowledge of their attributes.

The classical paradigms used while testing attributional models of achievement do not allow for the operation of a mechanism which punishes misinvestments of time. In addition, they do not allow for the compensation of weaknesses. Persons who persist for a long time at the experimental task almost automatically attain a better result than persons who give up easily.

Försterling and Morgenstern (2002) introduced a paradigm in which participants worked on different subtasks in order to maximize overall performance: tasks from different areas were presented and overall performance consisted of the sum of the correct solutions at these different areas. Under such conditions, we expected that participants who realistically attributed their performances at the various subtasks would achieve better overall performance than those who made unrealistically positive or negative attributions for outcomes at the individual subtasks.

Försterling and Morgenstern (2002) experimentally induced realistic and unrealistic attributions and assessed overall performance. In a preliminary stage of the experiment, participants worked on subtasks out of different areas (sentence completions, word selection, anagrams, analogies, and figure matching). During this pretest period, information relevant for attributions during the second stage of the experiment was assessed: Performances at the various subtasks (distinctiveness) in relation to their peers (consensus).

In the second stage, half of the participants received realistic (attributionally relevant) information about their performances at the various task areas at pretest (i.e., the correct number of items they solved at the various subtasks (distinctiveness) as well as the correct mean number of tasks solved correctly by their peers (consensus). The remaining participants received unrealistic information about their performances at pretest. Their feedback consisted of the inverse number of correct solutions at the various subtasks actually achieved. For instance, a participant who solved 8 items at sentence completion and 3 anagrams was told that she had solved 3 items at sentence completion and 8 anagrams. Both groups received this information (consensus and distinctiveness) in a tabular form at the beginning of the second stage of the experiment, which was conducted about a week after the first stage.

After receiving the (realistic vs. unrealistic) feedback about pretest performances at the beginning of the second stage of the experiment, participants had once more to work on the four different subtasks for 20 minutes. During this second stage of the experiment they could decide themselves how much time they wanted to spend with each subtask. They were asked to try to maximize overall performance (i.e., the sum of correctly solved tasks out of the various subtasks). The participant with the best performance was promised a reward of approximately 25 Euro. With regard to the dependent variable, we assessed the attributions for hypothetical failure at tasks out of each of the task areas and how much time each participant spent at each task area. The overall performance (the sum of the correctly solved tasks across all 5 task areas) served as the main dependent variable.

As predicted, participants who were realistically informed about their pretest performances showed better overall performance at posttest than individuals who received unrealistic pretest information. In addition, internal analyses revealed that the superior performance of the realistically informed subjects was attributable to the postulated mechanisms. Compared to the unrealistically informed participants, realistically informed individuals spent more time during posttest with tasks areas in which they had done well during pretest and less time at the tasks at which they had low performance during the first stage of the experiment. In addition, further internal analyses showed that this ability-sensitive allocation of time of the realistically informed group was responsible for their superior posttest performance: We calculated for each individual participant the correlation between the amount of correctly solved items at pretest across the 5 task areas with the amount of time spent at each of the respective 5 task areas at posttest. When holding this intraindividual correlation constant, the difference in overall performance at posttest between the realistically and unrealistically informed participants was no longer significant.

To summarize: Our studies on the veridicality of attributions in the achievement context revealed that realistic covariation information and realistic attributions, respectively, can have a performance-enhancing effect. They guide us to invest the available time into those areas where our strengths are and help us to not waste time in areas in which one is weak. This, in turn, leads to a maximization of overall performance. These advantages of realistic attributions could not be detected with the experimental designs previously used, as these only assessed performances on tasks from a single area.

The veridicality of attributions of depressives

The studies which applied the integrative attributional model to depression and depressive realism start with the assumption that depression is a dysfunctional reaction; at least, many clinical psychologists consider this affective state to require therapeutic intervention. If the assumption of the integrative attributional model that realistic attributions lead to dysfunctional reactions was correct, we could make the reversed conclusion that depression (a dysfunctional state) should be triggered by unrealistic attributions. To test this prediction, we used the definition and operationalization of veridicality of attributions as described while reporting the research by Försterling and Morgenstern (2002) to investigate depressives' causal attributions. In contrast to the studies in the achievement context, in which we assessed the functionality of a reaction as the dependent variable (i.e., overall performance), the studies investigating depressive realism used already existing interindividual differences in depression as the quasi independent variable.

In these studies, we use four different strategies for investigation. (1) We experimentally provided participants with (hypothetical) covariation information and assessed how depressives' and non-depressives' causal ascriptions are influenced by this information. We also investigated (2) whether there are differences between the different mood groups regarding perceived covariation information and to what extent the resulting attributions reflect this information. Moreover, we compared attributionally relevant variables with "objective" standards. We assessed (3) to what degree depressives and non-depressives have a realistic understanding of how their heterosexual partners causally explain their own (i.e., the depressive's and non depressive's) behavioral outcomes (i.e., meta-attributional veridicality). Finally (4), we investigated to what extent depressives' and non-depressives' subjectively perceived covariation information realistically reflects objective covariation information.

Experimentally induced covariation information

Försterling, Bühner, and Gall (1998) used the Beck Depression Inventory (Beck, Ward, Mendelson, Mock, & Erbaugh, 1961) to separate participants into non-depressives and (moderately) depressives via a median split. Participants were subsequently confronted with hypothetical scenarios, for instance, "imagine you fail an important exam..." In addition, participants were provided with covariation information. One group received covariation information designed to lead to depressogenic failure attributions (internal, stable, and global) and the remaining individuals received information designed to lead to antidepressogenic causal ascriptions (external, variable, and specific). For instance, in order to induce depressogenic failure attributions, participants were asked to imagine that most of their classmates succeeded at the test (low consensus), that they also failed at tasks out of similar areas (high consistency), and that they had failed at tasks out of other areas (low distinctiveness). It was assessed to what extent depressives and non-depressives attributed the imagined failure to internal, stable, and global factors.

Depressives attributed negative events (more internal, stable and global) than non-depressives (i.e., there was a main effect for depression) and also covariation information had a significant influence on attributions in the expected direction. However, we did not find a significant differential influence of covariation information on depressives' and non-depressives' causal attributions; the interaction between depression and covariation information failed to reach significance (see Försterling et al. 1998, Experiments 1–3).

This pattern of data suggests that depressives and non-depressives do not differ regarding the veridicality of their causal attributions when the sensitivity of the attribution to covariation information is taken as a criterion for defining veridicality. However, given identical covariation information, depressives make more internal, stable, and global attributions for failure than non-depressives. These somewhat ambiguous results could be traced back to various causes. First, our experimental participants were moderately dysphoric college students and not clinically depressed patients. Hence, the assumption that we assessed a truly dysfunctional reaction with the depression inventory might be false. In addition, the hypothetically presented covariation information might not have been personally relevant to the participants and therefore might not have triggered depressogenic schemata. We followed up on these possible explanations for our failure to find a Depression × Covariation Information interaction in two further studies.

Perceived covariation information and attributions

Försterling et al. (1998, Experiment 4) and Försterling and Bühner (2003) investigated whether (clinically and non-clinically) depressed individuals differ from nondepressives with regard to their implicit assumptions about covariation information. Do depressives possibly assume that there is, for instance, generally low consensus with regard to negative events and this is the reason why their attributions differ from non-depressives? To test these possiblities we assessed – in addition to depression and causal attributions – perceived covariation information. Participants imagined negative events (e.g., to have failed an important exam) and marked on scales – as in the previous studies – to what extent the cause for this event was internal, stable, and global. In addition, participants were asked how many other individuals would probably experience this negative event (perceived consensus), how the participant did in other areas (e.g., how s/he performed at other tasks: perceived distinctiveness), and how they did in comparable situations in the past (perceived consistency).

In all three studies, depressives did not only make more internal, stable, and global attributions than non-depressives but they also assumed covariation information which was entirely consistent with these attributions: they assumed – more so than non-depressives – that there is low consensus with regard to the negative event (e.g., "only very few others in addition to myself have failed the exam"), as well as high consistency (e.g., " I also failed similar tests in the past"), and low distinctiveness (e.g., "I also fail exams in other areas"). This finding points to the possibility that depressives have actually collected different covariation information than non-depressives. Hence, the differences in attributional style between the mood groups might be based on differences in depressives' vs. non-depressives' reality and not in different information processing.

However, such possible differences in actual experiences of the mood groups do not fully explain the mood differences in attributions as depressives also make more internal, stable, and global attributions even when holding self-perceived covariation information constant. For instance, in all studies an aggregated difference score (attribution minus perceived covariation information) was higher for depressives than for non-depressives.

Similarly, when statistically partialling out perceived covariation information, the correlation between depression and a depressogenic attributional style remained significant. These findings suggest that depressives and non-depressives have a general tendency to make internal, stable, and global attributions even when perceived covariation is held constant. Hence, these studies yield findings consistent with the results of the studies in which covariation information is experimentally induced (in the latter type of study depressives made more internal, stable, and global attributions than non-depressives regardless of the induced covariation information). However, these difference scores and analyses with partial correlations involving perceived covariation, depression, and attributions are based on aggregated scores and hence are not informative with regard to the question of how sensitively the attributions reflect perceived covariation information.

To determine whether depressives' or non-depressives' attributions more closely reflect self-perceived covariation information, we calculated intraindividual correlations between attributions and self-perceived covariation information, individually for each participant across 8 situations of the questionnaire assessing attributional style and perceived covariation information. A high positive correlation resulted: internal, global, and stable failure attributions go hand in hand with the assumption that failure covaries with the person, whereas external, variable, and specific attributions are made in connection with the assumption that failure covaried with the circumstances. By contrast, negative correlations result when a participant makes an internal, stable, and global attribution and simultaneously voices the assumption that failure covaried with the circumstances, whereas external, variable, and specific attributions are made together with the assumption that failure covaried with the person. For instance, a negative correlation will result when a person attributes failure to external, variable, and specific causes (i.e., "failure was due to bad luck") and simultaneously assumes that s/he is the only one who fails at this task, that s/he had repeatedly failed at this task, and that s/he fails at other tasks as well (low consensus, high consistency, and low distinctiveness).

In all three studies, the mean correlation between self-perceived covariation information and attributions was higher for depressives than for non-depressive participants. This finding is consistent with the hypothesis of "depressive realism" and, at first glance, it is not compatible with our integrative attributional model.

Taken together, the studies in which the attributions of depressives and non-depressives were compared to experimentally induced and self-perceived covariation information, revealed the following findings: There is a general tendency that depressives make more internal, stable, and global attributions for failure than non-depressives, even when covariation information is experimentally controlled or statistically held constant. However, it is not clear whether the depressive or the non-depressive style is "closer to reality." Moreover, the mood groups appear to be comparably sensitive to experimentally induced covariation information. In addition, depressives were somewhat more sensitive in their causal judgments with regard to their self-perceived covariation information than non-depressives (however, this effect was rather small). Hence, the difference in attributions between depressives and non-depressives seems to concern an attribution bias rather than a difference in information processing. Or, to put it somewhat metaphorically: depressives and non-depressives seem to see reality in a similar way but through colored glasses. It remains to be determined whether the bias reflects depressives' dark glasses or non-depressives' rose-colored glasses.

Hence, our findings lead to two questions: The first question is whether the attributions of depressives or non-depressives constitute a bias? And, secondly, to what extent is self-perceived covariation information of depressives and non-depressives realistic?

Meta-attributional veridicality: Attributions within dyads

With regard to the first question, Försterling, Schuster, and Morgenstern (2005) conducted a study in which an "objective" standard for the detection of the direction of an attribution bias was assessed. Participants were members of heterosexual couples who had already spent a considerable amount of time with each other and hence should have had a good knowledge of their respective partner. In addition to measures of depression (Beck Depression Inventory), assessments of the following variables were taken from each participant. As in the previously reported studies, each participant made, in an attributional style questionnaire, attributions for their individual behavioral outcomes (e.g., "you fail an important exam; how do you explain that?"). In addition, participants made attributions about the same behavioral outcomes of their partner (e.g., "your partner fails an important exam; how do you explain that?"). Finally, participants were asked for their expectations as to how their partner would explain their behavioral outcome (e.g., "you fail an important exam; how would your partner explain that?"). The simultaneous assessment of the attributions which the partner actually made for the behavioral outcome of the participant and the attribution which the participant expected from the partner provides an objective criterion for the veridicality of the attribution. More specifically, we could determine whether depressives or non-depressives deviate more, and in what direction, with regard to their expectations of their partner's attributions from the attribution which the partner actually made. We found that depressive participants expected their partners to be making more internal, stable, and global attributions for their (i.e., the participant's) failure than the partners actually made. In contrast, non-depressives were more realistic in the judgment as to how their partners explain their (i.e., the non-depressives') failures. This finding about the meta-attributional veridicality suggests that depressives' pessimistic attributions are indeed more unrealistic than the attributions of non-depressives.

Veridicality of subjectively perceived covariation information

As already indicated, we did not only find differences between depressives and non-depressives with regard to their attributions but also with regard to self-perceived covariation information. When depressives fail a task, they not only assume that failure was due to internal, stable, and global causes, but they also believe that only few other individuals failed the task (low consensus), that they failed this type of task in the past as well (high consistency), and that they had also failed different tasks in the past (low distinctiveness). These mood-group differences with regard to self-perceived covariation information are entirely consistent with the differences in attributions between depressed and non-depressed individuals. Therefore, Försterling and Binser (2002) extended the question of whether depressives are more or less realistic in their causal judgments than non-depressives and investigated whether the mood groups differ in the veridicality of subjectively perceived covariation information.

An area in which both objective and subjective covariation information are readily available is the school context. Pupils receive grades in a certain field (e.g., mathematics) at different points of time (consistency information), their performances are graded in other areas as well (e.g., German and English: distinctiveness), and their peers receive grades too (consensus). These different types of grades (covariation information) are objectively available in the school records and they are (subjectively) available in the memory of the pupils. And a comparison of the subjective and the objective representations allows an assessment of the veridicality of perceived covariation.

Försterling and Binser (2002) assessed depression scores (Beck Depression Inventory) of 183 pupils as well as their memories of their report-card grades in the areas of mathematics, German, and English. In addition, pupils were asked to indicate what they perceived to be the average class grade in these three areas. In a next step, the objective grades were retrieved from the archive.

We found that depressive students had worse grades than nondepressives. This indicates that the objective covariation (i.e., the situation) is in fact more disadvantageous for depressives than for non-depressives. Regarding the veridicality of the subjectively perceived covariation information, we found that pupils generally have a quite realistic assessment of their past grades, however, there was a significant tendency to recall one's grades as somewhat better than they actually were. Most interestingly, the tendency to positively distort memories of school grades was more pronounced among depressed pupils than among non-depressives. This means that, in this study, depressives distorted the objective covariation (distinctiveness and consistency) more than non-depressives in a positive direction. With regard to perceived consensus information (i.e., the estimated average grades), we did not find differences between the mood groups.

Taken together, the application of the integrative attributional model to the analysis of the cognitive components of depression allowed differentiated conceptualizations and investigations of the question of whether depressives are more or less realistic than non-depressives. Our studies assessed mood differences with regard to objective and subjective covariation information, and they have asked how causal attributions are made in response to both subjective and objective covariation information. Finally, we have introduced the concept of meta-attributional veridicality, and we have shown that the internal, stable, and global attributions which depressives expect their partners to be making about themselves (i.e., the depressives) are unrealistic.

The general message of our findings is that depressives make more internal, stable, and global attributions for failure than non-depressives, and that this bias reflects non-veridicality of the depressives. However, the sensitivity of the attribution for covariation information might even be slightly more pronounced for the depressives than for the non-depressives. This pattern of findings, which might appear at first glance paradoxical, is compatible with the assumption that depression might be triggered by unrealistic appraisals (e.g., attributional biases), but that this affective "disorder" leads to increased cognitive examinations of these appraisals, possibly with the goal of recalibration of these causal theories (see Cosmides & Toby, 2000). Hence, a temporal sequence might exist in which unrealistic assumptions lead to depression, depression, in turn, leads to a more elaborated information processing, which, in turn, leads to more realistic appraisals and hence to an amelioration of depression. Naturally, longitudinal designs would be necessary to investigate this question.

Summary and final discussion

The studies described in the present chapter tested a model which integrates conceptions about the antecedents of causal attributions with those about attributional consequences. In these studies, we used operationalizations of veridicality, which were derived form the integrative model. The integrative model was applied to achievement-related behavior and to the analysis of depression. In the achievement context, it was shown that participants who made realistic attributions performed better than individuals who made unrealistic causal ascriptions. These results were obtained with a new experimental paradigm, which implies that overall performance consists of the sum of the performances at subtasks. The findings indicate that the assumption of unambiguous advantages of high ability self-perceptions, which is central to most motivational theories being based on self-concepts of ability and attributions, might need to be revised: unrealistically high self-concepts of ability or an unrealistic tendency to attribute failure to non-ability causes might have disadvantageous effects. In addition, the model's predictions and our results are consistent with the central assumption of theories about the antecedents of causal attributions, that the motive to gain realistic knowledge of one's personal attributes and the environment has a high functional value.

With regard to the attributional analysis of depression we have demonstrated that the model can be used to investigate the question as to whether depressives are more realistic than non-depressives. Our studies on depression revealed that depressives use experimentally induced covariation information for their causal inferences in the same way as non-depressives do (Försterling et al., 1998, Experiments 1–3). The studies in which assessed rather than experimentally induced covariation information was used revealed a (weak but) consistent tendency indicating that depressives' causal inferences more closely reflect self-perceived covariation information (i.e., higher intraindividual correlations) than nondepressives' attributions (Försterling et al., 1998 Experiment 4; Försterling & Bühner, 2003, Study 1 and 2). These results are inconsistent with the hypothesis that depressives are more unrealistic than non-depressives. At least, depressives do not exhibit a (covariation) information processing deficit. However, all studies revealed that, given identical (experimentally induced or self-perceived) covariation information, depressives make more internal, stable, and global attributions than non-depressives. These results probably reflect a pessimistic bias of depressives, i.e., a pessimistic constant factor, which is added in each configuration of covariation information (see Försterling et al., 2005). Taken together, our studies investigating the veridicality of depressives' attributions revealed that depressives do not process covariation information inaccurately, but possibly even more accurately. However, their inferences from covariation information have a (constant) unrealistic pessimistic bias.

The finding that depressives' information processing with regard to covariation information is not deficient when compared to non-depressives seems, at first glance, inconsistent with our model, which suggests that dysfunctional reactions are caused by unrealistic attributions. However, our data might be compatible with a temporal sequence model of depression. This temporal sequence could imply that depression is triggered by unrealistic cognitions and that depression is a self-repair mechanism leading to more realistic thoughts by inducing the individual to process information more analytically. This, in turn, might lead to more realistic appraisals. However, a test of such a model would require longitudinal studies.

References

Abramson, L. Y., Seligman, M. E. P., & Teasdale, J. D. (1978). Learned helplessnesss in humans. *Journal of Abnormal Psychology, 87,* 49–74.

Beck, A. T., Ward, C. H., Mendelson, M., Mock, J., & Erbaugh, J., (1961). An inventory for measuring depression. *Archives of General Psychiatry, 4,* 561–571.

Buss, D. M. (1995). Evolutionary psychology: A new paradigm for psychological science. *Psychological Inquiry, 6,* 1–30.

Cosmides, L. (1989). The logic of social exchange: Has natural selection shaped how humans reason? Studies with Wason selection task. *Cognition, 31*(3), 187–276.

Cosmides, L. & Toby, J. (2000). Evolutionary psychology and emotions. In M. Lewis, & J. M. Haviland-Jones (Eds.) *Handbook of Emotions: Second Edition* (pp. 91–115). New York: The Guilford Press.

Dweck, C. S., & Leggett, E. L. (1988). A Social-cognitive approach to motivation in personality. *Psychological Review, 95,* 256–273.
Dweck, C. S., Chiu, C., & Hong, Y. (1995). Implicit theories and their role in judgements and reactions: A world from two perspectives. *Psychological Inquiry, 6(4),* 267–285.
Försterling, F. (1985). Attributional retraining: A review. *Psychological Bulletin, 98,* 495–512.
Försterling, F. (1986). Attributional conceptions in clinical psychology. *American Psychologist, 41,* 275–285.
Försterling, F. (1988). *Attribution theory in clinical psychology*. Chichester, UK: John Wiley & Sons.
Försterling, F. (1989). Models of covariation and causal attribution: How do they relate to the analogy of analysis of variance? *Journal of Personality and Social Psychology, 57,* 615–625.
Försterling, F. (1992). The Kelley Model as an analysis of variance analogy: How far can it be taken? *Journal of Experimental Social Psychology, 28,* 475–490.
Försterling, F. (1994) The functional value of realistic causal attributions. In W. Stroebe & M. Hewstone (Eds.) *European Review of Social Psychology* (Vol. 5, pp. 151–179). Chichester, UK: Wiley.
Försterling, F. (2001). *Attribution: Theory, research and practice*. Social Psychology: A Modular Course. Hove, UK: Psychology Press.
Försterling, F., & Binser, M. (2002). Depression, school performance, and the veridicality of perceived grades and causal attributions. *Personality and Social Psychology Bulletin, 28,* 1441–1449.
Försterling, F., & Bühner, M. (2003). Attributional veridicality and evaluative beliefs: How do they contribute to Depression? *Journal of Social and Clinical Psychology, 22,* 369–392.
Försterling, F., Bühner, M., & Gall, S. (1998). Covariation information, attributions and depression: A test of depressive realism. *Journal of Personality and Social Psychology, 75,* 1047–1061.
Försterling, F., & Morgenstern, M. (2002). Accuracy of self-assessment and task performance: Does it pay to know the truth? *Journal of Educational Psychology, 94,* 576–585.
Försterling, F., & Rudolph, U. (1988). Situations, attributions and the evaluation of behavior. *Journal of Personality and Social Psychology, 54,* 225–232.
Försterling, F., Schuster, B., & Morgenstern, M. (2005). Perspectives of causal attributions: A study of couples and depression. *Journal of Social and Clinical Psychology, 24,* 767–784.
Heider, F. (1958). *The psychology of interpersonal relations*. New York: Wiley.
Kelley, H. H. (1967). Attribution theory in social psychology. In D. Levine, *Nebraska Symposium on Motivation, Vol. 15* (pp. 192–238). Lincoln, NE: University of Nebraska Press.
McArthur, L. A. (1972). The how and what of why: Some determinants and consequences of causal attributions. *Journal of Personality and Social Psychology, 22,* 171-193.
Meyer, W.-U. (1973). *Leistungsmotiv und Ursachenerklärung von Erfolg und Mißerfolg* [Achievement motive and causal explanations for success and failure]. Stuttgart, Germany: Klett.

Schuster, B., Rudolph, U., & Försterling, F. (1998). Attributions or covariation information: What determines behavioral reaction decisions? *Personality and Social Psychology Bulletin, 24,* 838–854.

Weiner, B. (1986). *An attributional theory of motivation and emotion*. New York: Springer.

Weiner, B., Russell, D., & Lerman, D. (1978). Affective consequences of causal ascriptions. In J. H. Harvey, W. J. Ickes, & R. F. Kidd (Eds.), *New directions in attribution research, Vol. 2* (pp. 59-90). Hillsdale, NJ: Erlbaum.

Self-Management Training (SMT)

Theoretical and Empirical Foundations for the Development of a Metamotivational and Metavolitional Intervention Program

Hugo M. Kehr & Lutz von Rosenstiel

Introduction

"Cui bono?" asked the reviewers from the German Research Foundation when they evaluated our research proposal about theoretical and empirical examinations of motivational and volitional processes among managers. Shortly after, personnel officers contacted about arranging our empirical studies also asked "Cui bono?" So from the beginning of this research we were concerned with possible applications. We soon realized that development of a self-management training program might be a suitable response to the understandable call for application of our motivational and volitional research.

This chapter presents the key achievements of our endeavor. We start by reviewing the literature on self-management and self-management training and by identifying some limitations of existing approaches. We then sketch the basic version of the compensatory model of work motivation and volition (Kehr, 2004b), a theoretical framework for integrating recent research developments in dual system theories of motivation and volitional self-regulation. This framework is then used to derive the metamotivational and metavolitional intervention concept and develop the self-management training (SMT).

SMT involves six training modules: (1) goal setting and reducing goal conflicts, (2) increasing awareness of implicit motives, (3) enhancing volition, (4) reducing overcontrol, (5) enhancing organismic congruence and intrinsic motivation, and (6) identifying and overcoming barriers to action. We end the chapter with a detailed description of the six training modules. For each module, we provide a literature review, supplemented with illustrative data from our research with managers. We also explain the intervention goals, and describe the methods and didactics used.

A short literature review

From the perspective of motivational psychology (e.g., Heckhausen, 1984), *self-management* involves the ability to systematically enhance one's motivation and volition and to overcome barriers to action (Kehr, 2001). With clinical applications in mind, Kanfer and Karoly (1982) proposed a more elaborate definition:

> Self-management, while covering a wide range of processes, generally signifies the gradual assumption of control by the individual over cueing, directing, rewarding, and correcting his or her own behavior. The term suggests active client participation in goal setting and evaluation, in attention to internal and external responses, and in the use of cognitive processes to increase adaptive effectiveness. (p. 576)

Being narrower than the definition of Baltes, Smith, and Staudinger (1992), yet broader than the conceptualizations of Brigham (1982), Carver and Scheier (1982), and Kossek, Roberts, Fisher, and Demarr (1998), this definition fits the theoretical concept underlying our approach to self-management. In particular, Kanfer and Karoly's (1982) definition differentiates between internal and external processes, combines motivational and volitional elements, and conceptualizes self-regulation as an evolving ability. We adopt it in part because it does not dichotomize "existent" and "non-existent" aspects, which is important for intervention.

Numerous approaches have been proposed for enhancing self-management (e.g., Brigham, 1982; Carver & Scheier, 1982; Hackman, 1986; Kanfer & Schefft, 1988; Manz, 1986; Mills, 1983; Neck & Manz, 1992). An early example is Florin and von Rosenstiel's (1976) program aimed at increasing self-management among students with test anxiety and achievement deficits. This program embraces ten flexibly combinable modules including time management, goal setting, and cognitive as well as systematic desensitization techniques to counteract test anxiety. The theoretical background for these self-management interventions are Bandura's (1988, 1989; Bandura & Schunk, 1981) theories on self-regulation, Mahoney's (1972; Mahoney & Thoresen, 1974) work on self-reinforcement, and Kanfer's (Kanfer & Gaelick, 1986; Kanfer & Karoly, 1982) cognitive self-management therapy.

Goals of self-management interventions are diverse and include enhancing control of emotional reactions, fear, intrusive thoughts, conflicting life situations, negative self-reactions, and unwanted desires (Kanfer & Karoly, 1982). Such diverse goals require a variety of methods. Karoly (1995) listed over 50 methods for self-management interventions. Most of these combine some of the following elements: goal setting (Bandura, 1988; Locke & Latham, 1990), self-observation and self-reinforcement (Kanfer & Gaelick, 1986), imagination (Meichenbaum, 1978; Neck & Manz, 1992), and cognitive strategies to increase self-efficacy (Bandura & Schunk, 1981; Schwarzer, 1992).

Kanfer and Gaelick (1986) asserted that clients, not trainers or therapists, are the most effective agents to change dysfunctional cognitions and behaviors. Trainers and therapists should support self-awareness and change by offering guidance and feedback. Self-observation and behavior modification are difficult and unpleasant, and thus require a strong training motivation on the behalf of the client and stable alliances between client and trainer. A self-management intervention should not be restricted to resolving specific actual problems, but should aim to increase general competencies.

There has been little work on assessing self-management interventions. The work of Frayne and Latham (1987; Latham & Frayne, 1989) is an oft-cited exception. This study showed that self-management training that integrated Locke and Latham's (1984) goal setting and Bandura's (1988, 1989) approach to self-regulation increased job attendance among unionized government employees. With a similar intervention based on goal setting and self-efficacy, Frayne and Geringer (2000) improved objective and subjective job performance of salespeople. In contrast, an intervention on career self-management by Kossek et al. (1998) was unsuccessful and even decreased career-oriented self-management. However, the scope of career self-management, "the degree to which one regularly gathers information and plans for career problem solving and decision making" (Kossek et al., 1998, p. 938), is narrower than the concept of self-management proposed here.

Wexley and Baldwin (1986) demonstrated that cognitive training interventions including goal setting are more successful than training lacking this element. Gist, Bavetta, and Stevens (1990) examined whether this success depends on goal setting per se or on *interactions* of goal setting with other self-management techniques. The authors concluded that an integrative approach is preferable, particularly for innovative tasks in unstructured environments.

Which elements should be involved in such an integrated approach? Some authors suggest new agendas for self-management to complement existing approaches and overcome their limitations. Kanfer (1990) proposed that self-management interventions should not only support cognitive mechanisms relevant for motivation – virtually all prior approaches include this aspect -, but also focus on *affective components* of motivational processes. Karoly (1993) suggested *internal conflicts* should get more attention in endeavors to enhance self-management. Kanfer and Heggestad (1997) say new approaches to self-management should not only involve internal conflicts but also *self-regulatory mechanisms of conflict-resolution*. They also advocate a *differential approach* to self-management intervention, with training tailored to the individual client's personality structure, particularly to the person's motivational traits and skills (Kanfer & Heggestad, 1997). Recently, Comelli and von Rosenstiel (2001) advocated a comprehensive approach to self-management, which involves, in addition to the concepts cited above, role (re-) interpretation, development of visions, reduction of over-motivation, maintaining equilibrium between job and private life, and workplace redesign.

Earlier approaches to self-management, however, were predominantly concerned with specific psychological phenomena that are easily consciously accessible and affected by straightforward cognitive interventions (e.g., the relatively clear *goal* construct and goal setting interventions). Some earlier approaches were atheoretical or based on "mini-theories," resulting in simplistic recipes instead of being founded on a closely knit body of knowledge suitable for differential intervention.

These early approaches left little room for the observation of affective, subconscious, and dynamic processes, intrapersonal conflicts, and corresponding self-regulatory conflict-resolution strategies. One likely reason for the limitations of earlier self-management concepts is that theoretical developments in basic psychological research during the last two decades have not been fully incorporated into applied approaches to self-management. Two key research trends are dual system approaches to motivation (Brunstein, Schultheiss, & Grässmann, 1998; Deci & Ryan, 2000; Emmons & McAdams, 1991; McClelland, Koestner, & Weinberger, 1989) and approaches to volitional self-regulation (Karoly, 1995; Kuhl, 2000; Metcalfe & Mischel, 1999; Muraven & Baumeister, 2000; Sokolowski, 1993). Attempts to develop self-management interventions that overcome the limitations of earlier approaches should be based on a comprehensive model that integrates these two research trends.

The compensatory model of work motivation and volition

Overview of the model

The compensatory model of work motivation and volition (Kehr, 2004b) combines two previously unrelated lines of research: the dual system approach to human motivation and research on volitional self-regulation. A detailed description of this model and its precursors can be found in Kehr (1999, in 2004b, c). Here, we summarize the model and its background.

Figure 1 illustrates the compensatory model of work motivation and volition in its basic version[1] (see Kehr, 1999, 2004c). Structural components of the model, the implicit motive system and the explicit motive system, are represented as two circles. The dark circle on the right represents the explicit motive system, in particular explicit goals, and the bright circle on the left represents the implicit motive system.

The intersection of the two circles in Figure 1 suggests partial overlap of implicit and explicit motive systems. This intersection is associated with the absence of intrapersonal conflict. Hence, volitional conflict-resolution is unnecessary. Instead, congruence of implicit and explicit motives is associated with intrinsic motivation.

Figure 1. Compensatory model of work motivation and volition (basic version).

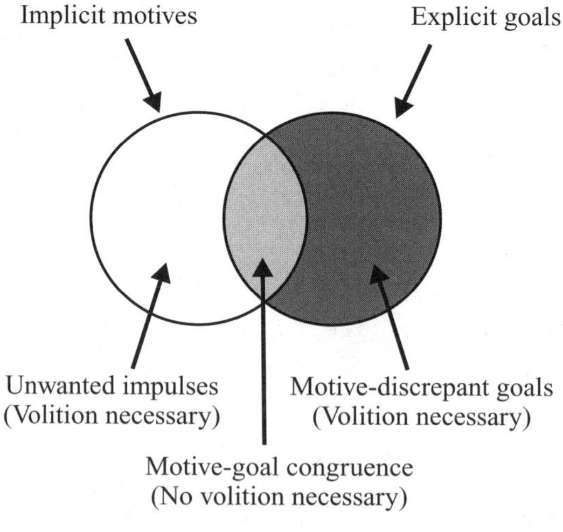

[1] The comprehensive version of this model (see Kehr, 2004b) also considers perceived abilities as an additional structural component of the model and problem solving (supplementing insufficient abilities) as an additional functional property. For self-management interventions, however, we focus on implicit motives and explicit goals, the basic structural components of the model (see Kehr, 1999, 2004c).

In contrast, the non-overlapping sections of the two circles represent a discrepancy between implicit motives and explicit motives, where volitional regulation is necessary. The two non-overlapping sections in Figure 1 suggest a twofold function of volition. One function of volition supports explicit motives discrepant from implicit needs and motives (this corresponds to the outer sector of the dark circle). The second function of volition suppresses behavioral tendencies from aroused implicit motives incongruent with consciously represented, explicit motives (this corresponds to the outer sector of the bright circle). The following sections explain the components of the model and its functional properties in more detail.

Implicit and explicit motive systems

Dual system approaches to human motivation distinguish between implicit and explicit motive systems (Brunstein et al., 1998; Deci & Ryan, 2000; Emmons & McAdams, 1991; McClelland et al., 1989). The distinction can be traced to pioneering work by Lewin (1926), Michotte and Prüm (1910), and Wundt (1896/1907). As early as 1910, Michotte and Prüm, the first experimentors on the issue, contrasted intrinsic motives (*motifs intrinsèques*) and extrinsic motives (*motifs extrinsèques*).

Based on extensive earlier work (Koestner, Weinberger, & McClelland, 1991; McClelland, 1985; McClelland, Atkinson, Clark, & Lowell, 1953; McClelland et al., 1989), McClelland (1995) isolated the differences between implicit and explicit motives. *Implicit motives* are associated with task-intrinsic interest and spontaneous behavior (Koestner et al., 1991). Because implicit motives are not consciously represented (McClelland et al., 1953), assessment requires projective measurement techniques such as the Thematic Apperception Test (TAT; Murray, 1943). According to McClelland (1995), the "big three" implicit motives are power, achievement, and affiliation. The power motive relates to dominance and social control (e.g., a manager having lunch with the CEO). The achievement motive arises when personal performance standards must be met or exceeded (e.g., a worker trying to increase output). Finally, the affiliation motive involves establishing and intensifying social relationships (e.g., an employee extending the break to finish a talk with a new colleague). Researchers also differentiate hope (i.e., approach) and fear (i.e., avoidance) motives (Atkinson, 1964; Higgins, 1998; Kanfer & Heggestad, 1997; Sokolowski, Schmalt, Langens, & Puca, 2000). Conceptually, implicit motives relate to constructs such as *basic* and *organismic needs* (Ryan & Deci, 2000; Sheldon & Kasser, 1995), *immediate-return needs* (Martin, 1999), and *auto-motives* (Bargh, 1990).

In contrast, *explicit motives* are the reasons people self-attribute for their actions (McClelland et al., 1989). Explicit motives are strongly influenced by social demands (Koestner et al., 1991) and often appear as goals or duties (McClelland et al., 1989). Being consciously accessible, explicit motives can be assessed with questionnaires such as the Personality Research Form (PRF; Jackson, 1984). Among the constructs related to explicit motives, *goals* have received the most attention in the literature (Farr, Hofmann, & Ringenbach, 1993; Hollenbeck & Klein, 1987; Locke & Latham, 1990; von Rosenstiel, Kehr, & Maier, 2000) and hence this chapter primarily focuses on the goal construct.[2]

---

2 Precisely, explicit goals are not identical to explicit motives, because explicit motives must combine with perceived abilities in order to instigate explicit goals (see Kehr, 2004b). For the purpose of the present article, however, it is sufficient to treat the two constructs as identical.

Here, *explicit goals* represent other constructs rooted in the explicit motive system, such as *strivings* (Emmons, 1986), *intentions* (Gollwitzer, 1993), and *self-concepts* (Markus & Wurf, 1987).

Regarding empirical support for the overlap section in Figure 1, several authors reported small empirical correlations between implicit and explicit motive systems (Brunstein et al., 1998; Cantor & Blanton, 1996; Emmons & McAdams, 1991; King, 1995; Sokolowski et al., 2000). Despite these correlations, there is general agreement that implicit and explicit motives are conceptually distinct and functionally independent (Brunstein et al., 1998; McClelland et al., 1989), because they relate to different aspects of the person (Spangler, 1992). Being largely independent of each other, implicit and explicit motives give rise to behavioral tendencies that may conflict. Accordingly, McClelland et al. (1989) noted, "Whatever the reasons for discordance between implicit and explicit motives, it can certainly lead to trouble" (p. 700).

To-date, there is ample evidence that discrepancies between implicit and explicit motive systems can cause psychological conflicts and may result in impaired psychological well-being and physical health problems (Brunstein et al., 1998; Kehr, 2004a; McClelland et al., 1989; Ryan & Deci, 2000; Ryan, Sheldon, Kasser, & Deci, 1996). In contrast, congruence of implicit and explicit motive systems is intrinsically motivating, free of conflict, and fulfilling, hence establishing preconditions for happiness, well-being, and health (Brunstein et al., 1998; Deci & Ryan, 2000; Kehr, 2004c; Mischel, 1999; Ryan & Deci, 2000; Sheldon & Elliot, 1999; Sheldon & Kasser, 1995).

The larger the discrepancy between implicit and explicit motives (i.e., the smaller the overlap of the circles in Figure 1), the more behavioral conflict and dysfunctional consequences one may expect. Simply put, the less I know about my deeper needs and implicit motives, the higher the chances I will develop goals discrepant from my deeper needs and suffer from resulting conflicts.

Volitional regulation

How do people handle and resolve such behavior-related conflict? Here, volitional self-regulation comes into play. Several researchers analyzed action-related, intrapersonal conflict and volitional conflict-resolution strategies that may resolve such conflict (Ainslie & Haslam, 1992; Bazerman, Tenbrunsel, & Wade-Benzoni, 1998; Kehr, 2004c; Kuhl, 1985, 2000; Kuhl & Goschke, 1994; Loewenstein, 1996; Metcalfe & Mischel, 1999; Mischel, Cantor, & Feldman, 1996; Sokolowski, 1993). The idea common to most volitional regulation approaches is that intrinsically motivated behavior (i.e., behavior in accord with basic needs and motives; Deci & Ryan, 2000) does not need volitional regulation (Karoly, 1995). In contrast, volition is needed to act *against* intrinsically motivated behavioral tendencies or to act *in the absence of* intrinsic motivation (Kehr, 2004c; Kuhl & Goschke, 1994; Sokolowski, 1993). Because volition *compensates* for insufficient motivation, the model is called the compensatory model.

Sokolowski (1993) made the distinction between motivation and volition explicit by contrasting "motivational regulation" and "volitional regulation." Sokolowski speaks of motivational regulation if behaviors accord with the person's actually aroused implicit motives. In contrast, behaviors not in accord with the person's actually aroused implicit motives require volitional regulation. Using different terminology, Kuhl and Fuhrmann (1998) proposed a similar concept when they contrasted "self-organization" (behavior energized by implicit motives) from "self-regulation" (behavior insufficiently energized by implicit motives and requiring volitional support).

Constructs closely related to our concept of volition are *willpower* (Metcalfe & Mischel, 1999; Mischel, 1996), *motivational skills* (Kanfer & Heggestad, 1997), and *self-control* in its narrow sense (e.g., control to override or inhibit competing urges; Muraven & Baumeister, 2000; Rachlin, 1995). However, volition as used here is narrower than Binswanger's (1991) volition or Latham and Locke's (1991) *self-regulation*, because the latter terms subsume every goal-related effort (not just cases where internal conflicts must be resolved or unwanted impulses overridden).

Some researchers suggested coalescing dual system theories of motivation with approaches to volitional self-regulation and proposed that volitional regulation might be needed to handle discrepancies between implicit and explicit motive systems (Brunstein, Schultheiss, & Maier, 1999; Emmons, 1999; Epstein, 1998; Kehr, 1999, 2004c; Ryan et al., 1996). Ryan et al. (1996) noted that extrinsic actions resulting from goals discrepant to basic needs require volitional initiation. Conversely, Karoly (1995) maintained that volitional regulation is unnecessary if there are no such discrepancies. He wrote, "Clearly, if a person's actions automatically or naturally matched her or his intentions, there would be little need for a process model of volition" (Karoly, 1995, p. 262).

Figure 1 suggests volitional regulation has two functions: to *support* motive-discrepant goals (corresponding to the outer sector of the dark circle) and to *suppress* unwanted implicit impulses from aroused implicit motives (corresponding to the outer sector of the bright circle). Several lines of evidence suggest such a distinction (Atkinson & Birch, 1970; Forgas, Johnson, & Ciarrochi, 1998; Mischel, 1996; Norman & Shallice, 1986). Atkinson and Birch (1970), for example, contrasted "inhibitory" forces that suppress behavioral impulses and "instigating" forces that enforce activated goal representations.

For this twofold task, an array of volitional strategies can be employed (Kehr, 2004c; Kuhl, 1985; Kuhl & Fuhrmann, 1998; Metcalfe & Mischel, 1999). These include *motivation control* (i.e., developing positive goal-related fantasies in the face of difficulties; see Lewin, 1926; Mischel, 1996; Oettingen, Pak, & Schnetter, 2001), *emotion control* (i.e., adjusting emotional states to the demands of the current intention; see Bagozzi, Baumgartner, & Pieters, 1998; Erber, 1996; Forgas et al., 1998; Gross, 1999) *attention control* (i.e., focusing attention on aspects of the situation relevant to the current intention; see Atkinson & Birch, 1970; Egeth & Yantis, 1997; James, 1890/1981; Norman & Shallice, 1986), and *decision control* (i.e., employing mechanisms to decide quickly and avoid rumination; see Koole, Smeets, van Knippenberg, & Dijksterhuis, 1999; Michotte & Prüm, 1910; Tyszka, 1998).

Like other psychological processes, volitional regulation may have deficiencies. Volition (a) can be ineffective, (b) consume resources, (c) have unwanted side-effects, and (d) be dysfunctionally associated with rigid self-control. With respect to (a), it was found that emotions (Morris & Reilly, 1987) and attentional processes (Wegner, 1994) are often uncontrollable. With respect to (b), recent experiments show that after volitional acts (e.g., eating radishes rather than chocolates), subsequent acts of volition (e.g., persisting in unsolvable puzzles) are more likely to fail (Baumeister, Bratslavsky, Muraven, & Tice, 1998; Muraven & Baumeister, 2000). This led to a resource-based concept of "volitional strength," where volitional acts consume and ultimately deplete volitional strength. Regarding (c), Kanfer and Ackerman (1989) proposed that volitional activities block cognitive capacities and make them unavailable for other task-related activities. Negative side-effects of volition include strain, emotional distress, maladaptive behavior, and behavioral excesses after relapse (Cantor & Blanton, 1996; Polivy, 1998). This leads to (d), the hazards of rigid self-control ("overcontrol"; Asendorpf & Van Aken, 1999). People who constantly overemphasize goals, ignore deeper needs, and use dysfunctional volitional strategies (e.g., negative fantasies, extreme internal pressure) may suffer from impaired well-being and alienation (Deci & Ryan, 2000; Kuhl & Fuhrmann, 1998; Polivy, 1998).

Empirical support for the compensatory model

Recent studies (Kehr, 2004a, 2003a) tested a crucial proposition of the compensatory model. The twofold function of volition suggests volitional self-regulation is needed to bridge discrepancies between implicit and explicit motives or suppress unwanted impulses from implicit motives. The first function of volition was examined by Kehr (2004a) and the second function of volition was the objective of Kehr (2003a).

The underlying idea of Kehr (2004a) was that discrepancies between implicit and explicit motives cause behavioral conflict requiring conflict-regulation by volitional mechanisms. Adopting a resource-based concept of volition (Baumeister et al., 1998; Muraven & Baumeister, 2000), it may be expected that discrepancies between implicit and explicit motives require volitional resources, which may ultimately lead to a "depletion" (Baumeister et al., 1998; Muraven & Baumeister, 2000) of the person's volitional resources.

Kehr's (2004a) study used a longitudinal design to strengthen causal inference. Study participants were managers from several companies representing diverse industries. Implicit motives were measured using the Multi-Motive Grid (MMG; Sokolowski et al., 2000), a semi-projective diagnostic tool measuring the "big three" (McClelland, 1995) implicit motives: achievement, affiliation, and power/dominance (Sokolowski et al., 2000). Similar to the TAT, the MMG uses pictorial stimuli. In contrast to picture-story tests such as the TAT, the MMG does not require participants to write stories, but to choose statements fitting a particular picture. Motive scores are the sum of scores for 14 pictures. Reliability, validity, and acceptance of the MMG, which has a relatively long research tradition (Schmalt, 1976), are satisfactory (Sokolowski et al., 2000). MMG scores predict task enjoyment and intrinsic motivation (see Sokolowski et al., 2000, for a summary), so it seems safe to conclude that the MMG relates to the implicit, not the explicit, motive system (see McClelland et al., 1989).

Explicit motives were assessed by three subscales of the Personality Research Form (PRF; Jackson, 1984): dominance, affiliation, and achievement. PRF uses self-ascriptions (e.g., "I try to control others rather than permit them to control me") related to the explicit motive system (McClelland, 1985; McClelland et al., 1989). Dependent measures were volitional strength (measured with subscales of the Volitional Components Inventory, VCI; Kuhl & Fuhrmann, 1998) and subjective well-being (using a composite of positive and negative affect; see Brunstein, 1993).

Kehr's (2004a) results can be summarized as follows: Discrepancies between the managers' implicit and explicit motives were associated with reduced volitional strength. Structural equation modeling confirmed that the discrepancy/well-being relation was fully mediated by reduced volitional strength.

Another longitudinal field study with managers (Kehr, 2003a) intended to replicate these findings and extend their scope to implicit fear motives. The idea was that implicit fear motives might cause avoidance-related behavioral impulses that conflict with other approach-related goals of the person and thus require suppression, the second function of volition.

Implicit fear motives were measured with an aggregate of the three fear-related subscales of the MMG (i.e., fear of failure, fear of rejection, and fear of loss of control). As predicted, managers high on implicit fear motives had reduced volitional strength and subsequently decreased well-being. Structural equation modeling again showed that the reduction in volitional strength fully mediated the effects of fear motives on decreased well-being.

The results corroborate the basic proposition of the compensatory model: Dysfunctional motive constellations – be it implicit/explicit motive discrepancies as in Kehr (2004a) or implicit fear motives as in Kehr (2003a) – require volitional support and deplete the person's volitional resources. Taken together, the studies substantiate the twofold function of volition, an essential element of the compensatory model.

Deriving the concept of self-management training (SMT) from the model

Self-management training (SMT), based on the compensatory model of work motivation and volition, is primarily employed in management training programs (Kehr, 2001, 2003d) but can also be used for self-instruction (Kehr, 2002).

We explain how the concept of metamotivation and metavolition, underlying the SMT, was derived from the compensatory model and then describe how the concept of metamotivation and metavolition was transformed into the six training modules of the SMT. Finally, we describe the training procedure.

Metamotivation and metavolition

Metacognitive processes assist people in improving behavioral competencies (Brown; 1978; Heckhausen, 1984; Kuhl & Kraska, 1989). Because metacognition covers a wide range of phenomena, it is necessary to focus on metaprocesses pertaining to motivational approaches to self-management (see Heckhausen, 1984).

According to the compensatory model of motivation and volition, behavior is either intrinsically motivated or requires volitional support, in line with Sokolowski's (1993) distinction between motivational regulation and volitional regulation. Analogously, metamotivational and metavolitional processes may be contrasted. In a first terminological approximation, *metamotivation* denotes metacognitive strategies to improve motivational processes, and *metavolition* refers to metacognitive strategies to improve volitional processes.

More specifically, metamotivational strategies aim to increase intrinsic motivation by reducing discrepancies between implicit and explicit motives (Schultheiss & Brunstein, 1999) and to enhance the person's "organismic congruence" (Sheldon & Kasser, 1995; cf. Ryan et al., 1996). For example, a person high on implicit affiliation motive may be encouraged to develop career goals involving extensive contact with other people. In contrast, metavolitional techniques aim to enhance effectiveness of volitional strategies and reduce their resource consumption and negative side-effects. For example, people may be encouraged to develop positive instead of negative self-regulatory fantasies (see Kehr, 2003c).

Metavolitional strategies thus support goals and enforce goal implementation, often by suppressing competing behavioral impulses (Gollwitzer & Bayer, 1999) originating in aroused implicit motives (McClelland et al., 1989). Metamotivational strategies, in contrast, support implicit motives and organismic needs and increase the chances of need satisfaction. This may require changing or reprioritizing goals, particularly goals that are primarily socially determined (Koestner et al., 1991) and externally regulated (Deci & Ryan, 2000). By increasing thematical congruence between implicit and explicit motives (the overlap section in Figure 1), metamotivation decreases the probability that volitional regulation will be needed to overcome future conflicts from discrepancies between implicit and explicit motives. So, metavolition *improves* volitional strategies to handle behavioral conflict, whereas metamotivation *avoids* behavioral conflict and the necessity of volition. Hence, metamotivation is the more fundamental and far-reaching strategy.

However, achieving perfect integration of implicit and explicit motives is unlikely. Even people with relatively high integration occasionally experience situations requiring volitional support. In these situations, it is advantageous to use a flexible array of volitional strategies and to be aware of costs and drawbacks associated with these strategies. Thus, metavolition complements any metamotivational approach.

Historically, the distinction between metavolition and metamotivation can be traced to Ach (1935) and Lindworsky (1923a). Ach (1935) contrasted "volitional effort" and "modification of goals", and Lindworsky (1923a) proposed that interventions to enhance willpower will only be successful if accompanied by systematic development of the person's goals. A similar account for the interplay of metamotivation and metavolition can be found in Polivy (1998), who wrote, "The goal is twofold; one should act in accordance with one's motives, while balancing any conflicting desires or external constraints" (p. 185). Additional concepts similar to the distinction between metamotivation and metavolition are offered by Neck and Manz (1996), who discriminated between establishing new self-directions on the one hand and self-motivational strategies on the other, or by Rosenbaum (1998), who differentiated between opening and closing skills.

Overview of the concept of self-management training (SMT)

Here, we discuss how SMT relates to the compensatory model and the concept of metamotivation and metavolition, and we give an overview of SMT and the six training modules [3] that comprise it. A more thorough description of the theoretical and empirical background of each module will be given in the next section.

The six SMT modules are: (1) goal setting and reducing goal conflicts, (2) increasing awareness of implicit motives, (3) enhancing volition, (4) reducing overcontrol, (5) enhancing organismic congruence and intrinsic motivation, (6) identifying and overcoming barriers to action.

[3] Training *modules* permit breaking up the training program and using separate modules according to specific training needs (see Tannenbaum & Yukl, 1992). However, similar to the findings of Gist et al. (1990), pretests that isolated single modules proved to be is less effective than an integrated program (for a related argument, see Frayne & Geringer, 2000). We attribute the superiority of the integrated program to the fact that an integrated program allows better overview and insight into interrelations of motivational and volitional processes, an important precondition for an effective intervention into these processes.

Figure 2 illustrates how these six modules relate to the compensatory model. SMT starts by introducing the basic model (Figure 2a) to the participants. Instead of using the terms implicit and explicit motives, the concept is introduced with the metaphor of "head" and "heart" (see Epstein, 1994; see also Weiner, 1992, p. 343 f., for the benefits of metaphors). In general, "head" is associated with rational thoughts, whereas "heart" is associated with feelings and emotions. This closely resembles the underlying concept of explicit and implicit motives.[4]

Participants are then asked in which direction they would shift the two circles in Figure 2a (i.e., what these circles represent), if this were possible. Most people say one of the circles (or both) should be moved towards the other; intuitively, the intersection seems to promise positive outcomes with respect to personal success and well-being. Participants are also asked how they would realize this intended change. Most participants agree that the initial step should be to analyze what the two circles represent, in order to more fully understand the actual situation.

This is exactly what is intended with the first two training modules. Modules 1 and 2 concentrate on structural components of the compensatory model. Module 1 (*explicit*

Figure 2. The six training modules of SMT.

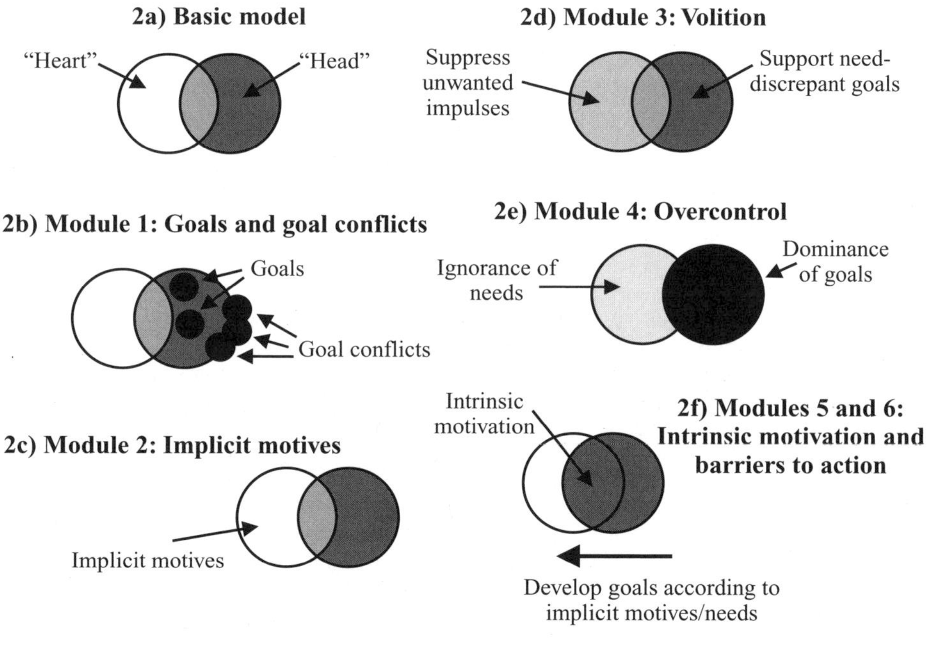

[4] SMT was originally invented in Germany. The German language contains the metaphor of "Kopf" (head) and "Bauch" (literally: stomach), conveying the distinction between implicit and explicit motive systems better than Epstein's (1994) "head" and "heart" metaphor. This is because "Bauch" in German is not only associated with feelings and emotions (the connotation of "heart"), but additionally transmits the idea of intuition (i.e., "gut feeling").

goals; see Figure 2b) comprises goal setting techniques (Bandura, 1988; Latham & Locke, 1991), and identification and resolution of goal conflicts by reprioritizing goals (Cantor & Blanton, 1996; Emmons, King, & Sheldon, 1993). Module 2 (*implicit motives*; see Figure 2c) aims at enhancing awareness of implicit motives, consistent with the view that implicit motives should not be ignored (Bazerman et al., 1998; Deci & Ryan, 2000; McClelland et al., 1989).

Modules 3 and 4 correspond to the concept of metavolition. Module 3 (*volition*; see Figure 2d) discusses motive-goal discrepancies and the twofold function of volition. Survey feedback is given regarding the participant's volitional strength (Kuhl & Fuhrmann, 1998) and various exercises and homework assignments are recommended to enhance volition (see Erber & Erber, 2000; Mischel, 1996; Kuhl, 1998). Module 4 (*overcontrol*; see Figure 2e) illuminates rigid self-control, the "dark side" of volition. Survey feedback is given regarding the person's inclination to rigid self-control (Kuhl & Fuhrmann, 1998), and exercises are employed to counteract this inclination and enhance self-determination (Deci & Ryan, 2000).

Finally, Modules 5 and 6 epitomize the concept of metamotivation. Module 5 (*organismic congruence and intrinsic motivation*; see Figure 2f) intends to enhance intrinsic motivation by achieving "organismic congruence" (Sheldon & Kasser, 1995). Visualization techniques (Schultheiss & Brunstein, 1999) are employed that, metaphorically speaking, aim at enlarging the overlap in Figure 2f. If this endeavor meets difficulties, Module 6 (*overcoming barriers*) provides analysis of whether intrapersonal conflict or external causes are responsible. Appropriate strategies are developed to overcome these difficulties.

Training procedure

SMT covers three training phases: (1) preparatory phase, (2) training phase, and (3) transfer phase.

Preparatory phase

Informal interviews with personnel managers and potential participants establish a first impression of current training needs. Potentials and limits of SMT are explained to provide realistic training preview (Hicks & Klimoski, 1987). Systematic assessment of training needs (Hesketh & Bochner, 1994; Tannenbaum & Yukl, 1992) is achieved from pre-training questionnaires distributed about four weeks prior to SMT. The questionnaires assess goals (Brunstein et al., 1998), goal conflicts (Emmons & King, 1988; Kehr, 2003b), implicit motives (Sokolowski et al., 2000), volitional strength and overcontrol (Kuhl & Fuhrmann, 1998), and expectations regarding SMT (Tannenbaum & Yukl, 1992). This assessment sensitizes participants about issues relevant to SMT, which is known to enhance training motivation (Smith-Jentsch, Jentsch, Payne, & Salas, 1996).

Training phase

SMT is conducted as a two- or three-day program. Training length depends on client preferences, prior experiences of participants with respect to personality trainings, and the need for practical exercises. Optimal group size is between eight and twelve participants. Participants typically hold management positions in various companies from diverse sectors, and are often heterogeneous with regard to age, gender, educational background, function, and hierarchical level.

SMT starts with a mutual presentation and warm-up, followed by a general introduction to motivational psychology. To establish realistic expectations for training (Kanfer, Reinecker, & Schmelzer, 1996, p. 183), pre-training expectations are discussed, the roles of trainers and participants are clarified, and training contents and procedures are outlined.

Enhancing client insight and self-awareness by lecturing and providing supplementary exercises, the trainer's role is that of a "catalyst" (Kanfer et al., 1996, p. 156), triggering cognitive and behavioral changes in the client. SMT aims at enhancing problem awareness, motivation for change, and strategy knowledge. In all these processes, self-observation is vital (Bandura & Schunk, 1981; Brigham, 1982; Carver & Scheier, 1982; Snyder, 1974). To improve these skills and to sensitize for particular problems, SMT contains several self-observation exercises, mostly as homework assignments (Epstein, 1998; Kanfer et al., 1996) and diary methods (Conway & Briner, 2002). Training contents are transmitted by metaphors and practical examples, without sacrificing the scientific foundation of the intervention. Multiple methods intensify the training, including lectures, plenary discussions, small group exercises, case studies, and simulations.

Modules 1 to 4 provide individual and confidential feedback of questionnaire results. Several studies show training motivation is enhanced if participants perceive the measurements as accurate (see Tannenbaum & Yukl, 1992, for an overview), so instruments are carefully explained and average scores from earlier surveys are provided for comparison purposes. As suggested by Meichenbaum (1993), individual scores are interpreted by stressing the adaptive potential, avoiding pathological distortions or catastrophic interpretations.

After Module 4, time is set aside for self-study and individual exercise, with opportunity for individual consultation with the trainer. This leaves room for private themes less suited for plenary discussion. To stay on track, the trainer tries to avoid departing from the theoretical background of the compensatory model and the empirical data provided by the client's questionnaire results.

Modules 5 and 6 include a comprehensive visualization exercise to integrate earlier elements of the training (see below for details). Then, a summary of the SMT is given, using Figure 2 to illustrate the main themes of the training. Participants are encouraged to build training alliances (Hesketh & Bochner, 1994) and develop personal transfer intentions, to increase training transfer (Hesketh, 1997). Satisfaction with training and transfer intentions are assessed with a post-training questionnaire.

Transfer phase

Training transfer depends on practice with the learned exercises and techniques (Priemuth, 2002). However, there can be resistance to self-management exercises, even those experienced as beneficial (see, Heatherton & Vohs, 1998). Generally, personality intervention requires high motivation for change (Kanfer et al., 1996), and, at the same time, may induce stress (Weinberger, 1994) and resistance (Kanfer et al., 1996; Pervin, 1994), decreasing the needed motivation. This is a dilemma, because it is difficult to control and regulate the aftertreatment phase, and external control is incompatible with the liberal and egalitarian concept of self-management (Kanfer et al., 1996).

Some measures help alleviate the dilemma. The training manual, provided at the onset of the training, summarizes the theory and contains all SMT exercises. It is particularly relevant to the participants, because it bears their personal notes and individual results from the pre-training questionnaires, increasing the chances that it will be used in the transfer phase. Then, about three month after SMT, a follow-up questionnaire is distributed, containing instruments similar to the pre-training questionnaire. Commitment to transfer intentions is higher if a follow-up survey is expected (Baldwin & Magjuka, 1991), so this follow-up is announced at the end of the training program. With a second feedback on individual results, participants are confronted again with the contents of the training. In addition, they may analyze changes between pre- and post-training measures, the relation between changes and the exercises employed, and the desirability of additional exercises. In addition, summary analyses of pre-and post-training results assist the personnel department in evaluating the training program (Hesketh, 1997).

The six SMT modules in detail

The remainder of this chapter describes the six SMT modules in detail. For each module, we review related literature, provide data from our management studies, and explain intervention aims, methods, and didactics employed. Although the compensatory model and supporting studies (Kehr, 2003a, 2004a) pertain to all SMT modules, each module represents a particular perspective on self-management and involves a specific theoretical background requiring separate explication. In addition, we review research demonstrating the relevance of each module for management behavior. However, space restrictions prevent explanation of intervention techniques in full detail. Ready-to-use descriptions of SMT intervention techniques are offered in Kehr (2002), and academic references for these techniques can be found in Kehr (2004c).

Module 1: Goal setting and reducing goal conflicts

Module 1 combines elements of goal setting theory (Locke & Latham, 1990) and approaches to goal conflicts (Emmons & King, 1988; Kehr, 2003b).

Literature

The notion that specific and challenging goals are associated with increased output (when compared to diffuse or do-best goals) is common to goal research (Locke & Latham, 1990; Locke & Kristof, 1996; Wegge, 1998). Less is known about goal conflict. However, because people generally strive for more than one goal at a time (Broadbent, 1985), conflict among goals is common (Emmons & King, 1988). Goal conflicts may have detrimental consequences for goal attainment (Cantor & Blanton, 1996; Emmons & King, 1988).

Four mechanisms, in particular, may account for the negative relation between goal conflict and goal attainment. First, conflicting goals compete for the person's resources

(Cantor & Blanton, 1996; Carver & Scheier, 1990; Emmons & King, 1988; Miller, Gallanter, & Pribram, 1960; Sheldon & Kasser, 1995), so fewer resources remain for any particular goal. Second, goal conflicts may trigger dysfunctional thought processes (Emmons & King, 1988, Study 3) that occupy cognitive capacity. Third, conflicting goals can directly impair each other (Carver, 1996; Miller, 1944), increasing the probability that, even if one goal is successfully pursued or reached, progress on the remaining goals may suffer (Harlow & Cantor, 1994). Fourth, goal conflicts can lead to reprioritization (Campion & Lord, 1982; Cropanzano, Citera, & Howes, 1995; Klein, 1989), decreasing the chances of achieving any particular goal.

Negative influences of goal conflicts on goal attainment are likely to be mirrored in the person's well-being, and there is evidence for negative effects of goal conflict on well-being (Emmons, 1986; 1999; Emmons & King, 1988). However, some authors speculated that goal conflict can also activate cognitive and motivational mechanisms to pave the way for creative solutions (Sheldon, 1995), or prompt reprioritizing processes or plan revision (Cropanzano et al., 1995; Klein, 1989). If these processes help resolve initial goal conflicts, well-being might not be impaired at all. Accordingly, Emmons (1999) and Emmons and King (1988) recognized positive and negative affective consequences of goal conflicts.

Empirical data from the management domain

We felt no need to study the well-sustained main propositions of goal setting theory (Locke & Latham, 1990), but Kehr (2003b) studied effects of goal conflict among managers on goal attainment and well-being.

The notion that goal conflicts inhibit attainment of the goals causing the conflict (Emmons & King, 1988; McKeeman & Karoly, 1991) seems highly plausible if not tautological, given the definition of goal conflict as a situation where "achieving one valued goal inhibits achieving another desired goal" (Lee, Locke, & Latham, 1989, p. 300). To strengthen the argument for inhibiting effects of goal conflicts and avoid tautological reasoning, the principle aim of the Kehr (2003b) study was to show that *preexisting* goal conflicts also inhibit progress toward *newly* set goals. An additional aim was to explore the relation between goal conflict and well-being.

A longitudinal field study was conducted with managers from different companies. The main results were that preexisting goal conflict significantly impaired attainment of newly set goals, but goal conflict had no negative effect on well-being. Nevertheless, there was a significant interaction of goal conflict and goal attainment on changes in positive affect. High initial goal conflict shielded people against declines in positive affect after failure and after enduring conflict. The findings suggest that high goal conflict may be associated with lower expectations regarding goal attainment. This is consistent with the notion of a buffering effect (see Linville, 1987) where goal conflicts provide a buffer against fluctuations in well-being. This supports the idea that goal conflicts have a double-edged character (see Emmons & King, 1988; King, 2001).

Intervention

After the head and heart metaphor is introduced, it is explained that goals only pertain to the explicit motive subsystem ("head") and are thus not the only behaviorally relevant agent (see Figure 2b).

As in earlier training programs (Bandura, 1988; Frayne & Latham, 1987; Neck & Manz, 1992), SMT includes a goal setting exercise. In line with Cantor and Blanton (1996), both private and professional goals are considered. Participants are confronted with their goals expressed in the pre-training questionnaire. After some theoretical input (most participants are already familiar with the basics of goal setting theory), participants analyze, individually and then with a partner, whether their personal goals are sufficiently specific, challenging, and realistic. If necessary, specification and reformulation of goals are encouraged.

Consistent with the literature (Cantor & Blanton, 1996; Emmons et al., 1993; Kanfer et al., 1996; Norman & Shallice, 1986; Reither & Stäudel, 1985), Module 1 also aims to identify and reduce goal conflict by reprioritizing goals. Using research on assessment of goal systems (Brunstein, 1993; Emmons & King, 1988; Wadsworth & Ford, 1983), a method was developed to diagnose goal conflict (for a more precise description, see Kehr, 2004c). After ranking goals for subjective importance, participants arrange their goals in a two-dimensional matrix and quantify all intergoal effects.

This instrument serves as a heuristic for identifying reprioritization needs. Sums of rows represent the average effects of a particular goal on the other goals. Goals with a positive sum in the row support, on average, the other goals ("supporter"), while goals with a negative sum in the row inhibit other goals ("troublemaker"). People are invited to devote more resources (money, time, or attention) to supporters and less resources to troublemakers.

Goals with a positive sum in the column are supported by the other goals ("favorite"), and goals with a negative sum in the column are inhibited ("victim"). A case by case analysis clarifies whether it is advantageous to dedicate less attention to favorites (because they might be sufficiently supported by the other goals) or to take advantage of the favorable situation and devote more resources to reaching the favorite. Likewise, victims may be postponed or even abandoned or, conversely, if sufficiently important, given additional assistance to shield against the detrimental influence of the other goals.

However, since goal conflicts may have positive effects (e.g., to buffer against emotional suffering after failure; Kehr, 2003b), it is explained that it is not necessary to completely resolve goal conflict (which may be illusionary), but just to identify particularly inhibiting conflict situations and develop suitable strategies for handling them.

Module 2: Increasing awareness of one's implicit motives

Module 2 aims to improve self-awareness about implicit motives by comparing self-attributed motives with implicit motives as assessed with a semi-projective instrument.

Literature

The literature on discrepancies between implicit and explicit motives was reviewed in the theoretical section of this chapter. The general notion was that implicit and explicit motive systems are conceptually distinct and discrepancies between these systems negatively influence health and personal well-being (Brunstein et al., 1998; Kehr, 2004a; McClelland et al., 1989; Deci & Ryan, 2000; Ryan et al., 1996). Moreover, the empirical overlap between implicit and explicit motives is small (Brunstein et al., 1998; Cantor &

Blanton, 1996; Sokolowski et al., 2000) or non-existent (Spangler, 1992), indicating people are not completely aware of implicit motives underlying their actions.

Empirical data from the management domain

Studies reported earlier in this chapter as supporting the compensatory model show that, consistent with basic research on implicit/explicit motive discrepancies, empirical overlap between implicit and explicit motives among managers is small (Kehr, 2004a). Furthermore, discrepancies between implicit and explicit motives (Kehr, 2004a), as well as implicit fear motives (Kehr, 2003a), exert negative influences on well-being, mediated by depletion of volitional strength.

An additional study (Sokolowski & Kehr, 1999) explored the relevance of implicit motives for managerial success. This longitudinal study was conducted in the course of "Management by Objectives" (MbO; see, Rodgers & Hunter, 1991) training program. Here, executive personnel are instructed in different social and communication skills, which should help them influence their staff to carry out the firm's objectives. Influencing subordinates primarily relates to the power motive (instead of the affiliation or the achievement motive), and it was expected that managers high on implicit power motive would profit more from MbO training and have greater training transfer. Implicit motive scores (MMG) were obtained four weeks prior to training.

In line with predictions, the managers' implicit power motive was positively associated with satisfaction with training, intrinsic and extrinsic motivation for training transfer, and subjectively measured success of training. Conversely, neither the achievement motive nor the affiliation motive significantly influenced training transfer, despite high intercorrelations among motive scores. Hence, implicit motives, despite being substantially intercorrelated, may have differential and substantial effects on behavioral correlates of managers.

Intervention

To begin with, it is explained that implicit motives, while not being (fully) consciously accessible (McClelland et al., 1989), are still of great behavioral relevance (see Figure 2c). We often simply don't know why we like or dislike certain tasks more than others, but such predilections are clearly influential in determining our courses of action.

Because self-awareness is supported by systematic personality diagnosis (Baumgardner, 1990), self-ascriptions (assessed by straightforward questions, e.g., "How strong is your achievement-motive?") are compared with the implicit motive scores of the MMG (Sokolowski et al., 2000). In case of discrepancies between implicit and self-ascribed motives, McClelland and his colleagues advocated self-observation. They wrote, "We also believe [...] that through self-observation and analysis, greater congruence between the two types of motives can be achieved" (McClelland et al., 1989, p. 700). Accordingly, to increase self-awareness of implicit motives, self-observation of implicit impulses, temptations, and task enjoyment is encouraged (McClelland et al., 1989). However, the effectiveness of techniques for increasing self-awareness is limited. Epstein (1998) noted (with some irony), "To the extend that insight is helpful in this endeavor, it is therapeutic. If it is not, it may simply succeed in making a neurotic without insight into one with insight"

(p. 14). Hence, Module 5 (see below) returns to the issue of implicit/explicit motive discrepancies and introduces a more direct intervention technique to establish coherence.

Module 3: Enhancing volition

Module 3 offers survey feedback on individual strengths and weaknesses regarding volitional strategies and contains several exercises to enhance volitional strength (see Erber & Erber, 2000; Kuhl, 1998; Mischel, 1996).

Literature

The literature on volitional self-regulation was reviewed earlier, when the compensatory model was introduced.

Empirical data from the management domain

Kehr's (2003a, 2004a) studies, reviewed above in support of the compensatory model, illustrate the mediating function of volition on the relation between dysfunctional motive constellations and well-being.

In addition, Kehr, Bles, and von Rosenstiel (1999a) longitudinally examined the effects of volitional self-regulation on success of insurance managers in a training context. The predictor, volitional self-regulation, was measured at the onset of the training program with the self-regulation scale of the Volitional Components Inventory (VCI; Kuhl & Fuhrmann, 1998). As dependents, several subjective transfer-related measures were taken. In line with predictions, volitional self-regulation longitudinally predicted training success and transfer-related emotions.

As these effects were restricted to subjective measures, an additional study (Kehr 2003c) examined whether positive effects of volitional self-regulation are confirmed by more objective criteria. Kehr (2003c) focused on one specific volitional strategy, positive self-regulatory fantasies. This is essentially equivalent to what Kuhl (1985; Kuhl & Fuhrmann, 1998; cf. Kanfer & Heggestad, 1997) called "motivation control." Motivational control has been characterized as one of the principal volitional strategies (Beckmann, 1999; Kanfer & Heggestad, 1997). The Kehr (2003c) study showed that positive self-regulatory fantasies (assessed with the motivation control subscale of the VCI) predicted the sales performances of insurance managers (assessed one year after the predictors had been taken). Hence, positive effects of volitional strength can also be found when objective performance measures are considered.

Intervention

For introductory purposes, the twofold function of volitional self-regulation is explained: supporting need-discrepant goals and suppressing unwanted behavioral impulses origi-

Table 1. Exercises to enhance volition

Scale[1]	**Exercises**
Motivation control	Development of positive self-regulatory fantasies (Kanfer et al., 1996, p. 369; Kanfer & Ackerman, 1989; Mischel, 1996; Oettingen, 1996) Expressive talking about positive experiences (Langston, 1994) Reframing (Polivy, 1998)
Emotion control	Creating and enhancing functional emotions (Josephson et al., 1996; Mischel et al., 1996; Strack et al., 1985) Suppressing and toning down dysfunctional emotions (Erber, 1996; Metcalfe & Mischel, 1999; Strack et al., 1985) Enhancing emotional self-awareness (Salovey & Meyer, 1990; Sokolowski, 1993)
Decision control	Separation of information collection and information evaluation (Kehr, 2002, in press-c)
Activation control/calming	Progressive muscle relaxation (Jacobson, 1938)
Activation control/activating	Reference to Module 1 (setting of realistic goals and reduction of goal conflict via reprioritization)
Attention control	Concentration and mediation exercises (Karoly, 1995; Klinger, 1982)

Notes. [1] The scales were extracted from Kuhl and Fuhrmann's (1998) VCI.

nating in implicit motives (see Figure 2d). Feedback is given on individual strengths and weaknesses regarding volitional strategies (e.g., motivation control), using several subscales of the VCI (Kuhl & Fuhrmann, 1998). Since volition may be enhanced by training (Kuhl, 1998; Kuhl & Kraska, 1989; Lindworsky, 1923b; Muraven, Baumeister, & Tice, 1999), various exercises and homework assignments are recommended (see Erber & Erber, 2000; Kuhl, 1998; Mischel, 1996), depending on the training needs diagnosis. Table 1 gives lists volitional strategies and exercises employed in SMT.

These exercises are described in detail in Kehr (2002, 2004c). For example, to enhance emotional self-awareness (i.e., the ability to recognize one's emotional states, categorize them, and act appropriately; see Salovey & Meyer, 1990; Sokolowski, 1993), a diary exercise is used. Some questions assist in self-observation: In which situation did I experience emotions today? What kind of emotions were they? (A list of emotions is provided to choose from.) What caused these emotions? How did I handle these emotions? In particular, did I suppress the emotions, or did I act them out? Am I pleased with how I handled these emotions? Participants are encouraged to keep this diary for at least four weeks.

Module 4: Reducing overcontrol

Module 4 establishes awareness of overcontrol, provides feedback on personal inclination to overcontrol, and contains exercises to counteract and reduce overcontrol.

Literature

There is evidence for dysfunctional effects of rigid self-control ("overcontrol"; Asendorpf & Van Aken, 1999) on psychological and physiological well-being (e.g., Deci & Ryan, 1987; Kuhl, 2000; Polivy, 1998). Kuhl's (2000; Kuhl & Fuhrmann, 1998) approach provides a theoretical framework for this research. Kuhl distinguishes two modes of volition, which he calls "self-regulation" and "self-control." In his terminology, self-regulation is a self-integrating ("democratic") style of action control and self-control is a self-disciplined ("authoritarian") style of action control. In particular, self-regulation is the person's ability to form goals in accordance with the individual need structure and flexibly use self-regulatory strategies to resolve conflicts among behaviorally relevant subsystems (Kuhl & Goschke, 1994). Thus, Kuhl's (2000) self-regulation is a merger of what we call "volition" and "meta-motivation" in this chapter.

Kuhl's (2000) self-control, on the other hand, refers to the ability to pursue goals with a high priority that are not embedded in the personal need structure. This is typically the case of goals imposed by others. Implementing other-imposed goals may require the ability to overcome tempting alternatives, and this is the adaptive aspect of moderate and temporary forms of self-control (Kuhl & Fuhrmann, 1998). Nevertheless, operating in the self-control mode can be maladaptive (Kuhl & Fuhrmann, 1998; cf. Deci & Ryan, 2000). According to Kuhl (2000), the self-control mode activates the punishment system, involving negative emotions and a high amount of conscious effort, so goal achievement becomes stressful.

Ignoring "unwanted" and distracting behavioral impulses, means the person foregoes opportunities to satisfy his or her needs; unwanted impulses and temptations often originate in aroused implicit motives and organismic needs and may indicate opportunities to satisfy one's needs. As a consequence, by constantly suppressing such impulses, the person is alienated from his or her implicit need structure (Kuhl, 2000; cf. Ryan & Deci, 2000).

According to Kuhl and Fuhrmann (1998), self-control comprises, among others, impulse control (i.e., suppressing implicit impulses), external control (deference to social constraints; see Deci & Ryan, 2000), intention control (constantly thinking about intentions), planning (an overemphasis on planning courses of action), and negative self-regulatory fantasies.

It is not clear if self-control is an autonomous mode of action control, as Kuhl (2000; Kuhl & Fuhrmann, 1998) theorizes, or just too much of a good thing, as Kehr (2004c) and Polivy (1998) argue. In this chapter, we defined a two-fold function of volitional self-regulation: to either support need-discrepant goals or suppress unwanted behavioral impulses. With this definition in mind, Kuhl's concept of self-control is an overemphasis on volitional self-regulation rather than a specific and distinct mode of action-regulation.

In support of this view, several authors emphasized the janus-headed character of self-control, and identified disadvantages of too much or too little self-control (Asendorpf & van Aken, 1999; Baumeister & Heatherton, 1996; Block & Block, 1980; Funder & Block, 1989; Gramzow, Sedikides, Panter, & Insko, 2000). For example, "over-planning"

(Dörner, 1985), which Kuhl and Fuhrmann (1998) subsumed under self-control, seem to be one pole of the planning dimension. The opposite pole of this dimension is "short-cut behavior" (Dörner, 1985), with insufficient consideration of long-term consequences indicative of a planning deficit (see Frese, Stewart, & Hannover, 1987). In sum, there is reason to assume a curvilinear relation of self-control and behavioral success (see Kehr, Bles, & von Rosenstiel, 1998).

Empirical data from the management domain

The Kehr et al. (1999a) study, summarized earlier in this chapter, contained several self-control related subscales of Kuhl and Fuhrmann's (1998) VCI to see if negative effects of self-control pertain to success among managers. As expected, inclination to rigid self-control negatively influences subjective criteria such as well-being, self-ascribed behavioral success, and goal attainment. With respect to more objective criteria, Kehr (2003c) reported that negative self-regulatory fantasies, the principal component of Kuhl and Fuhrmann's self-control construct, may counteract positive effects of positive self-regulatory fantasies on sales performance of insurance managers.

Intervention

Because of the dysfunctional effects of over- or undercontrol (Asendopf & van Aaken, 1999), intervention efforts aim at finding a "balance" (Epstein, 1998; Polivy, 1998) and achieving a "healthy" (Kuhl, 1998) equilibrium.

For introductory purposes, Figure 2e is used to illustrate overcontrol as over-emphasis on explicit goals and ignorance or suppression of implicit motives and organismic needs (see Deci & Ryan, 2000). In general, participants' problem awareness for overcon-

Table 2. Exercises to counteract overcontrol

Scale[1]	**Exercises**
Impulse control	Diary: identification and management of temptations (Kehr, 2002, in press-c)
External control	Identification of external control (Kuhl, 1998) and discrimination of degrees of external control (Kehr, 2002, in press-c; Ryan & Deci, 2000) Self-determination (Kuhl, 1998)
Intention control	Relief of intention memory by the aid of planning instruments
Planning	Generation of unplanned test situations
Negative self-regulatory fantasies	Development of positive self-regulatory fantasies (Kanfer et al., 1996, p. 369; Kanfer & Ackerman, 1996; Mischel, 1996; Oettingen, 1996)

Notes. [1]The scales were extracted from Kuhl and Fuhrmann's (1998) VCI.

trol is low and sometimes virtually non-existent ("No pain, no gain," is a typical motto of people high on self-control). To establish problem awareness, empirical studies are reviewed to illustrate negative effects of over- (and under-) control on well-being and, what managers often consider as even more important, on personal success.

In analogy to Module 3, personal feedback is given from the respective subscales of the VCI. Table 2 gives an overview of the exercises used to counteract the inclination to overcontrol (for details, see Kehr, 2002, 2004c). Most of these exercises employ diary methods (see Conway & Briner, 2002), where particular themes (e.g., daily temptations) are analyzed and documented (see Pennebaker, 1997). The general objective is to improve self-observation and self-awareness (see Pennebaker, 1980), because inadequate self-awareness is common among people tending to overcontrol (Kuhl, 2000; Kuhl & Fuhrmann, 1998; Deci & Ryan, 2000). Ultimately, these exercises enhance the ability to perceive one's implicit needs and desires and counteract the tendency to overemphasize goals (Loewenstein, 1996; Polivy, 1998; Deci & Ryan, 2000).

Module 5: Enhancing organismic congruence and intrinsic motivation

Module 5 aims at enhancing congruence of implicit and explicit motives by adjusting the person's goals (the principal component of the explicit motive system) to his or her implicit motive base, which increases intrinsic motivation.

Literature

There is insufficient space to review the voluminous literature (see Vallerand, 1997) on intrinsic (and extrinsic) motivation here. However, we discuss how the compensatory model helps clarify the concept of intrinsic motivation. According to Kehr (2004c), the necessary condition for intrinsic motivation of behavior is *thematical congruence with the person's aroused implicit motives*. The additional sufficient condition for intrinsic motivation is the *absence of discrepant cognitive preferences*. Hence, intrinsic motivation is expected for behaviors that thematically fall in the overlap section in Figure 1, where both the necessary and the sufficient conditions for intrinsic motivation are met. Conversely, extrinsic motivation is assumed if cognitive preferences (e.g., goals) are to be supported that are discrepant with the implicit motives (this corresponds to the outer sector of the dark circle in Figure 1).

Prior approaches on intrinsic motivation rely on the distinction between means and ends. Higgins and Trope (1990) wrote that approaches to intrinsic motivation "emphasize the classic distinction between engaging in an activity as an end in itself (intrinsic motivation) and engaging in an activity as a means to an end (extrinsic motivation)" (p. 232). However, this means-ends distinction raises conceptual concerns. Because of the complex structure of means-ends relations (Stern, 1935/1950) and their inherently subjective quality (Brunstein, 1993), conceptions of intrinsic motivation based on a means-ends relation seem vague and arbitrary. They are ambiguous on whether a particular behavioral act is a means or an end. It is not clear, for example, whether writing a chapter is intrinsically motivated (because it marks the end of an interesting research project), or whether it is extrinsically motivated (because it is a step in an academic career).

Our approach does not require the means-ends distinction. If we observe children playing, it is evident that intrinsic motivation does not depend on the existence of a goal. However, as highlighted by the present approach, intrinsic motivation requires the *absence* of thematically incongruent, cognitive preferences. Conversely, if cognitive preferences conflict with implicit motives, intrinsic motivation cannot be experienced, because the person will strive to suppress the momentarily unwanted implicit impulses.

Our approach offers an explanation for inconsistencies in the literature regarding the corruption of intrinsic motivation by extrinsic rewards (Deci, Koestner, & Ryan, 1999). Many authors found a corruption effect, but some authors found that extrinsic rewards did not weaken, but even enhanced intrinsic motivation (see Deci et al., 1999; Rigby, Deci, Patrick, & Ryan, 1992).

Based on the compensatory model, extrinsic rewards only corrupt intrinsic motivation if they activate cognitive preferences incongruent with the intrinsically motivated activity. In contrast, extrinsic rewards that do not activate incongruent cognitive preferences, or that activate cognitive preferences thematically *congruent* with the intrinsic motivated behavior, will not result in corrupted intrinsic motivation, but rather enhance pre-existing motivation.

Empirical data from the management domain

There is abundant literature on the advantages of intrinsic motivation as compared to extrinsic motivation. Sokolowski and Kehr (1999) found that this applies to the management domain, where intrinsic motivation mediates the relation between implicit motives and goal attainment. A recent experiment on effects of aroused achievement motives (Puca & Schmalt, 1999) had similar findings. Path analyses in the Sokolowski and Kehr study confirmed that intrinsic motivation (operationalized as task enjoyment), but not extrinsic motivation (operationalized as goal commitment), mediated the implicit power motive-goal attainment relation.

The present approach also proposes that congruence between implicit and explicit motives (the overlap section in Figure 1) positively relates to intrinsic motivation. The Kehr (2004a) studies indirectly support this proposition, if we consider subjective well-being as a proxy for intrinsic motivation (see Sheldon & Houser-Marko, 2001). Kehr (2004a) found indirect relations between implicit/explicit motive congruence and subjective well-being, and Kehr (2004c; Study 5) also found significant correlations between implicit/explicit motive congruence and a generalized measure of intrinsic motivation.

Intervention

Module 5 introduces the notion that volition is the second-best solution for dealing with incongruent implicit motives and explicit goals, and that more profound solutions involve enhancing congruence (see Figure 2f).

Congruence between implicit and explicit (e.g., goals) motive systems may be achieved by adjusting implicit motives or goals, respectively. Changing implicit motives, however, is difficult (McClelland, 1972) and ethically questionable (see Kehr, 2004c, for a critical review on attempts to modify implicit motives).

Therefore, Module 5 chooses the alternative of assisting people in setting and pursuing goals that are maximally need-congruent. Using the visualization technique of Schultheiss and Brunstein (1999), goals are subdivided into action steps, and the realization of each step is visualized. This visualization triggers anticipative affective reactions useful for orientation (Mischel et al., 1996; Schwarz & Bohner, 1996). To increase motive-goal congruence, participants are encouraged to choose action alternatives triggering positive affect during visualization, because positive affect indicates congruence with implicit motives (Schultheiss & Brunstein, 1999; Schwarz & Bohner, 1996).

Module 6: Identifying and overcoming barriers to action

If the visualization technique of Module 5 generates negative affect, Module 6 analyzes whether these are due to anticipated future difficulties and whether the difficulties are rooted in causes internal to the person or in external barriers. Participants are instructed to develop appropriate behavioral strategies to overcome these difficulties.

Literature

Generally, negative emotions signal behavioral difficulties (Carver & Scheier, 1990; Simon, 1967). Mellers, Schwartz, and Ritov (1999) also showed that anticipated emotions are reliable predictors for actually experienced emotions. Hence, negative anticipations signal (Schwarz & Bohner, 1996) future difficulties. Wheeler and Janis (1980, p. 21) cautioned that it can be maladaptive to disregard such signals. In support of this view, Oettingen et al. (2001) showed that imagined future success is less helpful for self-regulatory purposes if difficulties are disregarded.

What is the advantage of the anticipation of difficulties? Rubinstein (1940/1984) theorized that anticipating difficulties may reinforce commitment. In Gollwitzer's (1993) terminology, anticipation of difficulties supplements goal intentions with more specific implementation intentions. More precisely, implementation intentions enhance accessibility of representations of appropriate mental knowledge structures and create situational contingencies by attaching initiation of the intention to specific situational cues (Gollwitzer, 1993). As a result, implementation intentions augment chances for successfully enacting the intention (Gollwitzer, 1999). Mischel (1996), for example, showed that children with specific plans for overcoming obstacles were more successful in delaying gratification.

In sum, it is advantageous to anticipate, analyze, and prepare for future difficulties. In this respect, it is important to draw a sharp line between intra-personal or extra-personal causes for behavioral difficulties (Kannheiser, 1983; Kehr, 2004c; Kuhl & Goschke, 1994; Lazarus, Kanner, & Folkman, 1980; Metcalfe & Mischel, 1999; Sokolowski, 1993), in analogy to the distinction of internal and external influences on behavior (Epstein, 1998; Kuhl & Goschke, 1994; Leventhal & Scherer, 1987; Metcalfe & Mischel, 1999). For conceptual clarity, we follow Sokolowski's (1993) holding that internal barriers require volitional self-regulation (James, 1890/1981; Kehr, 2004c), and external barriers require problem-solving (loosely defined as activation of problem solving routines, search for previously unknown solutions, or acquisition of knowledge and task-specific skills; see Ackerman, 1987; Nair, 2000; Smith, 1997).

Empirical data from the management domain

Two studies have particular relevance for Module 6. The first, a longitudinal study in the context of a management training program (Kehr, Bles, & von Rosenstiel, 1999b), examined a principle notion underlying Module 6: negative anticipatory emotions are good predictors for failure. As expected, negative affective anticipations predicted subsequent failure of training transfer.

The second study (Kehr, 2004c; Study 3) explored subjective theories about the difference between volition and problem-solving. From a research review, several problem-solving strategies (e.g., search for information, organizing technical support, and improving communication; see Ackerman, 1987; Dörner, Reither, & Stäudel, 1983; Frese et al., 1987; Nair, 2000; Smith, 1997) and volitional strategies (e.g., positive and negative self-regulatory fantasies; see Kehr, 2003c; Kuhl, 1985) were extracted. It was expected that subjective theories, like scientific theories, would assign problem-solving strategies to external barriers and volitional strategies to internal barriers. Similar to Kuhl and Kraska (1989), two scenarios were developed. One scenario described an internal barrier to action, whereas the other scenario described an external barrier to action. Study participants were public relation employees from several automobile companies. Each participant was given both scenarios and a list of five volitional and five problem solving strategies.

Participants were asked to rate the suitability of each strategy for each scenario. Volitional strategies were preferred for internal barriers, and problem solving strategies were preferred for external barriers. Consistent with Sokolowski's (1993) proposition, employees' subjective theories clearly discriminate between volition and problem solving and appropriately assign the respective strategies to internal and external causes, respectively.

Intervention

Miller et al. (1960) suggested that checking the feasibility of plans and error detection is facilitated by simulation. These ideas have influenced several more recent approaches employing imagination exercises and subsequent development of cognitive strategies to overcome anticipated barriers (Bennett & Cautela, 1981; Skovholt, Morgan, & Negron-Cunningham, 1989; Taylor & Schneider, 1989). In Kanfer's self-management therapy (Kanfer et al., 1996), for example, detailed analysis of alternative pathways to a goal and anticipation of possible barriers to action are important elements of "prospective self-regulation."

The SMT procedure adopts these suggestions. Module 6 instructs participants to analyze all action steps that triggered negative affective responses during visualization (see Module 5) to see if internal causes (e.g., goal conflicts, aroused fear motives, temptations) or external causes (e.g., lacking support by supervisors or subordinates, lacking skills, technical difficulties) result in the negative anticipations. Participants prepare for these difficulties by building implementation intentions of the type "when situation *x* arises, I will do *y*" (Gollwitzer, 1999, p. 494) using volitional strategies for intrapersonal conflicts and problem solving strategies for external difficulties. This procedure increases the chances that the person will successfully meet anticipated future difficulties.

If developing proactive strategies does not eliminate negative affective toning of the envisioned behavior, plan revision (Brandtstätter, Wentura, & Rothermund, 1999;

Cropanzano et al., 1995) or disengagement (Klinger, 1975) is suggested. While it is often difficult to disengage from action plans (Klinger, 1975), it can be a wise strategy because it avoids depletion of resources (Schönpflug, 1985), rumination (Beckmann, 1998), and the risk of learned helplessness reactions (Martin & Tesser, 1989).

Conclusion

Most of the intervention techniques used in SMT are by no means new. Quite the contrary, SMT draws heavily on existing literature and research. Consider, for example, Emmons and King's (1988) assessments of goal systems, McClelland's idea to increase self-awareness on implicit motives by self-observation (McClelland et al., 1989), Kuhl's (1998) or Mischel's (1996) exercises to increase willpower, Polivy's (1998) suggestions against rigid self-control, Schultheiss and Brunstein's (1999) visualization technique to enhance organismic congruence, and the notion of prospective self-regulation to overcome difficulties by Kanfer et al. (1996).

SMT integrates these diverse intervention techniques into a consistent approach. While some preliminary evaluation studies have been conducted (Kehr, 2004c, Studies 7.1 and 7.2; Priemuth, 2002), it is still too early for conclusive reports on SMT effectiveness. Evaluation designs must be strengthened, and one discouraging preliminary result must be addressed (Priemuth, 2002, reported that SMT had the expected effects on the first wave of training groups but not on the second wave). However, most of the previous evaluation results were encouraging, indicating that SMT significantly enhances self-management-related knowledge, volitional strength, and affective well-being, and decreases overcontrol, stress, and energy-deficit (Kehr, 2001, 2003d, 2004c, Studies 7.1 and 7.2).

The main advantage of SMT is that it builds on coherent theory. The compensatory model of work motivation and volition coalesces dual system theories of motivation and approaches to volitional self-regulation, two previously unrelated approaches to human motivation. Both theoretically and empirically, important advances have been recently made in these two lines of research. Integrating these research trends, the compensatory model provides a conceptual framework for intrinsic motivation (in case of congruence between the two systems) and, conversely, for intrapersonal conflict and volitional conflict-resolution (in case of discrepancies). SMT permits practitioners, trainers, and applied researchers to take advantage of this scientific progress. In effect, this extends earlier approaches to self-management, which were largely confined to goal setting and self-efficacy training (e.g., Frayne & Geringer, 2000; Latham & Frayne, 1989) and thus much narrower in focus than the SMT.

Furthermore, SMT is based on empirical research relevant for its target group. The empirical research was conducted primarily with management samples. It seems doubtful that manager motivation could be validly assessed by experimenting solely on freshmen and sophomores of introductory psychology classes. Clearly, confronted with "real" managers participating in SMT, the ability to fill the framework provided by the compensatory model with empirical results actually relevant for managers, adds credence to the approach.

Finally, it is of particular advantage that a simple Venn diagram (Figure 1) can convey the theoretical underpinning of the compensatory model in a way quick to grasp and easy to remember. The head and heart metaphor (Epstein, 1994) is as an additional didactic device. For practical application, the Venn diagram allows diagnosis of a large variety of self-management-related situations (see Figures 2a–2f).

To emphasize this and increase accessibility of the SMT contents with a practical exercise, participants are instructed at the very end of a SMT course to use their hands to form two circles; thumb and forefinger of each hand form a circle. The trainer then demonstrates how to move both hands together so that eventually the two circles overlap. SMT is concluded with the trainer's advice, "Keep it in your minds, it is always in your hands."

Acknowledgments

The research reviewed in this chapter was generously supported by grants of the German Research Foundation (DFG). An earlier version of this paper has been nominated by the Academy of Management (Section Management Education and Development) for the 2003 William H. Newman Award.

We are grateful to Joachim Brunstein, Julius Kuhl, Richard Ryan, and Kurt Sokolowski for helpful comments on our theoretical and empirical research.

References

Ach, N. (1935). Analyse des Willens [Analysis of volition]. In E. Abderhalden (Ed.), *Handbuch der biologischen Arbeitsmethoden. Vol. VI*. Berlin: Urban & Schwarzenberg.

Ackerman, P. L. (1987). Individual differences in skill learning: An integration of psychometric and information processing perspectives. *Psychological Bulletin, 102,* 3–27.

Ainslie, G., & Haslam, N. (1992). Self-control. In G. Loewenstein & J. Elster (Eds.), *Choice over time* (pp. 177–209). New York: Russel Sage Foundation.

Asendorpf, J. B., & Van Aken, M. A. G. (1999). Resilient, overcontrolled, and undercontrolled personality prototypes in childhood: Replicability, predictive power, and the trait-type issue. *Journal of Personality and Social Psychology, 77,* 815–832.

Atkinson, J. W. (1964). *An introduction to motivation*. Princeton, NJ: Van Nostrand.

Atkinson, J. W., & Birch, D. A. (1970). A dynamic theory of action. New York: Wiley.

Bagozzi, R. P., Baumgartner, H., & Pieters, R. (1998). Goal-directed emotions. *Cognition and Emotion, 12,* 1–26.

Baldwin, T. T., & Magjuka, R. J. (1991). Organizational training and signals of importance: Linking pretraining perceptions to intentions to transfer. *Human Resources Development Quarterly, 2,* 25–36.

Baltes, P. B., Smith, J. & Staudinger, U. M. (1992). Wisdom and successful aging. In J. J. Berman & T. B. Sonderegger (Eds.), *Nebraska Symposium on Motivation* (Vol. 39, pp. 123-167). Lincoln: University of Nebraska Press.

Bandura, A. (1988). Self-regulation of motivation and action through goal systems. In V. Hamilton, G. H. Bower, & N. H. Frijda (Eds.), *Cognitive perspectives on emotion and motivation* (pp. 37-61). Dordrecht, The Netherlands: Kluwer.

Bandura, A. (1989). Self-regulation of motivation and action through internal standards and goal systems. In L. A. Pervin (Ed.), *Goal concepts in personality and social psychology* (pp. 473–479). Hillsdale, NJ: Lawrence Erlbaum Associates.

Bandura, A., & Schunk, D. H. (1981). Cultivating competence, self-efficacy, and intrinsic interest through proximal self-motivation. *Journal of Personality and Social Psychology, 41,* 586–598.

Bargh, J. A. (1990). Auto-motives: Preconscious determinants of social interaction. In E. T. Higgins & R. M. Sorrentino (Eds.), *Handbook of motivation and cognition: Vol. 2. Foundations of social behavior* (pp. 93–130). New York: Guilford.

Baumeister, R. F., Bratslavsky, E., Muraven, M., & Tice, D. M. (1998). Ego depletion: Is the active self a limited resource? *Journal of Personality and Social Psychology, 74,* 1252–1265.

Baumeister, R. F., & Heatherton, T. F. (1996). Self-regulation failure: An overview. *Psychological Inquiry, 7,* 1–15.

Baumgardner, A. H. (1990). To know oneself is to like oneself: Self-certainty and self-affect. *Journal of Personality and Social Psychology, 58,* 1062–1072.

Bazerman, M. H., Tenbrunsel, A. E., & Wade-Benzoni, K. (1998). Negotiating with yourself and losing: Making decisions with competing internal preferences. *Academy of Management Review, 23,* 225–241.

Beckmann, J. (1998). Intrusive thoughts, rumination, and incomplete intentions. In M. Kofta, G. Weary & G. Sedek (Eds.), *Personal control in action: Cognitive and motivational mechanisms* (pp. 259–278). New York: Plenum.

Beckmann, J. (1999). Persönlichkeit, Motivation und Leistung: Die Wechselwirkung von Persönlichkeitseigenschaften und Aufgabenmerkmalen bei der Erbringung von Leistung unter belastenden Bedingungen [Personality, motivation, and achievement: Interrealtions of personality traits and task characteristics in achievement-related situations under strain]. In M. Jerusalem & R. Pekrun (Eds.), *Emotion, Motivation und Leistung* (pp. 169–181). Göttingen, Germany: Hogrefe.

Bennett, A. K., & Cautela, J. R. (1981). The use of covert conditioning in the modification of pain: Two experimental tests. *Journal of Behavior Therapy and Experimental Psychiatry, 12,* 315–320.

Binswanger, H. (1991). Volition as cognitive self-regulation. *Organizational Behavior and Human Decision Processes, 50,* 154–178.

Block, J. H., & Block, J. (1980). The role of ego-control and ego-resiliency in the organization of behavior. In W. A. Collins (Ed.), *Development of cognition, affect, and social relations* (pp. 39–101). Hillsdale, NJ: Erlbaum.

Brandtstädter, J., Wentura, D., & Rothermund, K. (1999). Intentional self-development through adulthood and later life. In J. Brandtstädter & R. M. Lerner (Eds.), *Action & self-development* (pp. 373–400). London: Sage.

Brigham, T. (1982). Self-management: A radical behavioral perspective. In P. Karoly & F. H. Kanfer (Eds.), *Self-management and behavior change* (pp. 32–59). New York: Pergamon.

Broadbent, D. E. (1985). Multiple goals and flexible procedures in the design of work. In M. Frese & J. Sabini (Eds.), *Goal directed behavior: The concept of action in psychology* (pp. 285–294). Hillsdale, NJ: Erlbaum.

Brown, A. L. (1978). Knowing when, where and how to remember: A problem of metacognition. In R. Glaser (Ed.), *Advances in instructional psychology*. Hillsdale, NJ: Erlbaum.

Brunstein, J. C. (1993). Personal goals and subjective well-being: A longitudinal study. *Journal of Personality and Social Psychology, 65,* 1061–1070.

Brunstein, J. C., Schultheiss, O. C., & Grässmann, R. (1998). Personal goals and emotional well-being: The moderating role of motive dispositions. *Journal of Personality and Social Psychology, 75,* 494–508.

Brunstein, J. C., Schultheiss, O. C., & Maier, G. W. (1999). The pursuit of personal goals. In J. Brandtstädter & R. M. Lerner (Eds.), *Action & self-development* (pp. 169–196). London: Sage.

Campion, M. A., & Lord, R. G. (1982). A control systems conceptualization of the goal setting process. *Organizational Behavior and Human Performance, 2,* 258–275.

Cantor, N., & Blanton, H. (1996). Effortful pursuit of personal goals in daily life. In J. A. Bargh & P. M. Gollwitzer (Eds.), *The psychology of action: Linking cognition and motivation to behavior* (pp. 338-359). New York: Guilford.

Carver, C. S. (1996). Some ways in which goals differ and some implications of those differences. In P. M. Gollwitzer & J. A. Bargh (Eds.), *The psychology of action: Linking cognition and motivation to behavior* (pp. 645–672). New York: Guilford.

Carver, C. S., & Scheier, M. F. (1982). An information-processing perspective on self-management. In P. Karoly & F. H. Kanfer (Eds.), *Self-management and behavior change: From theory to practice* (pp. 93–127). New York: Pergamon.

Carver, C. S., & Scheier, M. F. (1990). Origins and functions of positive and negative affect: A control-process view. *Psychological Review, 97,* 19–35.

Comelli, G., & Rosenstiel, L. v. (2001). *Führung durch Motivation* [Leadership by motivation]. München: Vahlen.

Conway, N., & Briner, R. B. (2002). A daily diary study of affective responses to psychological contract breach and exceeded promises. *Journal of Organizational Behavior, 23,* 287–302.

Cropanzano, R., Citera, M., & Howes, J. (1995). Goal hierarchies and plan revision. *Motivation and Emotion, 19,* 77–98.

Deci, E. L., Koestner, R., & Ryan, R. M. (1999). A meta-analytic review of experiments examining the effects of extrinsic rewards on intrinsic motivation. *Psychological Bulletin, 125*, 627–668.

Deci, E. L., & Ryan, R. M. (1987). The support of autonomy and the control of behavior. *Journal of Personality and Social Psychology*, *53*, 1024–1037.

Deci, E. L., & Ryan, R. M. (2000). The "what" and "why" of goal pursuits: Human needs and the self-determination of behavior. *Psychological Inquiry, 11*, 227–268.

Dörner, D. (1985). Verhalten, Denken und Emotionen [Behavior, cognition, and emotions]. In L. H. Eckensberger & E. D. Lautermann (Eds.), *Emotion und Reflexivität* (pp. 157–181). Munich, Germany: Urban & Schwarzenberg.

Dörner, D., Reither, F., & Stäudel, T. (1983). Emotion und problemlösendes Denken [Emotion and problem solving cognitions]. In H. Mandl & G. L. Huber (Eds.), *Emotion und Kognition* (pp. 61–84). Munich, Germany: Urban & Schwarzenberg.

Egeth, H. E., & Yantis, S. (1997). Visual attention: Control, representation, and time course. *Annual Review of Psychology*, *48*, 269–297.

Emmons, R. A. (1986). Personal strivings: An approach to personality and subjective well-being. *Journal of Personality and Social Psychology*, *51*, 1058–1068.

Emmons, R. A. (1999). *The psychology of ultimate concerns: Motivation and spirituality in personality*. New York: Guilford.

Emmons, R. A., & King, L. A. (1988). Conflict among personal strivings: Immediate and long-term implications for psychological and physical well-being. *Journal of Personality and Social Psychology*, *54*, 1040–1048.

Emmons, R. A., King, L. A., & Sheldon, K. (1993). Goal conflict and the self-regulation of action. In D. M. Wegner & J. W. Pennebaker (Eds.), *Handbook of mental control* (pp. 528–551). Englewood Cliffs, NJ: Prentice-Hall.

Emmons, R. A., & McAdams, D. P. (1991). Personal strivings and motive dispositions: Exploring the links. *Personality and Social Psychology Bulletin, 17*, 648–654.

Epstein, S. (1994). Integration of the cognitive and the psychodynamic unconscious. *American Psychologist, 49*, 709–724.

Epstein, S. (1998). Personal control from the perspective of cognitive-experiential self-theory. In M. Kofta, G. Weary, & G. Sedek (Eds.), *Personal control in action: Cognitive and motivational mechanisms* (pp. 5–26). New York: Plenum.

Erber, R. (1996). The self-regulation of moods. In L. L. Martin & A. Tesser (Eds.), *Striving and feeling: Interactions among goals, affect, and self-regulation* (pp. 251–275). Mahwah, NJ: Erlbaum.

Erber, R., & Erber, M. W. (2000). The self-regulation of moods: Second thoughts on the importance of happiness in everyday life. *Psychological Inquiry, 11*, 142–148.

Farr, J. L., Hofmann, D. A., & Ringenbach, K. L. (1993). Goal orientation and action control theory: Implications for industrial and organizational psychology. In G. L. Cooper & I. T. Robertson (Eds.), *International Review of Industrial and Organizational Psychology* (Vol. 8, pp. 193–232). New York: Wiley.

Florin, I., & Rosenstiel, L. v. (1976). *Leistungsstörungen und Prüfungsangst* [Performance deficits and test anxiety]. München: Goldmann.

Forgas, J. P., Johnson, R., & Ciarrochi, J. (1998). Mood management: The role of processing strategies in affect control and affect infusion. In M. Kofta, G. Weary, & G. Sedek (Eds.), *Personal control in action: Cognitive and motivational mechanisms* (pp. 155–195). New York: Plenum.

Frayne, C., & Geringer, J. M. (2000). Self-management training for improving job performance: A field experiment involving salespeople. *Journal of Applied Psychology, 85*, 361–372.

Frayne, C., & Latham, G. P. (1987). Application of social learning theory to employee self-management of attendance. *Journal of Applied Psychology, 65*, 627–634.

Frese, M., Stewart, J., & Hannover, B. (1987). Goal orientation and planfulness: Action styles as personality concepts. *Journal of Personality and Social Psychology, 52*, 1182–1194.

Funder, D. C., & Block, J. (1989). The role of ego-control, ego-resiliency, and IQ in delay of gratification in adolescence. *Journal of Personality and Social Psychology, 57*, 1041–1050.

Gist, M. E., Bavetta, A. G., & Stevens, C. K. (1990). Transfer training method: Its influence on skill generalization, skill repetition, and performance level. *Personnel Psychology, 43*, 501–523.

Gollwitzer, P. M. (1993). Goal achievement: The role of intentions. In W. Stroebe & M. Hewstone (Eds.), *European Review of Social Psychology* (Vol. 4, pp. 141–185). Chicester, UK: Wiley.

Gollwitzer, P. M. (1999). Implementation intentions: Strong effects of simple plans. *American Psychologist, 54*, 493-503.

Gollwitzer, P. M., & Bayer, U. (1999). Deliberative versus implemental mindsets in the control of action. In S. Chaiken & Y. Trope (Eds.), *Dual-process theories in social psychology* (pp. 403–422). New York: Guilford.

Gramzow, R. H., Sedikides, C., Panter, A. T., & Insko, C. A. (2000). Aspects of self-regulation and self-structure as predictors of perceived emotional distress. *Personality and Social Psychology Bulletin, 26*, 188–205.

Gross, J. J. (1999). Emotion regulation: Past, present, future. *Cognition and Emotion, 13*, 551–573.

Hackman, J. R. (1986). The psychology of self-management in organizations. In M. S. Pollack & R. O. Perlfof (Eds.), *Psychology and work: Productivity change and employment* (pp. 85–136). Washington, DC: American Psychological Association.

Harlow, R. E., & Cantor, N. (1994). The social pursuit of academics: Side-effects and "spillover" of strategic reassurance seeking. *Journal of Personality and Social Psychology, 66*, 386–397.

Heatherton, T. F., & Vohs, K. D. (1998). Why is it so difficult to inhibit behavior? *Psychological Inquiry, 9*, 212–216.

Heckhausen, H. (1984). *Motivationspsychologische Metaprozesse in den verschiedenen Handlungsphasen* [Motivational metaprocesses in different action phases]. Unpublished manuscript, University of Bochum, Germany.

Hesketh, B. (1997). Dilemmas in training for transfer and retention. *Journal of Applied Psychology, 46*, 317–386.

Hesketh, B., & Bochner, S. (1994). Technological change in a multicultural context: Implications for training and career planning. In H. C. Triandis, M. D. Dunnette, & L. M. Hough (Eds.), *Handbook of industrial and organizational psychology* (Vol. 4, pp. 191–240). Palo Alto, CA: Consulting Psychologists Press.

Hicks, W. D., & Klimoski, R. J. (1987). Entry into training programs and its effects on training outcomes: A field experiment. *Academy of Management Journal, 30*, 542–552.

Higgins, E. T. (1998). Promotion and prevention: Regulatory focus as a motivational principle. *Advances in Experimental Social Psychology, 30*, 1–46.

Higgins, E. T., & Trope, Y. (1990). Activity engagement theory: Implications of multiply identifiable input for intrinsic motivation. In E. T. Higgins & R. M. Sorrentino (Eds.), *Handbook of motivation and cognition* (Vol. 2, pp. 229–264). New York: Guilford.

Hollenbeck, J. R., & Klein, H. J. (1987). Goal commitment and the goal-setting process: Problems, prospects, and proposals for future research. *Journal of Applied Psychology, 72*, 212–220.

Jackson, D. N. (1984). *Personality Research Form manual.* Port Huron, MI: Research Psychologists Press.

Jacobson, E. (1938). *Progressive relaxation.* Chicago: University of Chicago Press.

James, W. (1981). *The principles of psychology* (Vol. 2). Cambridge, MA: Harvard University Press. (Original work published 1890)

Josephson, B. R., Singer, J. A., & Salovey, P. (1996). Mood regulation and memory: Repairing sad moods with happy memories. *Cognition and Emotion, 10,* 437–444.

Kanfer, F. H., & Gaelick, L. (1986). Self-management methods. In F. H. Kanfer & A. P. Goldstein (Eds.), *Helping people change: A textbook of methods* (pp. 283–345). New York: Pergamon.

Kanfer, F. H., & Karoly, P. (1982). The psychology of self-management: Abiding issues and tentative directions. In P. Karoly & F. H. Kanfer (Eds.), *Self-management and behavior change: From theory to practice* (pp. 571–599). New York: Pergamon.

Kanfer, F. H., Reinecker, H., & Schmelzer, D. (1996). *Selbstmanagement-Therapie* [Self-management therapy]. Berlin: Springer.

Kanfer, F. H., & Schefft, B. K. (1988). *Guiding the process of therapeutic change.* Champaign, IL: Research Press.

Kanfer, R. (1990). Motivation theory and industrial and organizational psychology. In M. D. Dunnette & L. M. Hough (Eds.), *Handbook of industrial and organizational psychology* (Vol. 1, pp. 75–170). Palo Alto, CA: Consulting Psychologists Press.

Kanfer, R., & Ackerman, P. L. (1989). Motivation and cognitive abilities: An integrative/aptitude-treatment interaction approach to skill acquisition. *Journal of Applied Psychology, 74*, 657–690.

Kanfer, R., & Heggestad, E. D. (1997). Motivational traits and skills: A person-centered approach to work motivation. *Research in Organizational Behavior, 19*, 1–56.

Kannheiser, W. (1983). Theorie der Tätigkeit als Grundlage eines Modells von Arbeitsstreß [Theory of action as a foundation for a model of stress in working behavior]. *Zeitschrift für Arbeits- und Organisationspsychologie, 27*, 102–110.

Karoly, P. (1993). Mechanisms of self-regulation: A systems view. *Annual Review of Psychology, 44*, 23–52.

Karoly, P. (1995). Self-control theory. In W. O'Donoghue & L. Krasner (Eds.), *Theories of behavior therapy: Exploring behavior change* (pp. 259–285). Washington, DC: American Psychological Association.

Kehr, H. M. (1999). Entwurf eines konfliktorientierten Prozeßmodells von Motivation und Volition [Framework of a conflict-oriented process model of motivation and volition]. *Psychologische Beiträge, 41*, 20–43.

Kehr, H. M. (2001, November). *Bringing theories of motivation and volition into play: A new approach to self-management training*. Invited lecture presented at the Institute of Personality and Social Research Colloquium Series, University of Berkeley, CA.

Kehr, H. M. (2002). *Souveränes Selbstmanagement: Ein wirksames Konzept zur Stärkung von Motivation und Wille* [Self-management: An effective concept to enhance motivation and volition]. Weinheim, Germany: Beltz.

Kehr, H. M. (2003a). *Fear motives, intrusive thoughts, volitional depletion, and well-being among managers*. Manuscript submitted for publication.

Kehr, H. M. (2003b). Goal conflicts, attainment of new goals, and well-being among managers. *Journal of Occupational Health Psychology, 8*, 195–208.

Kehr, H. M. (2003c). *Interactions of positive and negative self-regulatory fantasies predict future sales in insurance managers.* Manuscript submitted for publication.

Kehr, H. M. (2003d, August). *Theoretical and Empirical Foundations of a Fresh Approach to Self-Management Training (SMT).* Paper presented at the Annual Meeting of the Academy of Management, Seattle.

Kehr, H. M. (2004a). Implicit/explicit motive discrepancies and volitional depletion among managers. *Personality and Social Psychology Bulletin, 30,* 315–327.

Kehr, H. M. (2004b). Integrating motives, goals, and abilities: The compensatory model of work motivation and volition. *Academy of Management Review* (Special issue: The future of work motivation theories)*, 29,* 479–499.

Kehr, H. M. (2004c). *Motivation und Volition: Funktionsanalysen, Feldstudien mit Führungskräften und Entwicklung eines Selbstmanagement-Trainings (SMT).* [Motivation and volition: Functional analyses, field studies with managers, and the development of self-management training (SMT)]. In J. Kuhl & F. Halisch (Series Eds.), Research on motivation. Göttingen, Germany: Hogrefe.

Kehr, H. M., Bles, P. & Rosenstiel, L. v. (1998, March). *Self-regulation improves while high degrees of self-control impede learning transfer in management training.* Paper presented at the 6th Workshop on Achievement and Task Motivation, Thessaloniki (GR).

Kehr, H. M., Bles, P., & Rosenstiel, L. v. (1999a). Self-regulation, self-control, and management training transfer [In M. Boekaerts (Ed.), Special issue on self-regulated learning], *International Journal of Educational Research, 31*, 487–498.

Kehr, H. M., Bles, P., & Rosenstiel, L. v. (1999b). Zur Motivation von Führungskräften: Zielbindung und Flußerleben als transferfördernde Faktoren bei Führungstrainings [Motivation and management training: Goal commitment and flow experience as training transfer enhancing factors]. *Zeitschrift für Arbeits- und Organisationspsychologie, 43*, 83–94.

King, L. A. (1995). Wishes, motives, goals, and personal memories: Relations of measures of human motivation. *Journal of Personality, 63*, 985–1007.

King, L. A. (2001). The hard road to the good life: The happy, mature person. *Journal of Humanistic Psychology, 41*, 51–72.

Klein, H. J. (1989). An integrated control theory model of work motivation. *Academy of Management Review, 14*, 150–172.

Klinger, E. (1975). Consequences of commitment to and disengagement from incentives. *Psychological Review, 82*, 1–25.

Klinger, E. (1982). On the self-management of mood, affect, and attention. In P. Karoly & F. H. Kanfer (Eds.), *Self-management and behavior change* (pp. 129–164). New York: Pergamon.

Koestner, R., Weinberger, J., & McClelland, D. C. (1991). Task-intrinsic and social-extrinsic sources of arousal for motives assessed in fantasy and self-report. *Journal of Personality, 59*, 57–82.

Koole, S. L., Smeets, K., Knippenberg, A. van, & Dijksterhuis, A. (1999). The cessation of rumination through self-affirmation. *Journal of Personality and Social Psychology, 77*, 111–125.

Kossek, E. E., Roberts, K., Fisher, S., & Demarr, B. (1998). Career self-management: A quasi-experimental assessment of the effects of a training intervention. *Personnel Psychology, 51*, 935–962.

Kuhl, J. (1985). Volitional mediators of cognition-behavior consistency: Self-regulatory processes and action versus state orientation. In J. Kuhl & J. Beckmann (Eds.), *Action control: From cognition to behavior* (pp. 101–128). Berlin: Springer.

Kuhl, J. (1998). *Was bedeutet Selbststeuerung und wie kann man sie entwickeln?* [What does self-regulation mean and how can we improve it?] Unpublished manuscript, University of Osnabrück, Germany.

Kuhl, J. (2000). A functional-design approach to motivation and self-regulation: The dynamics of personality systems and interactions. In M. Boekarts, P. R. Pintrich, & M. Zeidner (Eds.). *Handbook of self-regulation*. San Diego: Academic Press.

Kuhl, J., & Fuhrmann, A. (1998). Decomposing self-regulation and self-control: The volitional components inventory. In J. Heckhausen & C. S. Dweck (Eds.), *Motivation and self-regulation across the life span* (pp. 15–49). Cambridge, UK: Cambridge University Press.

Kuhl, J., & Goschke, T. (1994). A theory of action control: Mental subsystems, modes of control, and volitional conflict-resolution strategies. In J. Kuhl & J. Beckmann (Eds.),

Volition and personality: Action versus state orientation (pp. 93–124). Seattle: Hogrefe & Huber.
Kuhl, J., & Kraska, K. (1989). Self-regulation and metamotivation: Computational mechanisms, development, and assessment. In R. Kanfer, P. L. Ackerman, & R. Cudek (Eds.), *Learning and individual differences: Abilities, motivation, and methodology* (pp. 1–28). Hillsdale, NJ: Erlbaum.
Langston, C. A. (1994). Capitalizing on and coping with daily-life events: Expressive responses to positive events. *Journal of Personality and Social Psychology, 67,* 1112–1125.
Latham, G. P., & Frayne, C. A. (1989). Self-management training for increasing job attendance: A follow-up and replication. *Journal of Applied Psychology*, *72*, 411–416.
Latham, G. P., & Locke, E. A. (1991). Self-regulation through goal setting. *Organizational Behavior and Human Decision Processes*, *50*, 212–247.
Lazarus, R. S., Kanner, A. D., & Folkman, S. (1980). Emotions: A cognitive-phenomenological analysis. In R. Plutchik & H. Kellerman (Eds.), *Theory, research, and experience: Vol. 1. Theories of emotion* (pp. 189–217). New York: Academic Press.
Lee, T. W., Locke, E. A., & Latham, G. P. (1989). Goal setting theory and job performance. In L. A. Pervin (Ed.), *Goal concepts in personality and social psychology* (pp. 291–326). Hillsdale, NJ: Erlbaum.
Leventhal, H., & Scherer, K. (1987). The relationship of emotion to cognition: A functional approach to a semantic controversy. *Cognition and Emotion*, *1*, 3–28.
Lewin, K. (1926). Untersuchungen zur Handlungs- und Affekt-Psychologie. I.: Vorbemerkungen über die psychischen Kräfte und Energien und über die Struktur der Seele [Examinations on the psychology of action and affect. I: Preliminary remarks on psychological powers and energies and on the structure of the psyche]. *Psychologische Forschung*, *7*, 294–329.
Lindworsky, J. (1923a). *Der Wille: Seine Erscheinung und seine Beherrschung* [Volition: Its appearance and control]. Leipzig, Germany: Barth.
Lindworsky, J. (1923b). *Willensschule* [School of willpower]. Paderborn, Germany: Schöning.
Linville, P. W. (1987). Self-complexity as cognitive buffer against stress-related illness and depression. *Journal of Personality and Social Psychology*, *52*, 663–676.
Locke, E. A., & Kristof, A. L. (1996). Volitional choices in the goal achievement process. In P. M. Gollwitzer & J. A. Bargh (Eds.), *The psychology of action: Linking cognition and motivation to behavior* (pp. 365–384). New York: Guilford.
Locke, E. A., & Latham, G. P. (1984). *Goal setting: A motivational technique that works!*. Englewood Cliffs, NJ: Prentice Hall.
Locke, E. A., & Latham, G. P. (1990). *A theory of goal setting and task performance.* Englewood Cliffs, NJ: Prentice-Hall.
Loewenstein, G. (1996). Out of control: Visceral influences on behavior. *Organizational Behavior and Human Decision Processes*, *65*, 272–292.
Mahoney, M. J. (1972). Research issues in self-management. *Behavior Therapy*, *3*, 45–63.
Mahoney, M. J., & Thoresen, C. E. (1974). Behavioral self-control. In M. J. Mahoney & C. E. Thoresen (Eds.), *Self-control: Power to the person* (pp. 20–26). Monterey, CA: Brooks/Cole.
Manz, C. C. (1986). Self-leadership: Toward an expanded theory of self-influence processes in organizations. *Academy of Management Review*, *11*, 585–600.

Markus, H., & Wurf, E. (1987). The dynamic self-concept: A social psychological perspective. *Annual Review of Psychology, 38*, 299–337.
Martin, L. L. (1999). I-D compensation theory: Some implications of trying to satisfy immediate-return needs in a delayed-return culture. *Psychological Inquiry, 10*, 195–208.
Martin, L. L., & Tesser, A. (1989). Towards a motivational and structural theory of ruminative thought. In J. S. Uleman & J. A. Bargh (Eds.), *Unintended thought* (pp. 306–326). New York: Guilford.
McClelland, D. C. (1972). What is the effect of achievement motivation training in the schools? *Teachers College Record, 74*, 129–145.
McClelland, D. C. (1985). How motives, skills, and values determine what people do. *American Psychologist, 40*, 812–825.
McClelland, D. C. (1995). *Scientific psychology as a social enterprise.* Unpublished manuscript, University of Boston.
McClelland, D. C., Atkinson, J. W., Clark, R. A., & Lowell, E. L. (1953). *The achievement motive.* New York: Appleton-Century-Crofts.
McClelland, D. C., Koestner, R., & Weinberger, J. (1989). How do self-attributed and implicit motives differ? *Psychological Review, 96*, 690–702.
McKeeman, D., & Karoly, P. (1991). Interpersonal and intrapsychic goal-related conflict reported by cigarette smokers, unaided quitters, and relapsers. *Addictive Behaviors, 16*, 543–548.
Meichenbaum, D. (1978). Why does using imagery in psychotherapy lead to change? In J. L. Singer & K. S. Pope (Eds.), *The power of human imagination* (pp. 381–394). New York: Plenum.
Meichenbaum, D. (1993). Changing conceptions of cognitive behavior modification: Retrospect and prospect. *Journal of Consulting and Clinical Psychology, 61*, 202–204.
Mellers, B., Schwartz, A., & Ritov, I. (1999). Emotion-based choice. *Journal of Experimental Psychology, 128*, 332–345.
Metcalfe, J., & Mischel, W. (1999). A hot/cool-system analysis of delay of gratification: Dynamics of willpower. *Psychological Review, 106*, 3–19.
Michotte, A. E., & Prüm, E. (1910). Étude éxperimentale sur le choix volontaire et ses antécédents immédiats [Experimental study on volitional choice and its immediate antecedents]. In T. Flournoy & E. Claparède (Eds.), *Archives de Psychologie* (Vol. 10, pp. 119–299). Geneva, Switzerland: Librairie Kundig.
Miller, G. A., Galanter, E., & Pribram, K. H. (1960). *Plans and the structure of behavior.* London: Holt.
Miller, N. E. (1944). Experimental studies of conflict. In J. M. Hunt (Ed.), *Personality and the behavior disorders* (Vol. I, pp. 431–465). New York: Ronald.
Mills, P. K. (1983). Self-management: Its control and relationship to other organizational properties. *Academy of Management Review, 8*, 445–453.
Mischel, W. (1996). From good intentions to willpower. In J. A. Bargh & P. M. Gollwitzer (Eds.), *The psychology of action: Linking cognition and motivation to behavior* (pp. 197–218). New York: Guilford.
Mischel, W. (1999). Personality coherence and dispositions in a cognitive-affective personality (CAPS) approach. In D. Cervone & Y. Shoda (Eds.), *The coherence of personality: Social-cognitive bases of consistency, variability, and organization* (pp. 37–60). New York: Guilford.

Mischel, W., Cantor, N., & Feldman, S. (1996). Principles of self-regulation: The nature of willpower and self-control. In E. T. Higgins & A. Kruglanski (Eds.), *Social psychology: Handbook of basic principles* (pp. 329–360). New York: Guilford.

Morris, W. N., & Reilly, N. P. (1987). Toward the self-regulation of mood: Theory and research. *Motivation and Emotion, 11*, 215–249.

Muraven, M., & Baumeister, R. F. (2000). Self-regulation and depletion of limited resources: Does self-control resemble a muscle? *Psychological Bulletin, 126*, 247–259.

Muraven, M., Baumeister, R. F., & Tice, D. M. (1999). Longitudinal improvement of self-regulation through practice: Building self-control strength through repeated exercise. *Journal of Social Psychology, 139*, 446–457.

Murray, H. A. (1943). *Thematic Apperceptive Test Manual.* Cambridge, MA: Harvard University Press.

Nair, K. U. (2000). Cognitive maps of managers and complex problem solving. In T. K. Lant & Z. Shapira (Eds.), *Organizational cognition: Computation and interpretation:* 211–239. Mahwah, NJ: Erlbaum.

Neck, C. P., & Manz, C. C. (1992). Thought self-leadership: The influence of self-talk and mental imagery on performance. *Journal of Organizational Behavior, 13*, 681–699.

Neck, C. P., & Manz, C. C. (1996). Thought self-leadership: The impact of mental strategies training on employee cognition, behavior, and affect. *Journal of Organizational Behavior, 17*, 445–467.

Norman, D. A., & Shallice, T. (1986). Attention to action: Willed and automatic control of behavior. In R. J. Davidson, G. E. Schwartz, & D. Shapiro (Eds.), *Consciousness and self-regulation: Advances in research.* (Vol. 4, pp. 1–18). New York: Plenum.

Oettingen, G. (1996). Positive fantasy and motivation. In P. M. Gollwitzer & J. A. Bargh (Eds.), *The psychology of action: Linking cognition and motivation to behavior* (pp. 236–259). New York: Guilford.

Oettingen, G., Pak, H., & Schnetter, K. (2001). Self-regulation of goal-setting: Turning free fantasies about the future into binding goals. *Journal of Personality and Social Psychology, 80*, 736–753.

Pennebaker, J. W. (1980). Self-perception of emotion and internal sensation. In D. M. Wegner & R. R. Vallacher (Eds.), *The self in social psychology* (pp. 80–101). New York: Oxford University Press.

Pennebaker, J. W. (1997). Writing about emotional experiences as a therapeutic process. *Psychological Science, 8*, 162–166.

Pervin, L. A. (1994). Personality stability, personality change, and the question of process. In T. F. Heatherton & J. L. Weinberger (Eds.), *Can personality change?* (pp. 315–330). Washington: American Psychological Association.

Polivy, J. (1998). The effects of behavioral inhibition: Integrating internal cues, cognition, behavior, and affect. *Psychological Inquiry, 9*, 181–204.

Priemuth, K. (2002). *Motivation und Volition: Evaluation eines psychologischen Interventionsprogrammes* [Motivation and volition: Evaluation of a psychological intervention program]. Frankfurt, Germany: Lang.

Puca, R. M., & Schmalt, H.-D. (1999). Task enjoyment: A mediator between achievement motives and performance. *Motivation and Emotion, 23*, 15–29.

Rachlin, H. (1995). Self-control: Beyond commitment. *Behavioral and Brain Sciences, 18*, 109–159.

Reither, F., & Stäudel, T. (1985). Thinking and action. In M. Frese & J. Sabini (Eds.), *Goal directed behavior: The concept of action in psychology* (pp. 110–122). Hillsdale, NJ: Erlbaum.
Rigby, C. S., Deci, E. L., Patrick, B. C., & Ryan, R. M. (1992). Beyond the intrinsic-extrinsic dichotomy: Self-determination in motivation and learning. *Motivation and Emotion, 16*, 165–185.
Rodgers, R., & Hunter, J. E. (1991). Impact of management by objectives on organizational productivity. *Journal of Applied Psychology, 75*, 322–336.
Rosenbaum, M. (1998). Opening versus closing strategies in controlling one's responses to experience. In M. Kofta, G. Weary, & G. Sedek (Eds.), *Personal control in action: Cognitive and motivational mechanisms* (pp. 61–84). New York: Plenum.
Rosenstiel, L. v., Kehr, H. M., & Maier, G. W. (2000). Motivation and volition in pursuing personal work goals in the course of organizational socialization. In J. Heckhausen (Ed.), *Motivational psychology of human development* (pp. 287–305). North Holland: Elsevier.
Rubinstein, S. L. (1984). *Grundlagen der Allgemeinen Psychologie* [Foundations of general psychology]. Berlin: Volk und Wissen. (Original work published 1940)
Ryan, R. M., & Deci, E. L. (2000). Self-determination theory and the facilitation of intrinsic motivation, social development, and well-being. *American Psychologist, 55*, 68–78.
Ryan, R. M., Sheldon, K. M., Kasser, T., & Deci, E. L. (1996). All goals are not created equal: An organismic perspective on the nature of goals and their regulation. In P. M. Gollwitzer & J. A. Bargh (Eds.), *The Psychology of action: Linking cognition and motivation to behavior* (pp. 7–26). New York: Guilford.
Salovey, P., & Meyer, J. D. (1990). Emotional intelligence. *Imagination, Cognition, and Personality, 9*, 185–211.
Schmalt, H.-D. (1976). *Die Messung des Leistungsmotivs.* [Measurement of the achievement motive]. Göttingen, Germany: Hogrefe
Schönpflug, W. (1985). Goal directed behavior as a source of stress: Psychological origins and consequences of inefficiency. In M. Frese & J. Sabini (Eds.), *Goal directed behavior: The concept of action in psychology* (pp. 172–188). Hillsdale, NJ: Erlbaum.
Schultheiss, O. C., & Brunstein, J. C. (1999). Goal imagery: Bridging the gap between implicit motives and explicit goals. *Journal of Personality, 67*, 1–38.
Schwarz, N., & Bohner, G. (1996). Feelings and their motivational implications: Moods and the action sequence. In P. M. Gollwitzer & J. A. Bargh (Eds.), *The psychology of action: Linking cognition and motivation to behavior* (pp. 119–145). New York: Guilford.
Schwarzer, R. (1992). Self-efficacy in the adoption and maintenance of health behaviors: Theoretical approaches and a new model. In R. Schwarzer (Ed.), *Self-efficacy: Thought control of action* (pp. 217–243). Washington: Hemisphere.
Sheldon, K. M. (1995). Creativity and goal conflict. *Creativity Research Journal, 8*, 299–306.
Sheldon, K. M., & Elliot, A. J. (1999). Goal striving, need-satisfaction, and longitudinal well-being: The self-concordance model. *Journal of Personality and Social Psychology, 76*, 482–497.
Sheldon, K. M., & Houser-Marko, L. (2001). Self-concordance, goal attainment, and the pursuit of happiness: Can there be an upward spiral? *Journal of Personality and Social Psychology, 80*, 152–165.

Sheldon, K. M., & Kasser, T. (1995). Coherence and congruence: Two aspects of personality integration. *Journal of Personality and Social Psychology*, *68*, 531–543.
Simon, H. A. (1967). Motivational and emotional controls of cognition. *Psychological Review*, *74*, 29–39.
Skovholt, T. M., Morgan, J. I., & Negron-Cunningham, H. (1989). Mental imagery in career counseling and life planning: A review of research and intervention methods. *Journal of Counseling and Development*, *67*, 287–292.
Smith, G. F. (1997). Managerial problem solving: A problem-centered approach. In C. E. Zsambok & G. Klein (Eds.), *Naturalistic decision making* (pp. 371–380). Hillsdale, NJ: Erlbaum.
Smith-Jentsch, K. A., Jentsch, F. G., Payne, S. C., & Salas, E. (1996). Can pretraining experiences explain individual differences in learning? *Journal of Applied Psychology*, *81*, 110–116.
Snyder, M. (1974). Self-monitoring of expressive behavior. *Journal of Personality and Social Psychology*, *30*, 526–537.
Sokolowski, K. (1993). *Emotion und Volition* [Emotion and volition]. Göttingen, Germany: Hogrefe.
Sokolowski, K., & Kehr, H. M. (1999). Zum differentiellen Einfluß von Motiven auf die Wirkungen von Führungstrainings (MbO) [Differential impact of motive dispositions on the effects of management training (MbO)]. *Zeitschrift für Differentielle und Diagnostische Psychologie*, *20*, 192–202.
Sokolowski, K., Schmalt, H.-D., Langens, T. A., & Puca, R. M. (2000). Assessing achievement, affiliation, and power motives all at once: The multi-motive grid (MMG). *Journal of Personality Assessment*, *74*, 126–145.
Spangler, W. D. (1992). Validity of questionnaire and TAT measures of need for achievement: Two meta-analyses. *Psychological Bulletin*, *112*, 140–154.
Strack, F., Schwarz, N., & Gschneidinger, E. (1985). Happiness and reminiscing: The role of time perspective, affect, and mode of thinking. *Journal of Personality and Social Psychology, 49,* 1460–1469.
Stern, W. (1950). *Allgemeine Psychologie auf personalistischer Grundlage* [General psychology from a personalistic perspective]. (2nd ed.). Haag, The Netherlands: Martinus Nijhoff. (Original work published 1935)
Tannenbaum, S. I., & Yukl, G. (1992). Training and development in work organizations. *Annual Review of Psychology*, *43*, 399–441.
Taylor, S. E., & Schneider, S. K. (1989). Coping and the simulation of events. *Social Cognition*, *7*, 174–197.
Tyszka, T. (1998). Two pairs of conflicting motives in decision making. *Organizational Behavior and Human Decision Processes*, *74*, 189–211.
Vallerand, R. J. (1997). Toward a hierarchical model of intrinsic and extrinsic motivation. *Advances in Experimental Social Psychology*, *29*, 271–360.
Wadsworth, M., & Ford, D. H. (1983). Assessment of personal goal hierarchies. *Journal of Counseling Psychology*, *30*, 514–526.
Wegge, J. (1998). Die Zielsetzungstheorie: Ein kritischer Blick auf Grundlagen und Anwendungen [Goal setting theory: A critical view on foundations and applications]. In O. L. Braun (Ed.), *Ziele und Wille in der Psychologie: Grundlagen und Anwendungen* (pp. 3–50). Landau, Germany: Empirische Pädagogik.

Wegner, D. M. (1994). Ironic processes of mental control. *Psychological Review, 101*, 34–52.

Weinberger, J. L. (1994). Can personality change? In T. F. Heatherton & J. L. Weinberger (Eds.), *Can personality change?* (pp. 333–350). Washington: American Psychological Association.

Weiner, B. (1992). *Human Motivation: Metaphors, theories, and research.* Newbury Park, CA: Sage.

Wexley, K. N., & Baldwin, T. (1986). Post-training strategies for facilitating positive transfer: An empirical exploration. *Academy of Management Journal*, *29*, 503–520.

Wheeler, D. D., & Janis, I. L. (1980). *A practical guide for making decisions.* New York: Free Press.

Wundt, W. (1907). Grundriss der Psychologie [Sketch of psychology] (8th ed.). Leipzig, Germany: Engelmann. (Original work published 1896).

The Actiotope

A heuristic model for a research program designed to examine and reduce adverse motivational conditions influencing scholastic achievement

Albert Ziegler, Kurt A. Heller, Barbara Schober & Markus Dresel

Introduction

Since the onset of intellectual history, mankind has been interested in procuring details about the world in which it exists. This knowledge promises a basis for the potential actions which could lead to better environmental assimilation (Gruber, Mack, & Ziegler, 1999). However, it was soon clear that mankind is subject to perceptual limitation, a boundary which was primarily explained in mystical and religious terms. Through Plato, the idea was initially advanced that, as a matter of principle, objective access to the world is impossible; one cannot even rely on one's perceptive abilities. Nowadays the naïve realism or the conception that the world is commensurate with exactly our perceptions and beliefs about it no longer exists and is generally rejected. Admittedly, the evolution of epistemology is, from our perspective, a very constructive contribution to this problem in that it clearly points out that our apparatus for cognition would hardly have had a chance to develop if the information it was used to gather had not been rooted in reality (e.g., Plotkin, 1997; Vollmer, 1983). A plausible example, which is referred to time and time again, can be found in the form of a monkey who, in swinging from branch to branch, demonstrates the possession of a natural conception of distance, the lack of which would find him falling to the ground and exclude him from having been counted among our ancestors. This example attempts to express that human reality, although it is always a fabricated reality, must be quintessentially adaptive in order for a species to be able to successfully exist in its biotope, the habitat or living space utilized by types of plants and animals which require similar environmental conditions. From a psychological point of view, the concept of a *biotope* seems to be too crude to be able to account for individual actions. Furthermore, the concept of a *sociotope*, developed in the field of sociology, which refers to the living space of a specific social group (Muehlum, 1986), is too coarse to be of use here. Therefore, at this point we would like to introduce the term *actiotope* as the subjective living space with which a person comes to terms by means of his/her actions.

The concept of an actiotope

In contrast to biology and sociology, which conceptualize biotopes and sociotopes as the objective environmental conditions confronted by the active members of a species or social group, the actiotope is characterized by four components:

- action repertoire,
- subjective action space,
- goals, and
- environment.

We would like to substantiate these four components in the field of work favored by us: educational psychology. With *action repertoire* we are referring to the objectively ascertainable options for operation open to a person, which comprises the complete set of actions a person is, in principle, capable of carrying out, if (1) this option were to come under consideration, (2) the option is linked to an appropriate intention, and (3) the environment would permit the execution of this action. A demonstrative example for the relevance of this category of analysis can be found in the actions taken by girls gifted in the natural sciences and mathematics (Beerman, Heller, & Menacher, 1992). Despite being in possession of objectively equal talents, they demonstrate (1) a lower degree of confidence in their abilities than boys and (2) avoid engaging in activities corresponding to these fields, which is documented by, among other things, low participation rates. This can be traced back to their (3) learning environment, whereby parents and teachers accredited them with less abilities than boys (Ziegler & Schober, 1999). A significant fraction of the action repertoire is the *actualized action repertoire*, or the set of actions a person has actually carried out.

With the *subjective action space* we mean the entire set of operational and self-related cognitions which are determined by the subjective operational options available to a person. In order to illustrate what is meant here one often refers to the attributional styles engaged by boys and girls in subjects based on mathematics, the natural sciences, or technology. Whereas a girl would typically attribute a failure to her own lack of talent (and thereby falsely assume that a successful operation is not available in her action repertoire), boys typically make lack of effort or bad luck responsible for a failure. The attributional style favored by girls is therefore, from the point of view of operational functionality, much less suitable to spurring them on to learn, since their perceived lack of talent makes the corresponding efforts involved appear to them to be futile.

Goals allege the course of the actions taken, in other words they limit the repertoire of actions to those options which are suitable to securing the attainment of a specific objective (Locke & Kristof, 1996). However, sometimes we overestimate our abilities and set goals which are unreachable; sometimes we underestimate our abilities and set goals which are too low. The degree of specification of goals can vary considerably (Locke & Latham, 1994) and, in contrast to extremely concrete goals (e.g., motor functions), embrace very general objective targets, which can be expressed through motives or goal orientations.

The *environment* is, in the concept of an actiotope, a component which comprises a multitude of facets and, therefore, cannot be condensed into a homogenous entity. Included here are not only those situations in which the actions are to be conducted, but also those persons with which an individual interacts in these situations. Also it is necessary to make a differentiation here between an objective environment and a subjective environment. An objective environment refers to those aspects of the environment which the actor has not yet processed, examples here could be the personality characteristics of a person with which the actor is interacting (i.e., their intelligence) or properties of the room (size of the room), which a person finds himself. A subjective environment is understood as the environment which a person has already evaluated and for which this person has an internal representation. In this respect, an interaction partner, who is normally attributed with the characteristic "intelligent," can be seen as dumb by a particular actor; similarly, a room most persons consider to be large, could appear to be small to a particular actor.

An important advantage inherent in the concept of the actiotope in an educational context is that, analog to the conceptions of the biotope and sociotope, functionality analyses are supported which, in this case, are centered on the individual. In order to illustrate this, we would like to repeat an observation made by Covington (2000) in the terminology of the actiotope approach. Let us assume that a student always receives positive feedback from his environment when he performs well in school, and negative feedback when he performs poorly. Over the course of time, this student learns that his value as a person is contingent on the quality of his scholastic achievements. Furthermore, let us also assume that he couples his self-esteem to his scholastic achievements, but that at some time in his subjective action space there are no further representations of options available, with which he can (subjectively) fulfill the achievement expectations his environment makes on him with justifiable learning efforts and thereby maintain his self-esteem. Here it becomes clear that the knowledge of one's own action repertoire can be completely independent of the actual achievement opportunities. If this student were to pursue the goal of maintaining a positive self-esteem, then he could attain this by decoupling his self-esteem from his scholastic achievements, an example here would be the exercise of so-called self-handicapping strategies (Jones & Berglas, 1978). Prior to an important examination he intentionally spends little time preparing for the exam and goes out until late in the morning directly prior to the exam. Therefore, the resulting poor performance is not a reflection of his potential for achievement and is less damaging to his self-esteem than it would have been if he had attained a poor grade after an intensive learning effort. Interestingly, based on the actiotope concept, one can interpret this as a process of adaptation. Of course, within the framework of our institutionalized learning environments, learning standards are widely predetermined and measured against these standards; the actions taken by the student cannot be seen as being adaptive. Along these lines, the actiotopes of children in predetermined learning environments can, for heuristic purposes, be ordered along a continuum of maladaptive to adaptive actiotopes. Adaptive actiotopes are those in which the children maximally expand their action repertoires in accordance to the magnitude of their abilities in order to be able to sufficiently meet the defined demands made on them by their learning environments. These increments normally occur in the area of the subjective action space as well as that of goals, a consequence of which is that the actualized action repertoire is in accordance with the requirements made by the environment.

A research program based on the actiotope approach

Our previous investigations have been concerned with the behavior of girls in the areas of mathematics and the natural sciences. The actiotope approach does not intend to compensate for a psychological theory although, as a heuristic framework, it does point out the relevant components which a research program must take into account when attempting to come to terms with questions of this nature. The presentation of our empirical findings ensue in two sections, whereby in the first section the analyses of the situation being faced by girls will be broken down according to the four components of an actiotope. We will then introduce the various indicators which point out that the discrepancy between actual action repertoire and actualized action repertoire is greater for girls than it is for boys. We will further demonstrate that, consistent with this point, their subjective action space is more dysfunctional with respect to compliance with scholastic demands and, simultaneously, that they are more cautious when it comes to setting academic goals. In conclusion, we will submit findings which show that girls are indeed accorded lower levels of ability by their social environments than their male counterparts in the fields listed above. In the second section we will present training studies which should be able to help to improve the adaptivity of the actiotope in scholastic achievement contexts. The first approach is concerned with improving the learning environments of girls. A second group of studies was intended to expand the subjective action space. In addition, they also demonstrate that by an expansion of the action space attention must also be paid to the development of appropriate goals. In closing, a training will be delineated in which the action repertoire, the subjective action space, goals, and environment are all simultaneously modified.

An actiotope based analysis of the situation faced by girls

Actualized and actual action repertoire

In sorting through the extensive literature concerning the scholastic situation faced by girls in subjects dealing with mathematics and the natural sciences, one finds many indications that girls do not achieve as well as boys in these domains (e.g., Rustemeyer, 1999; Seegers & Boekaerts, 1996). This finding is independent of the type of school being attended and can be observed in most western industrialized countries. Overviews have been assembled by Beerman et al. (1992) as well as Middleton and Spanias (1999). Comprehensive achievement statistics have been compiled in the international scholastic achievement study Programme for International Student Assessment (PISA), which generated an independent gender variable effect (Deutsches PISA-Konsortium, 2001). Among the scholastic subjects considered, the gender differences in physics are the most extreme, while the differences in other subjects are not as exaggerated. Nevertheless, only in the "soft" natural science biology could no differences to the disadvantage to the girls be reported (Beerman et al., 1992). In the subject of mathematics, a subject which students study over the entire course of their schooling years, achievement differences favoring boys start to show up at the start of secondary school (Middleton & Spanias, 1999). For the natural sciences, which are taught somewhat later as independent subjects, our own studies have been able to show that achievement differences between the genders are present from the first classroom encounters (Broome, 1998; Ziegler, Broome, & Heller, 1999). Particularly striking are results which confirm that in primary school years, converse achievement differences are the norm, in other words girls perform better than boys (Marshall & Smith, 1987; Tiedemann & Faber, 1994). In one of our studies, we were able to confirm indications of the significance of the transgression from primary school into secondary school: Although achievement test scores obtained at the end of the 4th grade could not confirm significant differences, gender differences placing girls at a disadvantage could be observed at the start of the 5th grade within the same sample (Ziegler & Schober, 1996). In following up on the relevance of these indicators, we made a broader investigation of the role played by primary school transfer in the German state school system. The results infer that a multitude of changes in students' actiotopes can be traced back to this transfer phase (Finsterwald & Ziegler, 2001).

All theoretical concepts of scholastic achievement agree that scholastic achievement is to be understood as the result of a comprehensive and complex sequence of learning activities (Helmke & Weinert, 1997). Therefore, it can be viewed as an indicator of the current state of specific sectors of individual action repertoires. To start with, it can be confirmed that boys and girls can be differentiated with respect to their actualized action repertoire in the areas of mathematics and the natural sciences. Whether these differences also represent differences in objective action repertoires cannot be determined on the basis of scholastic achievement.

Cognitive abilities are considered to be more valid indicators of objective action opportunities in connection with academic learning (Heller, 2000, 2004, 2005; Heller, Perleth, & Lim, 2005). Innate talent differences have long been pertinent in the discussion attempting to explain the gender differences in scholastic achievement seen in the areas of mathematics and the natural sciences (Beerman et al., 1992). Supported by new empirical findings, however, criticism of such approaches to explain these phenomena has recently increased. In particular, the long predominant theory that the cognitive abilities of girls are generally lower has been fully rejected (e.g., Callahan, 1991). Furthermore, at the most, small gender differences in specific ability areas, for instance in spatial ability (Linn & Peterson, 1985), can hardly account for the achievement differences encountered. The longitudinal investigation of the cognitive abilities generated an epochal effect, whereby (in any case partial) gender differences are gradually reduced, and are therefore less likely to be able to contribute to the explanation of scholastic achievement differences (e.g., Feingold, 1988). In one of our own studies, we examined scholastic achievement at different ability levels (Ziegler, Heller, & Broome, 1996). Here – partially grave – achievement differences between girls and boys could be confirmed, who possessed comparative cognitive achievement prerequisites. Taken together, these are a strong indicator that gender differences can be confirmed in the actualization of action repertoires, although their cause cannot be traced to the objective action repertoire.

An alternative explanation for the deficient scholastic achievement of girls in domains related to the natural sciences is the hypothesis that boys, due to their more comprehensive volume of previous experience and larger degree of knowledge gathered prior to initial instruction in these domains, have access to a more extensive action repertoire (e.g., Olszewski-Kubilius, Kulieke, Shaw, & Kreasney, 1990). According to this explanation, these initial differences lead, over the course of instruction-based learning, to scholastic achievement differences. Here the focus is not on the differential actualizing of identical, but rather on the objectively different action repertoires. In a study based on the subject of physics we examined the prior experience deficit hypothesis (Dresel, Ziegler, Broome, & Heller, 1998). Among the 1,188 students in our study, significant gender differences in previous experience with and prior knowledge of physics could be shown prior to the start of 8th grade introductory physics instruction (see also Ziegler, Broome, Dresel, & Heller, 1996). However, it was also shown that the prior knowledge gathered outside of the classroom is irrelevant, in that it is incapable of accounting for gender differences in the acquisition of the basic concepts of physics. This can be founded on the fact that this prior knowledge is often faulty and that it must be corrected through a (costly) relearning process. In another investigation, based on the subject of chemistry, it could be demonstrated that the premises for the prior experience deficit hypothesis could not be met for this domain: Prior to the start of 9th grade introductory chemistry instruction, no gender differences regarding previous experience and prior knowledge in the subject of chemistry could be observed (Ziegler, Dresel, & Schober, 2000).

The findings presented here underline the previously mentioned suspicion that the causes for deficits of this type in female scholastic achievement are not to be traced back to qualitatively inferior objective action repertoires among girls. On the contrary, one can assume that girls are less effective than boys in actualizing their action repertoire, in other words are less likely to adequately put their existing abilities to use. Therefore, among girls one can observe a greater discrepancy between objective and actualized action repertoire than among boys.

Subjective action space

Confronted with the discrepancy described in the last section, one advances to the question of what actually causes this deficiency in actualizing action opportunities among girls. Promising explanatory approaches currently under discussion focus, in particular, on **motivational variables** and the relationship between **self-related knowledge** and behavior (e.g., Dweck, 1999). In other words, it is assumed that self-related cognitions, acquired over the course of the female socialization process, are frequently dysfunctional with respect to the demands and characteristics of academic subjects in the domains of mathematics and the natural sciences. Accordingly, this leads to the situation that objective opportunities in the subjective action space are not represented, thereby a functional action repertoire has just as little chance of developing as does the accumulation of action-related knowledge.

Indications that the self-related knowledge of girls and women in the area of mathematics and the natural sciences is indeed less favorable than that for boys can be found in many of the results obtained from relevant investigations. It has often been reported that girls are less confident in mathematics, articulate lower levels of success expectations, see themselves as being less talented, and tend to explain their successes and failures to causes which are significantly less supportive of self-worth and motivation, in other words they demonstrate a less favorable attributional style (Bettge, 1992; Beyer & Bowden, 1997; Eccles et al., 1985; Marsh, 1989; Mura, 1987; Rustemeyer & Jubel, 1996; Stipek & Gralinski, 1991; Tiedemann & Faber, 1995). Also, girls are significantly more likely to show symptoms of helplessness in dealing with episodes of failure as well as raised levels of the antecedal factors of this problem (Dweck, 1999).

One of the objectives we had in conducting our studies within the framework of an actiotope was to replicate the often only singularly engaged aspects of self-related knowledge concentrated results with a view towards the subjective action space in its entirety in different scholastic subjects. Conclusive insights regarding the constellation of relevant cognitions were also to be attained, whereby we were also interested in information regarding their relationships and the potential they have for explaining characteristics of high relevance such as confidence in one's own abilities. Furthermore, against the background of goal-relevant information for preventative and interventive measures, a central objective of the studies was to accumulate differentiated results regarding the development of dysfunctional subjective action spaces for girls. This concerns not only the temporal age at which they first appear, but also the point in time, with respect to how long the person has been occupied with the subject, at which they can be recognized.

With regard to the **age** at which a cramped subjective action space can be verified among girls, we were able to – concurrent with Tiedemann and Faber (1994) – find first indications among primary school age girls that they are less confident than boys although they have a comparably similar achievement history (Schober & Ziegler, 1998; Ziegler, Schober, & Dresel, 2005). A perusal of the entire constellation of motivationally relevant self-related cognitions unequivocally substantiates the unfavorable situation faced by girls making the transition into secondary education (start of the 5th grade) in the subject of mathematics: Girls possess a poorer ability self-concept, a lower level of aspiration, they attribute failures more frequently to lack of ability, show a lower level of control conviction, are less capable of dealing with feedback about failure, display a more stable implicit theory of their own abilities, and describe themselves at this point in time as being more helpless than boys (e.g., Ziegler & Schober, 1996, 1999; Schober, 2002). A comparable (when not completely identical) pattern of findings were isolated for girls in more advanced grades (e.g., Dresel, Heller, Schober, & Ziegler, 2001), whereby it could be shown that self-related knowledge among girls is more dysfunctional than that for boys for most relevant variables, not only for mathematics but also for the subjects of physics (Ziegler et al., 1999) and chemistry (Ziegler et al., 2000).

The results of studies on physics and chemistry were not only significant with respect to the differences between school subjects; efforts were also undertaken to determine the **point in time with the occupation** with a subject at which the differences emerge – an aspect which can only be clarified in scholastic mathematics under severe limitations. In both investigations, it could be shown that the constricted subjective action space of the girls had already been established prior to the first classroom instruction in each subject (Ziegler et al., 1999; Ziegler et al., 2000). Obviously, quite a number of attitudes and expectations come into play here, which themselves develop independently from concrete positive or negative experiences with a school subject. Furthermore, it is clear that prior knowledge, previous experience, the gender role specific casting of the subject as a "boy's subject," as well as a flexible view of one's own ability potential are important parameters in the explanation of anxiety regarding chemistry, raised levels of helplessness, and diminished ability self-concepts among girls. In addition to the demand for an alteration of unfavorable self-related knowledge derived from other studies, it can be said that (1) a well founded occupation with the natural sciences prior to introductory classroom instruction has a positive effect on self-confidence among girls, that (2) the impression that natural sciences are not for girls must be counteracted from the very beginning, and (3) the mediation of a flexible implicit theory of abilities and talents is a plausible interventive strategy.

Goals

In considering the goals held by girls in the area of mathematics and the natural sciences, both specific as well as general gender differences become apparent. This is only logical since the subjective action space for boys is itself different than that for girls. Specific goals, which are developed in interaction with domain-specific task demands, are **aspirations** or achievement quality levels, which are strived for. With respect to these types of goals, girls demonstrate significantly poorer achievement aspirations than boys in the domains surrounding mathematics and the natural sciences, and are also satisfied with lower levels of achievement (Beerman et al., 1992). Within the framework of our research program, we examined achievement aspirations as they unfolded over the course of introductory physics courses taught at German college preparatory high schools (Broome, 1998). Here it could be shown that girls, prior to introductory physics instruction, can be characterized by an aspiration level similar to that of boys, but that their goals after one semester of instruction fall to a level significantly lower than that of their masculine counterparts, and also that this situation does not improve by the end of the school year.

Indicative for global **life goals** are decisions made regarding course, university major, and career alternatives. Investigations undertaken, which are relative to the significance of the goal systems associated with such decisions, indicate that the predictive power of goals overbalances that of elements found in the subjective action space (Meece, Wigfield, & Eccles, 1990; Wigfield & Eccles, 1992; cf. Hannover, 1991). An example of gender-specific elective behavior can be observed in the course decision made by college-bound high school students: The proportion of girls attending the 13th (last) grade of high school in mathematics achievement courses in Bavaria during the 1998/99 school year was about 40%, in chemistry achievement courses 30%, and 14% in physics achievement courses (Bavarian Ministry of Education and Culture, personal communication, September 3, 1999). Low female participation rates continue to be noticeable when considering the participation rates regarding university majors and other forms of education programs related to the fields of mathematics and natural sciences. The proportion of female students attending Bavarian universities in the winter semester 1997/98 majoring in mathematics or natural science related fields came to an average rate of 33% and that for engineering science majors only 15% (Bavarian State Office for Statistics and Data Processing, 1998). Further illustration of this segregation can be found in Holz-Ebeling (2001) or Rustemeyer and Jubel (1996). This blatant low participation rate makes clear that girls and women pursue life goals which hinge on an occupation within the area of mathematics and the natural sciences less often than boys and men.

Significant gender differences can also be observed with respect to **interest** in mathematics and the natural sciences. Interest – conceptualized as a specific person-object relationship – can be theoretically separated from a goal system; they are, however, very closely linked to one another (Renninger, Hidi, & Krapp, 1992). It can be shown that a rather intense decline in interest in mathematics and natural sciences, which is first observed at primary school levels and accelerates during the secondary school years (Krapp, 1998), has a larger effect on girls than on boys (e.g., Hoffmann, Haeussler, & Peters-Haft, 1997). In addition, gender-specific interest patterns have also been documented (Hoffmann & Lehrke, 1986).

As a rule, the activation of goals is context specific. Nevertheless, those goals which persons pursue are not exclusively determined by situations. Put more simply, persons can be differentiated by the basic set from which their activated goals arise. These individually dependant basic sets are called **goal orientations**. One can differentiate between two types of goal orientations in educational achievement contexts (e.g., Nicholls, 1984; Dweck, 1986):

(1) Goals for which learning is in the foreground or where the acquisition of competence dominates are subsumed under the label of learning goal orientation.
(2) In contrast, goals which are dominated by the depiction of one's own competence or the recognition of abilities, and those which are focused on covering up ability deficits, are grouped under the label performance goal orientation.

Theoretical conceptions assume that goal orientations moderate the relationship between ability-related assumptions (of the subjective action space) and the execution of specific actions (Dweck, 1986, 1999; for a detailed theoretical and empirical explanation see Ziegler, 2001). So, for example, a strong learning goal orientation can safeguard against the negative effects a low ability self-concept can have on learning behavior (Dresel, 2000a). Investigations of gender-specific expressions of goal orientations have not been able to produce uniform findings (Midgley, Kaplan, & Middleton, 2001). Sometimes this can be attributed to the insufficient theoretical and methodological conceptualizations goal orientation as a construct suffers from due to its complexity. So the theoretically important differentiation between the search for desirable and the avoidance of undesirable states (e.g., Elliot & Harackiewicz, 1996) has, so far, seldom been taken into consideration and the differing salience of goal units regarding various significant others has never been taken into account. One conception, which takes the aspect of addressor specifity of goals into account, is being actualized within the framework of our research program with a questionnaire survey. The first investigations based on this show that boys in mathematics instruction are often more likely to pursue a learning goal orientation than girls; however, they also simultaneously cultivate more performance goals in the face of specific addressees such as parents, teachers, and peers (Stoeger, 2001).

Environment

To answer to the question of the genesis of functional or dysfunctional behavioral, factual and self-related knowledge one cannot avoid focusing on environmental influences and socialization agents. This has been dealt with by researchers such as Parsons, Adler, and Kaczala (1982), who see the adverse self-related cognitions found among students and the deficits in achievement behavior associated with them as being contingent on low expectations and ability evaluations on the parts of parents and teachers.

Although the principle relevance of assumptions and attitudes held by significant others is largely undisputed and has been widely documented through manifold indicators (e.g., Bornholt & Goodnow, 1999; Frome & Eccles, 1998; Ziegler, Kuhn, & Heller, 1998), it appears as though the tightness of the cohesion between the assumptions held by the socialization agents – in particular the parents – and the students, as well as the process involved in assimilating these cognitions has not been sufficiently clarified. Against the background of ambiguous findings and the important role expectations and assumptions play, the characteristics of **parental attitudes and expectations** as well as their relationships to those of their children were empirically scrutinized. This occurred with particular attention being paid to those aspects of self-related knowledge considered to be central to the aforementioned gender differences and the development of helpless behavior (see Beerman et al., 1992; Rustemeyer & Jubel, 1996; Tiedemann & Faber, 1994).

Studies conducted with students in the 5th, 7th, and 8th grades (Dresel et al., 2001; Ziegler et al., 1999; Ziegler & Schober, 1999) could confirm consistent gender-specific evaluations on the part of parents – in particular, those which take the form of low ratings of ability and talent, low aspiration levels, and adverse attributional patterns for girls, which were reflected in the corresponding self-evaluations made by their children. Conspicuous at this point are the differential effects of gender-related traditional reasoning made by parents. In all three studies the magnitude of parental gender-related traditional influenced the self-related knowledge of their children, whereby in two of the studies an explicit "enhancement effect" resp. "Golem effect" could be isolated (Dresel et al., 2001; Ziegler et al., 1999): Although the self-image of boys profited from the traditional attitude that mathematics and physics are boy subjects (enhancement effect), that of the girls was apparently impaired (Golem effect).

The analyses of the magnitudes of the cohesions and the relevant transfer mechanisms yielded only little evidence for direct forms of transmission from parent to child variables (Dresel et al., 2001; Ziegler & Schober, 1999). Substantially more explicit were those results which spoke for mediated impacts: Thus it could be demonstrated that adverse parental evaluations can be reflected in the maladaptive attributional styles of their child when he/she is already suffering from a low ability self-concept (Dresel et al., 2001). This infers that the influence of parental cognitions is mediated by the domain-specific self-concept of scholastic achievement behavior (Ziegler et al., 1999).

As already mentioned, the **expectations and attitudes held by teachers** represent a not to be underrated influential factor in the development of a functional resp. dysfunctional achievement-related action space. Rustemeyer (1999) was able to document the distinct manner in which these expectations are gender-specific in an investigation which confirmed that student teachers were already in the possession of explicit assumptions regarding the achievement, work, and learning strategies engaged by boys and girls in the subject of mathematics. Teachers also act on the assumption that girls find mathematics more difficult to manage than boys do (Tiedemann & Faber, 1995). Our studies conducted with mathematics and physics teachers show that every third teacher believes that boys are generally more talented in their subject than girls (Heller, Finsterwald, & Ziegler, 2000). When one also considers the tendency to give socially desirable answers to such questions, then the situation being portrayed here is presumably even more extreme. (By the way, no differences could be found in this study between male and female teachers or whether they were teaching in monoeducational or coeducational classes.) Exceptionally impressive was how the gender-specific expectations of their environment, with which the children were confronted via student-teacher interactions, were reflected in a sorting task involving the gender appropriateness of specific university majors (Heller et al., 2000; Lengfelder & Heller, 2002): Primary school teacher, language arts, and medicine were seen as particularly appropriate for girls; on the other hand mathematics and other subjects in the field of technology and the natural sciences were rated as commendable university majors for boys. Table 1 depicts the results obtained from mathematics teachers.

The third environmental aspect we examined in the context of our actiotope diagnosis for girls and boys in the area of mathematics, natural sciences, and technology pertained to **school books** and the question of to what extent guidelines are engaged in which reinforce traditional stereotypes (Joergens, Richter, Finsterwald, Raul, & Ziegler, 2001).

Table 1. Average positioning and standard deviations of suggested university majors assigned by mathematics teachers (1 *particularly appropriate* to 9 *particularly inappropriate*).

	Girls		Boys	
	M	*SD*	*M*	*SD*
Primary school education	1.4	0.9	7.5	2.6
Language arts	1.6	0.8	6.1	2.5
Medicine	2.9	1.4	4.9	1.8
Law	3.4	1.7	4.3	1.9
Economics	3.6	1.8	3.8	1.9
Mathematics	5.0	2.0	2.4	1.3
Physics	6.4	2.3	2.2	1.0
Engineering	7.2	2.7	1.1	0.7

In this study, 900 illustrations taken out of 43 books that are currently widely used in grades 1 through 6 of the German state school system were analyzed. The results of these analyses emphasize the urgent claim that in order to optimize female actiotopes – in particular, in the context of mathematics and the natural sciences – an intervention into the current environmental state appears to be absolutely indispensable.

Traditional roles are still being illustrated in these modern school books. Men were portrayed in career roles more often than women, and the latter were frequently found in household-related activities or in family circles. Men were often depicted performing outdoor activities, women indoor activities. The possession of or contact with technical accessories or status objects was more frequently masculine; the possession of household objects was more likely to be feminine.

Training studies to improve the actiotope

Through the points discussed so far it should be clear that action should be understood as the impact of a bundle of different causal agents, which exist within a system of constant exchange. An alteration in one of the elements of the system can therefore leave diverse effects and repercussions on an actiotope. In this manner, the alteration of a subjective action space – which could be triggered by an improvement in the ability self-concept – hopefully, can also bring about a change in goal determination (see Pintrich & Schunk, 1996).

Promoting the subjective environment

Separate instruction for boys and girls is not uncommon in German schools. Studies have proven this separation to be plausible for mathematics and natural science courses in particular. For example, girls who have been instructed in a monoeducational environment generate, on the average, better school grades, display more advantageous self-related cognitions (e.g., academic self-concept), and are more prone to consider pursuing a career in these areas than girls who attended coeducational classes. Expressed in the language of the actiotope concept, this infers that the actualized action repertoire, the subjective action space, and the goals pursued by girls instructed in monoeducational classes are expressed in more favorable terms. If one accepts the assumption that the objective action spaces of these girls are not differentiable, then it is primarily deviations in the environment which are responsible for the differences named above. An alteration in one of these components of the actiotope seems to have had far-reaching consequences for the entire actiotope. It is not, however, clear whether the causes are to be located in the subjective or objective environment.

There are several approaches which attempt to explain the positive effect of monoeducational instruction, but, of course, we are most interested in effects which generate the alteration of the **subjective** environment (Ziegler, Broome, & Heller, 1998). In one of our studies, girls who were being instructed in a coeducational system were informed at the end of the 7th grade that they would placed in either a single-sex or coeducational physics class in the new school year. The explanation given for this separation was that girls and boys have different types of interests with regard to physics, and that same gender instruction permitted the teachers to respond to these gender-specific interests. The actual assignment to coeducational or single-sex classroom was, however, purely random.

In fact, the announcement that they would be receiving same-gender instruction produced significantly more positive expectations about their class among the future female physics students than among the girls who were to receive coeducational instruction. Their motivational set as well as their self-confidence and their interest were improved by this prospect. These differences remained relatively stable after one semester of experiencing this type of instruction. Concurrently, a spectacular result could be demonstrated: The positive effects of monoeducational instruction could be, after one semester of instruction, attributed almost exclusively to the expectation effect measured prior to the start of physics instruction. In contrast, no remarkable effects of the monoeducational instruction itself could be isolated. What is the cause of this effect, which we labeled Pygmalion for the girls?

Our train of thought was that through the announcement that same-gender instruction the **subjective environment** of the girls could be changed to the extent that they could now act on the assumption of a good fit between their subjective action repertoires and their subjective environments. The fact that the girls perceive this fit to be so good, is reflected by a significant increase in their self-confidence, which in turn is an indication that they hold the conviction that they are more than capable of dealing with the demands the environment can make of them. Equivalently, raised levels of interest signal that these girls assume that the expected subjective environment would be more appropriate for their goals in this subject. Puzzling, and completely unexpected, was that these positive consequences were triggered through an alteration of the subjective environment and not the objective environment, as it is generally assumed. This state is not only an illustration of the basic premises of cognitive psychology, according to which specific behavioral sequences cannot be either initiated or inhibited by external environmental conditions, but rather that these effects are fundamentally procured through the intra-psychological processes engaged while information is being processed. In conjunction with the current state of research findings, it also provides a good argument for demanding that functional actualizations of objective action opportunities be immediately fixed on self- and task-related cognitions, if they are to be effective. The conceptions of all trainings which have been conducted within the framework of our research program have been, in a narrow sense, committed to this approach.

Promotion of the subjective action space and the role of goals

In our actiotope, cognitive concepts are represented through the subjective action space and the individual goal system. Wide ranging findings amassed in the literature pertaining to educational psychology have proven that in scholastic learning and achievement situations the extent and the quality of learning behaviors are determined, to a certain degree, by the success expectations and ability self-concept the student holds (summarized by Helmke, 1992). Widely undisputed is the fact that alterations in these two elements of the subjective action space can be traced to attributional processes, and are therefore key functions in the motivational process (e.g., Weiner, 1985).

In contrast to the weighty and undeniable relevance of subjectively perceived opportunities to act, personal goal systems can only garner a slight degree of attention when it comes to scholastic learning and achievement situations (Wigfield & Eccles, 1992). This becomes plausible when one keeps in mind that these situations are typically characterized by a sturdy structure in the form of external goal and activity guidelines. Based on the stronger significance it demonstrates, we first turned our investigative attention to the subjective action space in our attempt to promote a functional actiotope and investigated the role played by goals in later studies.

The causal predominance demonstrated by attributional processes suggests their possible value in a training content. As a matter of fact, in the clinical area, so-called **attributional retrainings** are counted among the better established and demonstrably more effective therapeutic measures (Foersterling, 1985). With these training methods, adverse causal explanations (e.g., associate X ignored me because I am unattractive) are replaced with favorable situational viewpoints (e.g., associate X ignored me because he was deep in thought). Despite the merits of this training approach (effective clinical application, economy of intervention, unobtrusive application), transfers into educational settings have, thus far, been less than satisfactory. Although attributional retrainings in scholastic achievement contexts have predominantly targeted improvements in the scholastic and instructional subjective action space, most of the training studies conducted with students have not occurred concurrent to instruction, but rather in settings far removed from the classroom (e.g., individual sessions with external trainers), and the exclusion of instructional measures in assessing the effectiveness of the trainings is extremely experimental in orientation (for an overview, see Dresel, 2001). Even when the training effects attained here can demonstrate the usefulness of this approach in the non-clinical area, no clear statements as to the effectiveness of attributional retrainings can be derived with respect to the specific conditions surrounding classroom instruction.

With our first intervention study (Ziegler & Heller, 1998; cf. Heller & Ziegler, 1996), we examined what chances an attributional retraining **implemented during regular classroom instruction** could offer students who were trained by their own teachers. We were also interested in the long-term effects of the training, a point which had formerly only been investigated in isolated experimental studies. In this investigation, in which 1,353

8th grade college preparatory students participated, physics teachers gave both verbal and written comments, with the desired attributions, on the achievements made by students in their physics classes over a period of 12 weeks. In cases of success, the explanations would primarily be associated with high levels of effort, in cases of failure they would be linked to external factors such as a high degree of task difficulty. In addition to this direct art of commentation with causal explanations, the exhibition of suitable types of covariation information (see Kelley, 1973) was also an attempt to indirectly influence the attributional styles of the students (an overview of the various techniques of attributional retraining which can be engaged in pedagogical contexts can be found in Ziegler & Schober, 2001). The attributional retraining was indeed capable of fostering the subjective action space of students with initially harmful attribution styles: They were more likely to attribute success to efforts made on their part and less like to attribute success to external factors such as luck or low task difficulty than students in the control group. Increases were also seen in the degree to which they ascribed failures to lack of effort and other attributions which are beneficial to self-worth, such as external factors. Training effects could be registered also regarding the indicators of the action repertoires: Those students who participated in the attributional retraining were able to generate better course grades and had a broader command over physics knowledge than those students assigned to the control group. These promotional effects, which could still be observed six months after the end of the training sessions, confirm that the deployment of attributional retrainings in the classroom is a promising prospect. Although the effects attained were consistent, they were of only moderate intensity and promotional effects regarding the meaningful ability attributions could not be obtained. On the one hand, practical reasons associated with interventions in general can be held responsible here. Delayed trainings effects, which could be observed for isolated variables, indicate that larger effects could have been attained with an extended and more intensive training.

On the other hand, theoretical arguments can also be cited here: Although one can directly deduce from attributional models that, in the case of failure, explanations made through inadequate effort have the most favorable consequences for motivation and self-worth (and that this is extremely well supported by empirical evidence; see Ziegler & Schober, 2001), the theoretical assertions made regarding attributions to success contradict one another (Covington & Omelich, 1984; Weiner, 1985). Correspondingly inconsistent is the current state of empirical research on the topic. Supposedly, there are ambivalent effects of the two most frequent spontaneously made attributions to success in achievement contexts (which were also most frequent applied in attributional retrainings), namely explanations made through high levels of effort and high ability levels. Success attributions to high levels of effort therefore could not only be producing the desired motivational effect, but also could possibly be interpreted as an indicator of poor competence levels through the perception of a compensatory link between ability and effort (Surber, 1984). Conversely, ability attributions could lead to dysfunctionally inflated estimations of ability and – in turn, through the perception of a compensatory scheme – to a reduction of learning efforts and would therefore be counterproductive. One could presume here that ambivalent effects of this nature carry a substantial proportion of the responsibility for the fact that attributional retrainings are only moderately effective.

In order to resolve the contradictory state of empirical findings and enlighten the short- and long-term consequences of ability and effort-based attributions, we conducted a further training study in which the attributional feedback the students received was varied systematically (Dresel, 2004). In addition to the theoretical gain, we were able to gather information regarding whether, when, and in which manner attributional feedbacks should be combined in order to compensate for reciprocal consequences. At this point in time, a few studies on this question had already been conducted, they were, however, plagued by contradictive and ecologically invalid findings which were not suitable to permit prognoses on long term-effects (e.g., Schunk & Rice, 1986). It seemed clear that the art in which the feedbacks were being sequenced played a significant role: The succession of feedbacks, in which first ability attributions and later effort attributions were to be engaged, generated different effects than the reverse order. The differences were, however, unsystematic.

For this study, in which a total of 981 7th grade college preparatory students participated, a computer-based motivational training (CBMT) for the subject of mathematics was developed, which permitted the controlled presentation of attributional feedback (Dresel, Ziegler, & Heller, 1999). This software, called *MatheWarp*, was used by 483 students outside of normal classroom instruction over the course of six one-hour sessions. The approximately 1,000 tasks and 80 lessons represented material repeated from the previous year's mathematics courses. After the completion of a block of several tasks, the students received a computer-generated causal explanation of their performance on that block (Example: "It is clear that you understand this topic. When you are finish the additional lesson, then it will be perfect"). In order to permit for the highest veridicality of these causal explanations, they were produced in accordance with individual achievement development and current task difficulty. Additionally, for ambivalent results the students received – as in the example – an attributional feedback for both the successful as well as the unsuccessful portions of their answers.

Through randomized allocation, a total of six experimental conditions were realized (see Table 2). After working through the tasks, the students were presented not only with feedback over the correctness of their solutions, but also causal explanations for the attainment of these results in five of these conditions. These conditions differed from one another in content and in the sequence of causal explanations offered after successes. Due to the explicit nature of the empirical findings reported regarding failure, explanations in this case were based on inadequate effort in these five experimental conditions. The participants in the placebo group simply obtained feedback on the correctness of their solutions.

Table 2. Experimental conditions used to investigate the effectiveness of attributional feedback, which were varied with respect to both content and sequence (Dresel, 2004).

	Success attribution		
Condition	Sessions 1–3	Sessions 4–6	Failure attribution
Ability only	ability	ability	effort
Effort only	effort	effort	effort
First ability then effort	ability	effort	effort
First effort then ability	effort	ability	effort
Ability and effort randomized	ability & effort randomized		effort
Placebo group	–	–	–

Note: Students were given feedback on the correctness of their work in all conditions.

In order to examine the effectiveness of the treatment, in addition to a pretest, two posttests were conducted one directly after the termination of the training and another five months later. In contrast to other trainings conducted outside the classroom (such as those conducted by Schunk), all constructs related to normal 7th grade mathematics instruction were operationalized and assessed with questionnaires. (Hereby different transfer effects, which Hager, Patry, & Brezing, 2000 have suggested examining, were also measured.) A multitude of attributional, motivational, and achievement measurements were surveyed. Presentation of all of these variables goes far beyond the scope of this chapter; we will therefore limit ourselves to one measurement of each of the actiotope components *subjective action space* (ability self-concept for mathematics as defined by Dweck, 1999), *goals* (value of mathematical achievement behavior as defined by Ziegler, Dresel, & Schober, 1998) and *action repertoire* (mathematical knowledge). For a more detailed portrayal of these results, see Dresel (2004).

Specific effects on the three components of an actiotope were expected for the types of attributional feedbacks we investigated. From exclusive ability feedbacks, it was expected that a directly positive effect on the subjective action space and goals would surface. Since it was assumed that this type of attribution to success would result in a reduction of effort, we presumed that this type of feedback would have an adverse effect on the action repertoire and that the promotional effects observed would not be permanent (see Helmke, 1992). The results obtained corresponded to these expectations. Unexpected, however, was the magnitude of these effects: exclusive ability feedback was able to cause a direct improvement in the ability self-concept of mathematics as well as the perceived value of mathematics. As suspected, this effect, due to the reduction in effort, is not a sustainable effect: Both variables sank drastically in the fifth month after the intervention, in part, to a point under the level demonstrated by the placebo group. For mathematical knowledge, it could be confirmed that uniform ability feedback does not have a promotional effect.

From exclusive effort feedbacks it was supposed that this could be used as an indicator of low ability levels, which is why no effect on the subjective action space was expected. Furthermore, we assumed that students who received these feedbacks would safeguard their self-worth by uncoupling their goal systems from mathematical activities (see Harter, 1986; Steele, 1988). However, we expected to find at least a short-term promotional effect on the action repertoire based on the strong influence effort was to exert on scholastic achievement. The negative effects exposed should prohibit any long-term improvement here. Also, these hypotheses could be confirmed: A uniform explanation of successes through high levels of effort was not capable of promoting an ability self-concept, neither directly nor with a delayed effect. Students who received these feedbacks showed less incentive for mathematical achievements at both posttests than those students who did not receive any attributional feedbacks at all. In mathematical knowledge, there was a weak advantage to be shown in contrast to the other attributional conditions, which is to be expected directly after the termination of an intervention.

Both short-term and long-term promotional effects were expected for all three actiotope components for the combined incorporation of ability and effort feedbacks, since the negative effects should act to mutually counter-balance one another. We expected the largest effects for the condition "first effort, then ability," since the students would be able to interpret the later reported messages of ability as a result of the previously stressed efforts undertaken. This focus on the growth of own abilities represents a beneficial motivational learning condition and an effective preventative measure against the symptoms of helplessness (Dweck, 1999). The lowest promotional effects were expected from the randomized incorporation of ability and effort attributions, since it was here assumed that the two causal factors would mutually devaluate one another and that the altered attributional style would not be able to sufficiently consolidate itself (see Ziegler & Heller, 1998). The combination of ability and effort feedbacks, whereby each one was presented over a longer period of time, was effective in directly promoting the ability self-concepts of the students exposed to it. An enduring effect was enjoyed by the feedback sequence "first effort, then ability," which was illustrated by a large advantage regarding ability self-concept with respect to the placebo group, and held constant over a period of five months. This condition was far and above all others at the third measuring point, including the other two combinations of ability and effort feedback. In particular – and contrary to expectations – the ability self-concepts of the students could not be positively influenced by the rapidly (randomized) changing sequence of ability and effort feedbacks, neither directly nor for the long run. The value of mathematical activities could be effectively encouraged with the sequence "first effort, then ability;" the other two combinations were not sufficiently capable of meeting up to this perception. The acquisition of mathematical knowledge during regular classroom instruction through randomized renditions could be promoted in the short-term, but not in the long-term. An inverted pattern of findings showed up for the other two combinational conditions: While directly following the termination of the training no expansions in knowledge could be confirmed, each student who was exposed to the ability and effort feedbacks in chronological sequence displayed more mathematical knowledge five months after the termination of the training than those students who had not been exposed to attributional feedback. Both feedback sequences were therefore more effective than all other experimental conditions, whereby the magnitude of the effect was particularly impressive for the condition "first effort, then ability."

In conclusion, it can be maintained that on the basis of their negative effects, neither unilateral ability nor unilateral effort feedbacks are suitable to sustainably promote the three actiotope components (subjective action space, goals, and actualized action repertoire) following experiences of success. The combination of the two attributions to success is more effective here. Differences are also to be noted in this conceptualization. The rapidly (randomized) changing sequence of ability and effort feedbacks was barely able to generate any promotional effects at all. This is revealing in light of the terms that this sequence can be understood as a model for attributional retrainings in which both types of attributions to success are engaged in the feedback component. It was seldom the case that this succession was controlled in previous studies. One reason for the sub-optimal effectiveness of previous trainings is to be found in the quickly changing rendition of different attributions to success. Substantially larger and longer-lasting promotional effects could be generated with the longer engagement of causal categories. In particular, the sequence which began with effort-related feedbacks and later switched to ability-related feedbacks was extremely effective, a result which can be interpreted as an ability growth experience. For the application of attributional feedbacks in classroom contexts, this implies that an agreement as to feedback sequence must be made during the didactic phases of the development of learning goals: The employment of attributions to effort would most reasonably occur during the early phases of instruction of a new topic of study, which ideally has the acquisition of specific knowledge, abilities, or competencies as its goal. A changeover should occur when the didactic phase of appropriation has been terminated and successes can already be cited in the phase of operative permeation. The appropriate competences can operate as the content of the ability feedbacks in this case. The differences in effectiveness, which have been demonstrated among the various sequences, theoretically implicate the existence of meanings and connections among attributional processes, which cannot be described through the dimensional characteristics of singular attributions alone (Dresel, Schober, & Ziegler, 2005), but are rather determined through antecedal causal explanations. The results indicate that attributional processes can be better described through the perspective of multiple causal explanations.

The exclusively effort-related feedback, which proved itself as relatively ineffective in the study just referred to, was subjected in an expansionary study whereby the component of the actiotope that has been the focus of our attention so far (subjective action space) was linked to that of the goals (Dresel, 2000b). In this training study, in which 92 students participated, teachers – similarly as in Ziegler and Heller (1998) – conducted an attributional retraining during regular 8th grade physics instruction, whereby attributions to effort were the only explanations made in response to success situations. In this study, the effect of the feedbacks was examined in conjunction with the goals pursued by the students. The expectation that these were moderating the training effects, based on the findings of Jagacinski and Nicholls (1984, 1987), was the key to the assumption that a compensatory connection between ability and effort only existed in conjunction with specific goal orientations, namely with a strong performance goal orientation or a weak learning goal orientation. Actually, the attributional retraining did have the desired promotional effect on preparedness to endeavor, personal importance of physics, attributional style, and scholastic achievement for students subscribing to specific goal orientations. For other goal orientations, the attributions to effort incited effects which were diametrically opposed to those intended. (Excluding regard for goal orientation, as in Dresel, 2004, no effects were to be observed.) The cultivation of a strong performance goal orientation, or the orientation on the presentation of individual abilities proved to be particularly adverse. An orientation on increasing learning and understanding, that is on learning goals was, in contrast, a promotional condition for the success of training. Finally, dependencies on a third class of goals were also demonstrated, namely those which are focused on insuring that the lowest possible degree of effort for scholastic demands is exerted. Such an orientation on avoiding effort prevents effort feedbacks received during the training from having any effect.

This study demonstrates that the negative effects of uniform attributional feedback can be dependant on the goals a student pursues in the classroom. (This is not to be expected for combined feedback since the negative effects here are compensated for by the other attributions.) In general, one can assume that the outcomes and their presumed causal antecedents are to be interpreted with respect to the goals that are being pursued through these activities. Though this window of interpretation, the related relevance of causal factors can correspondingly catch one's eye in different manners, which would imply the existence of different goal systems.

All in all, the findings of the intervention studies referred to so far demonstrate that the actiotope of students can be effectively promoted through a training operation based on the mediation of appropriate attributions, that is exclusively applied to the subjective action space. A necessary prerequisite for a sufficiently large effect is, however, the reflected engagement of attributional feedbacks, in particular, a close observation of the related relevance among specific attributions. Last but not least, on the basis of the confirmation of the moderator role played by goals, in addition and parallel to the differentiation of the approach of attributional retrainings, we pursued a second approach to the promotion of actiotopes in pedagogic contexts, namely the development of an intervention which simultaneously applies all components of the actiotope.

A fully integrated concept

Against the background of often only moderate (Ziegler & Heller, 1998) or differential effects (Dresel, 2000b) resulting from interventions that focus on single aspects of an actiotope, the concept of the Munich Motivational Training (MMT) attempts to realize an intervention which addresses all components of an actiotope (Schober, 2002). Precisely, this means that the intentions of the MMT are to optimize the objective action repertoire of students as well as its actualization, in that it is to promote knowledge concerning a specific domain as well as learning strategies which facilitate the effective application and autonomous enhancement of this knowledge. The alteration of self-related knowledge represents the next central building blocks of the MMT: The improvement of feedback processing, the modification of attributional style as well as the mediation of the understanding that one's own abilities are flexible (see Dweck, 1999). Thirdly, the MMT is directed towards a promotion of goals, which, in the terms of the Motivational Process Model developed by Dweck and Leggett (1988), attempt to relocate student motivational orientation towards learning goals through which students should be moved to pursue the ultimate intention of expanding their own competences. Finally, the realization of the MMT goals, which should simultaneously proceed on different levels, is unconditionally bound to an alteration of the environment (explicitly, e.g., through the discussion of specific topics of interest, implicitly through special achievement feedback offered by teachers and peers). Above all we are dealing with a training here which should ultimately find itself deployed in schools.

The MMT understands itself, within the framework of actitope terminology, not only as a fully integrated concept, but rather attempts not only to combine, theoretically as well as in practice, fruitful elements of previous motivational approaches to promotion, but also to optimize these elements according to the requirements made on scholastic interventions. The concrete theoretical framework of the MMT, which can be categorized somewhere between constructivism and social cognitive approaches (see Pintrich & Schunk, 1996) can be explicitly seen in Heckhausen's (1989) model of motivation and volition. In other words it attempts to positively and similarly influence processes and criteria which pertain to the implementation of, the maintenance of, and the assessment of activities related to learning and achievement. So the aim here is to combine knowledge about the "how" of an action with the motivational vision of the "why" of its results, and promote knowledge about one's self as well as factual information on various explicit and implicit levels. In conjunction with various theories and procedural approaches (e.g., measures founded in attributional theories with implications made by the central variables of the Dweck model, or consequences taken from the theory of self-determination), whereby a promotion on the levels of activities engaged, goals as well as needs would be plausible (for a detailed delineation of the theoretical background refer to Schober, 2002, or Ziegler and Schober, 2001).

The concrete goals pursued by the MMT pertain proximally to an augmentation of ability with regard to the constructive handling of failure or, to be more exact, their feedback, the functional attribution of achievement results, a heightened observation and strategic control over one's own learning processes, as well as the understanding that one's own abilities and deficits are flexible. Inherent in the MMT is also the desire to implicitly mediate a more solid orientation on learning goals, confidence in one's own abilities, as well as to increase in general control convictions and value regarding the domain in question and to decrease helplessness. Finally, an improvement in performance is the distal goal of the MMT. These modifying alterations to the entire process of action should be transferable over time, situation, and level of demand. This means that the MMT sees itself as a training whose effectiveness is not only short-term, but also long-term; this is not only applicable to the training material, but should also be reflected measurably in classroom instruction and the requirements found there.

The operationalization of the goals and the full theoretical conception of the MMT in corresponding training principles proceeds on several levels, and can be characterized from several perspectives. The principles and elements of the MMT can be primarily described through three central forms of procurement: (1) during the training sessions goal-specific intervention topics were worked through and the entire session was conducted in the context of this topic. For example, attributional styles were chosen as a central theme, discussed and, in group exercises, advantageous expressions of attributional styles were developed, applied in various manners, and practiced (**explicit** form of implementation). (2) Moreover, the training principles are **implicitly** integrated into the training schedule. For example, a project-oriented nature of the mathematics exercises should promote interest in mathematics and a learning goal orientation, or the opportunity to select the exercises to be completed instead of having them directly assigned should impart a sense of autonomy on the students. In particular, the procurement of a learning goal orientation comes to know an exclusively implicit implementation. This procedure is chiefly contingent on the fact that manipulation through mostly indirect, primarily instruction-based principles or achievement feedback also appears to be effective in explicit goal promotion programs (Ames, 1992). Implicit integration also implies that the trainers had to be constantly conscientious of their instructional activities regarding the explicit topics handled in each of the sessions, even when they were not the object of the current session and, thanks to accompanying measures, were always indirectly realized (e.g., the application of an individual reference norm, the bestowal of precise instructions, and the institution of goals which are specific and set in the not too distant future, or the emphasis on the relevance of the learning material). (3) Finally, the trainers officiated as **models** for the students. They demonstrated what was explicitly addressed in the goal-specific intervention topics and implicitly integrated in the training.

The training principles adhered to in the MMT can be understood beyond these three forms of procurement. Another interpretation can also be made in terms of an inegrated modification of different types of knowledge: from one perspective factual (e.g., mathematical) information and self-related knowledge are to be promoted simultaneously, from another perspective, knowledge should – as a central goal of the MMT – be supported in a manner which pays particular attention to the declarative, procedural, contextual, and meta-cognitive components of knowledge. The students should not just be afforded insights pertaining to general motivational relationships, they should also be learning how to appropriately utilize this information to their best interests and how to apply these constructs in relevant situations (e.g., when working on mathematical concepts and exercises during classroom instruction), and they should also actively learn how to reflect on themselves and their own knowledge.

Lastly, the building blocks of the MMT (and its individual sessions) in their combination essentially obey the principles of teaching functions (Klauer, 1985), resp. the nine teaching-learning steps (Gagné, 1985). More exactly, this means that in the MMT (with respect to each and every individual goal) (1) an attempt was made to win over and maintain the attention of the learners through the characterization of the training as a series of projects and by anchoring these projects in everyday life, (2) that the learners were always explicitly informed of the goals of the sessions, (3) that relevant prior knowledge was activated, (4) that both the mathematical and motivational materials were presented in such a manner that its significance was evident, (5) that the learning process was guided by various types of techniques (such as, for example, moderated and goal-directed problem discussions, self-awareness, role playing), (6) that the learners experience the desired behaviors through guided exercises (in the form of working through the mathematics projects), (7) that they receive information regarding the appropriateness of their behavior (primarily via oral and written feedbacks), (8) that their performances are appraised, and (9) that transfer is backed up in particular by the application to classroom instruction and the execution of peer-assisted learning, above all through peer feedback and peer monitoring (e.g., Henington & Skinner, 1998). The use of feedback plays a large and constructive role in the entire MMT, as large as the role small group work plays in a setting of cooperative learning, whereby beyond the feedback element the different facets of peer-assisted learning were of relevance (Topping & Ehly, 1998). The MMT can, to a certain degree, also be labeled a "feedback intervention" (Kluger & DeNisi, 1998), which takes place within the framework of project-oriented small groups and is also embedded in elements of discovery learning, communities of learners, problem-based learning, and application-based learning.

In order to clarify the question of whether, and to what extent, the MMT is capable of attaining its goals and thereby represents an advancement in motivational intervention, an assessment of its effectiveness was conducted within the framework of a pretest-posttest-follow-up experiment with comparison groups (Hager et al., 2000) which consisted of a training group, a placebo group, and a control group. A four-phase pretest-posttest design was put into operation; after a pretest the training group and the placebo group received a treatment. The direct effects were assessed with a posttest two weeks after the termination of the intervention; the long-term effects with a follow up survey conducted about six months later. A total of 818 students attending the 5th grade of college preparatory schools in the German state school system participated in the evaluation study, whereby the MMT was organized around the domain of mathematics (see Schober, 2002).

In this first evaluation, the MMT consisted of ten 60 minute long sessions, which took place on two afternoons per week. Each pair of sessions composed a thematic focal point so that the training was divided into five pairs of sessions. The particular "Math Clubs" were, as a rule, made up of six students and each club was headed by a tutor. The five explicit goals of the MMT each represented one of the "intervention topics" of a pair of sessions: "Feedback (also about errors) is informative and constructive" (Sessions 1–2), "Attributional styles which promote motivation" (Sessions 3–4), "The significance of learning strategies and manageable learning processes" (Sessions 5–6), "Flexibility of one's own abilities" (Sessions 7–8). Sessions 9–10 had repetition and the transfer to classroom instruction as their goals.

The success measurements chosen to be used here were those which allowed for the most direct operationalization of the goals formulated for the MMT. In addition, we attempted to comply with the requirements for the insurance of quality in an intervention and its evaluation formulated by Hager et al. (2000). Special consideration was given to that aspect of the transfer of the program in which measures were not formulated to evaluate the MMT and its content, but rather focused on the subject of mathematics in general and current instruction in this subject. Furthermore, no assessment of improvement in performance on the material which was worked through in the training was directly made; report card grades were used for this purpose. By making measurements based on classroom instruction (instead of within the framework of the training sessions) situational transfer could be accommodated, while temporal transfer was measured on the basis of the two measuring points. Since the choice of these criteria measures should allow for the detection of not only the proximal but also the indirect and distal as well as potentially sleeper and moderator effects, the variables recorded at all three measuring points, in addition to biographical data, included: management of mistakes, attributional patterns with respect to both success and failure, implicit personality theories on abilities in general and own deficits, motivational orientation, confidence in own abilities, helplessness, general control convictions, interest, and achievement (for more detail, refer to Schober, 2002; Schober & Ziegler, 2001).

Due to space limitations, it is not possible to report the results of this evaluation in detail here. In short it can be said that the MMT was able to effectively produce those short-term alterations one would expect from a motivational promotion in the vein of goal attainment in all of the competence areas on which it was focussed. For two of these areas, helplessness and interest, these effects could only be tenatively safeguarded. However, a more exacting consideration and localization of the findings led to a clear indication of the effectiveness of the training. Nonetheless, not all operationalizations of the various competences, however, could be modified and the question regarding short-term performance increases must remain unanswered due to the inaccessibility of the data material. Although one can certainly still discuss the failure of changes to materialize for some of the concrete measures, the short-term efficacy hypothesis, at least with respect to the central facets of the individual competences, can be considered to have been confirmed (see Schober, 2002). Figure 1 illustrates the direct training effects for four of the central training goal areas.

A glance at the long-term effects of the MMT shows that, for one thing, the distal goal of achievement increase at the third measurement point, although not unequivocal, nevertheless attains the designation of a desireable trend embedded in an overall rather drastic drop off in achievement recorded for all students. Nevertheless, it must be established that the MMT was only able to generate limited increases in the long-term outcomes for the average student in the domain of mathematics. In the face of blatant general worsening, this can be evaluated in a thoroughly positive light. All in all, the question as to what extent the MMT is suitable for generating changes in competences and performances, which can also be catgorized as temporally transferable, can be answered with a resounding yes.

Although one cannot deny that there are indications that a downward trend was beginning to formulate in at least some of the relatively favorable variables, practically all of the direct effects were still verifiable after a period of five months, and it came to isolated tendencies towards developmental impulse. In particular, these argued for the effectiveness and the transfer potential of the MMT, given the extracurricular conditions and the by and large negative development of motivational sets among fifth graders, which are by no means to be counted on.

The evaluation of the first implementations of the MMT confirmed its basic effectiveness. By all means, it is – as by all integrated promotional concepts – not possible at

Figure 1. Direct trainings effects of the MMT. Illustration of standardized intra-group differences (d) between pretest and posttest measurements for four central goal variables.k.

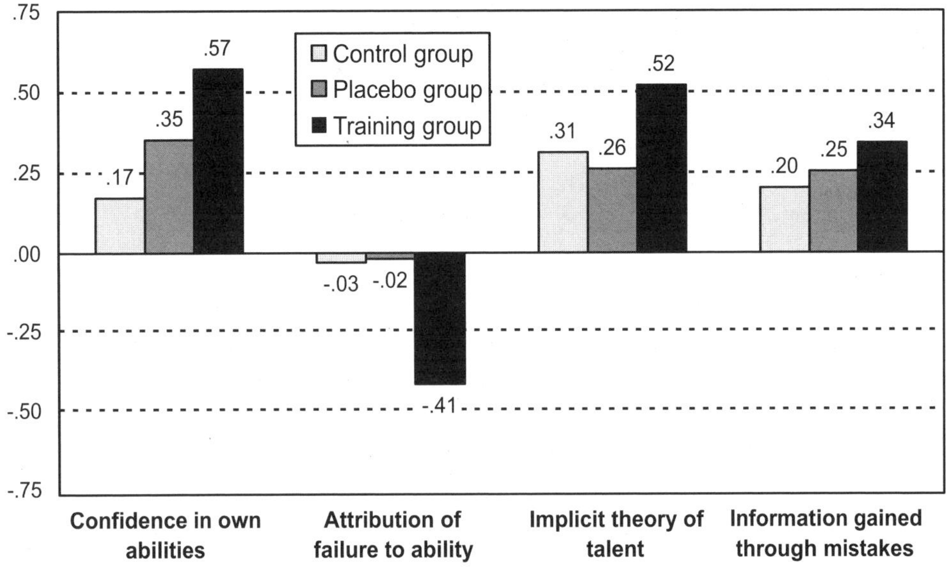

this time to specify whether all of the training components made a contribution to this success or if isolated components could be disposed of without going into further investigative detail. Further process-related and above all analytical evaluations would be without a doubt illuminating at this point.

When one considers the diagnosis of the effectiveness of the MMT in terms of the optimization of the central parameters of the relevant actiotope, it can be said, in short, that the approach being presented here is nothing if not fruitful: The actualized action repertoire is being improved or, at least, it finds itself in an improvement trend – the promotional effect on the subjective action space was unequivocal and it was possible to modify central goal areas. The alteration of the environment can only be considered to have been indirectly attained thus far (insofar as it can be seen as a condition for the implementation of the MMT) and remains unquestionably as a task to be confronted in the next step for implementation in the everyday learning context of the school.

Conclusions

The actiotope was developed as a heuristic framework model, on the basis of which we investigated questions related to the formation as well as the dismantling of gender differences in the area of mathematics and the natural sciences. In doing so, the actiotope approach does not and, of course, cannot replace any psychological theory. As a heuristic framework model, it does, however, indicate the relevant components of a research program that is engaged in problems of this nature needs to take into consideration. We hope that we have been able to show that our process, as a whole, has proven itself and we would like to now, in our closing remarks, discuss in which further areas of educational psychology we could envisualize a successful application of the actiotope concept.

An actiotope is comprised of two objective components which have not yet been subjected to interpretation: an objective action repertoire and an objective environment. If we are fully acquainted with all aspects of these two components, then we would be able to make a series of prognoses concerning the activities that a person would fundamentally be able to demonstrate. When we, for example, know all of the biometric measures such as the constitution of a runner's track – which represent the objective action repertoire in this simplified example –as well as the current weather conditions – which represent the objective environment – one would, more or less, be able to predict how quickly a person would, at best, be able to sprint over a specific distance. Of course, in most cases, the actualized action repertoire would lie under this maximum value since human potentials are rarely fully exhausted. In many cases, we, as educational psychologists, would find this discrepancy to be too large, and would want to reduce it. This can generate extremely different cases which, for example, range from extreme underachievement to the promotion of persons who have already demonstrated particularly high levels of achievement, even to those who are considered to be eminent in their field (Heller, Moenks, Sternberg, & Subotnik, 2000). If the discrepancies between the objective components of the actiotope and the actualized action repertoire are deemed to be significant, then we would consider it reasonable to make further analyses of the subjective action space, goals, and subjective environment. Wherever the particular opportunities for promotion in an actiotope may lie, it must be decided on a case-by-case basis. As demonstrated through the example of girls and women in mathematics and the natural sciences, the palette of encouraging singular components must encompass all components of an actiotope, also in terms of promotion.

Suggested Readings

Beerman, L., Heller, K. A., & Menacher, P. (1992). *Mathe: nichts für Mädchen? Begabung und Geschlecht am Beispiel von Mathematik, Naturwissenschaft und Technik* [Mathematics: Nothing for girls? Ability and gender with reference to mathematics, natural sciences, and technology]. Bern, Switzerland: Huber.

Dresel, M. (2004). *Motivationsfoerderung im schulischen Kontext: Effekte der Inhaltsvariation und Sequenzierung attributionalen Feedbacks* [Motivation in school: Effects of content varying and sequencing attributional feedback]. Goettingen, Germany: Hogrefe.

Heller, K. A., & Ziegler, A. (1996). Gender differences in mathematics and the natural sciences: Can attributional retraining improve the performance of gifted females? *Gifted Child Quarterly, 40*, 200–210.

Schober, B. (2002). *Entwicklung und Evaluation des Muenchner Motivationstrainings (MMT)* [Development and evaluation of the Munich Motivational Training]. Regensburg, Germany: Roderer.

Ziegler, A. (2005). The actiotope model of giftedness. In R. J. Sternberg & J. E. Davidson (Eds.), *Conceptions of giftedness* (2nd ed., pp. 411–436). New York: Cambridge University Press.

References

Ames, C. (1992). Classrooms: Goals, structures, and student motivation. *Journal of Educational Psychology, 84*, 261–271.

Bavarian State Office for Statistics and Data Processing (Ed.). (1998). *Statistisches Jahrbuch fuer Bayern* [Statistical year book for Bavaria]. Munich, Germany: Author.

Beerman, L., Heller, K. A., & Menacher, P. (1992). *Mathe: nichts fuer Maedchen? Begabung und Geschlecht am Beispiel von Mathematik, Naturwissenschaft und Technik* [Mathematics: Nothing for girls? Ability and gender with reference to mathematics, natural sciences, and technology]. Bern, Switzerland: Huber.

Bettge, S. (1992). Geschlechtsunterschiede in Erfolgserwartungen in Abhaengigkeit von der Formulierung von Mathematik-Textaufgaben [Gender differences in expectancies of success depending upon the wording of mathematical problems]. *Zeitschrift fuer Sozialpsychologie, 23*, 46–53.

Beyer, S., & Bowden, E. M. (1997). Gender differences in self-perceptions: Convergent evidence from three measures of accuracy and bias. *Personality and Social Psychology Bulletin, 23*, 157–172.

Bornholt, L. J., & Goodnow, J. J. (1999). Cross-generation perceptions of academic competence: Parental expectations and adolescent self-disclosure. *Journal of Adolescent Research, 14*, 427–447.

Broome, P. (1998). *Implizite Begabungstheorien und erlernte Hilflosigkeit* [Implicit theories of academic aptitude and learned helplessness]. Frankfurt/M., Germany: Lang.

Callahan, C. M. (1991). An update on gifted females. *Journal for the Education of the Gifted, 14*, 284–311.

Covington, M. V. (2000). Goal theory, motivation, and school achievement: An integrative review. *Annual Review of Psychology, 51,* 171–200.

Covington, M. V., & Omelich, C. L. (1984). Controversies or consistencies? A reply to Brown and Weiner. *Journal of Educational Psychology, 76*, 159–168.

Deutsches PISA-Konsortium (Ed.) (2001). *PISA 2000. Basiskompetenzen von Schuelerinnen und Schuelern im internationalen Vergleich* [PISA 2000. An international comparison of basic competences in school students]. Opladen, Germany: Leske & Buderich.

Dresel, M. (2000a). A longitudinal analysis of Dweck's motivational-process-model in the classroom. *Psychologische Beitraege, 43,* 129–152.

Dresel, M. (2000b). Der Einfluss der Motivationalen Orientierung auf den Erfolg eines Reattributionstrainings im Unterricht [Impact of students' motivational orientation on the effectiveness of attributional retraining in school settings]. *Zeitschrift fuer Entwicklungspsychologie und Paedagogische Psychologie, 4,* 192–206.

Dresel, M. (2001). Reattributionstraining [Attributional retraining]. In W. H. Honal (Ed.), *Handbuch der Schulberatung* (pp. 1–18). Landsberg, Germany: mvg.

Dresel, M. (2004). *Motivationsfoerderung im schulischen Kontext: Effekte der Inhaltsvariation und Sequenzierung attributionalen Feedbacks* [Motivation in school: Effects of content varying and sequencing attributional feedback]. Goettingen, Germany: Hogrefe.

Dresel, M., Heller, K. A., Schober, B., & Ziegler, A. (2001). Geschlechtsunterschiede im mathematisch-naturwissenschaftlichen Bereich: Motivations- und selbstwertschaedliche Einfluesse der Eltern auf Ursachenerklaerungen ihrer Kinder in Leistungskontexten [Gender differences in the area of mathematics and natural sciences: Detrimental influences of parents on causal attributions of their children]. In C. Finkbeiner & G. W. Schnaitmann (Eds.), *Lehren und Lernen im Kontext empirischer Forschung und Fachdidaktik* (pp. 270–288). Donauwoerth, Germany: Auer.

Dresel, M., Ziegler, A., Broome, P., & Heller, K. A. (1998). Gender differences in science education: The double-edged role of prior knowledge in physics. *Roeper Review, 21*, 101–106.

Dresel, M., Ziegler, A., & Heller, K. A. (1999). *MatheWarp. Ein Mathematik-Lern- und Uebungsprogramm mit integrierter Motivationsfoerderung. CD-ROM und Handbuch fuer Schueler(innen)* [MatheWarp: A mathematical learning software with an integrated motivation enhancement] [Computer Software]. Munich, Germany: BTA. Available: http://www.mathewarp.de

Dresel, M., Schober, B., & Ziegler, A. (2005). Nothing more than Dimensions? Evidence for a Surplus Meaning of Specific Causes in Students' Attributions. *Journal of Educational Research, 99,* 31–45.

Dweck, C. S. (1986). Motivational processes affecting learning. *American Psychologist, 41*, 1040–1048.

Dweck, C. S. (1999). *Self-theories: Their role in motivation, personality, and development.* Philadelphia, PA: Psychology Press.

Dweck, C. S., & Leggett, E. L. (1988). A social-cognitive approach to motivation and personality. *Psychological Review, 95*, 256–273.

Eccles [Parsons], J., Adler, T. F., Futterman, R., Goff, S. B., Kaczala, C. M., Meece, J. L., & Midgley, C. (1985). Self-perceptions, task perceptions, socializing influences, and the decision to enroll in mathematics. In S. F. Cipman, L. R. Brush & D. M. Wilson (Eds.), *Women and mathematics: Balancing the equation* (pp. 95–121). Hillsdale, NJ: Lawrence Erlbaum Associates.

Elliot, A. J., & Harackiewicz, J. M. (1996). Approach and avoidance goals and intrinsic motivation: A mediational analysis. *Journal of Personality and Social Psychology, 70*, 461–475.

Feingold, A. (1988). Cognitive gender differences are disappearing. *American Psychologist, 43,* 95–103.

Finsterwald, M., & Ziegler, A. (2001). *Entstehung und Foerderung von Leistungszielen zum Zeitpunkt des Uebertritts auf weiterfuehrende Schulen* [Development and enhancement of achievement goals at the time of transfer to secondary school] (Interim Report). Munich, Germany: University of Munich, Department of educational psychology.

Foersterling, F. (1985). Attributional retraining: A review. *Psychological Bulletin, 98*, 495–512.

Frome, P. M., & Eccles, J. S. (1998). Parents' influence on children's achievement-related perceptions. *Journal of Personality and Social Psychology, 74*, 435–452.

Gagné, R. M. (1985). *The conditions of learning and theory of instruction.* New York: Holt, Rinehart & Winston.

Gruber, H., Mack, W., & Ziegler, A. (Eds.) (1999). *Denken und Wissen* [Thinking and knowledge]. Opladen, Germany: Deutscher Universitaetsverlag.

Hager, W., Patry, J.-L., & Brezing H. (Eds.) (2000). *Evaluation psychologischer Interventionsmassnahmen: Standards und Kriterien: ein Handbuch* [Evaluation of

psychological intervention measures. Standards and criteria – A handbook]. Bern, Switzerland: Huber.
Hannover, B. (1991). Zur Unterrepraesentanz von Maedchen in Naturwissenschaften und Technik: Psychologische Praediktoren der Fach- und Berufswahl [Underrepresentation of girls in the natural sciences and technology: Psychological predictors of subject choice and for choice of occupation]. *Zeitschrift fuer Paedagogische Psychologie, 5*, 169–186.
Harter, S. (1986). Processes underlying the construction, maintenance and enhancement of the self-concept in children. In J. Suls & A. C. Greenwald (Eds.), *Psychological perspectives on the self* (Vol. 3, pp. 137–181). Hillsdale, NJ: Lawrence Erlbaum Associates.
Heckhausen, H. (1989). *Motivation und Handeln. Lehrbuch der Motivationspsychologie* [Motivation and action: Handbook of motivation psychology] (2nd ed.). Berlin: Springer.
Heller, K. A. (2000). Schuleignungsdiagnose und Schulerfolgsprognose [Prognosis and diagnosis of academic aptitude]. In K. A. Heller (Ed.), *Begabungsdiagnostik in der Schul- und Erziehungsberatung* (2nd ed., pp. 217–240). Bern, Switzerland: Huber.
Heller, K. A. (2004). Identification of gifted and talented students. *Psychology Science, 46,* 302–323.
Heller, K. A. (2005). The Munich Model of Giftedness and its impact on identification and programming. *Gifted and Talented International, 20,* 30–36.
Heller, K. A., Finsterwald, M., & Ziegler, A. (2000). Implicit theories of German mathematics and physics teachers on gender specific giftedness and motivation. In A. Ziegler (Ed.), *Antecedents of motivation and behavior. The role of implicit theories of intelligence* (pp. 172–189). Lengerich, Germany: Pabst.
Heller, K. A., Moenks, F. J., Sternberg, R. J., & Subotnik, R. F. (Eds.) (2000). *International handbook of giftedness and talent* (2nd ed.). New York, NY: Elsevier.
Heller, K. A., Perleth, Ch., & Lim, T. K. (2005). The Munich Model of Giftedness designed to identify and promote gifted students. In R. J. Sternberg & J. E. Davidson (Eds.), *Conceptions of giftedness* (2nd ed., pp. 147–170). New York, NY: Cambridge University Press.
Heller, K. A., & Ziegler, A. (1996). Gender differences in mathematics and the natural sciences: Can attributional retraining improve the performance of gifted females? *Gifted Child Quarterly, 40*, 200–210.
Helmke, A. (1992). *Selbstvertrauen und schulische Leistungen* [Self-confidence and academic achievement]. Goettingen, Germany: Hogrefe.
Helmke, A., & Weinert, F. E. (1997). Bedingungsfaktoren schulischer Leistung [Predictors of academic achievement]. In F. E. Weinert (Ed.), *Psychologie des Unterrichts und der Schule* (pp. 71–176). Goettingen, Germany: Hogrefe.
Henington, C., & Skinner, C. H. (1998). Peer monitoring. In K. Topping & S. Ehly (Eds.), *Peer-assisted learning* (pp. 237–253). Mahwah, NJ: Lawrence Erlbaum Associates.
Hoffmann, L., Haeussler, P., & Peters-Haft, S. (1997). *An den Interessen von Maedchen und Jungen orientierter Physikunterricht* [Physics instruction oriented at the interests of girls and boys]. Kiel, Germany: IPN Schriftenreihe.
Hoffmann, L., & Lehrke, M. (1986). Eine Untersuchung von Schuelerinteressen an Physik und Technik [A study on students' interest in physics and technology]. *Zeitschrift fuer Paedagogik, 32*, 189–204.

Holz-Ebeling, F. (2001). Koedukation [Coeducation]. In D. H. Rost (Ed.), *Handwoerterbuch Paedagogische Psychologie* (2nd ed., pp. 243–246). Weinheim, Germany: PVU.

Jagacinski, C. M., & Nicholls, J. G. (1984). Conceptions of ability and related affects in task involvement and ego involvement. *Journal of Educational Psychology*, *76*, 909–919.

Jagacinski, C. M., & Nicholls, J. G. (1987). Competence and affect in task involvement and ego involvement: The impact of social comparison information. *Journal of Educational Psychology*, *79*, 107–114.

Joergens, M., Richter, U., Finsterwald, M., Raul, T., & Ziegler, A. (2001). *Die Darstellung von Frauen und Maennern in Schulbuechern* [The protrayal of women and men in school books]. Poster presented at the 61. meeting of the Arbeitsgruppe Empirisch Paedagogischer Forschung (AEPF), Schwaebisch Gmuend, Germany.

Jones, E. E., & Berglas, S. (1978). Control attributions about the self through handicapping: The appeal of alcohol and the role of underachievement. *Personality and Social Psychology Bulletin, 4*, 200–206.

Kelley, H. H. (1973). The process of causal attribution. *American Psychologist*, *28*, 107–128.

Klauer, K. J. (1985). Framework for a theory of teaching. *Teaching and Teacher Education*, *1*, 5–17.

Kluger, A. N., & DeNisi, A. (1998). Feedback interventions: Toward the understanding of the double-edged sword. *Current Directions in Psychological Science*, *7*, 67–72.

Krapp, A. (1998). Entwicklung und Foerderung von Interessen im Unterricht [Development and promotion of interests in instruction]. *Psychologie in Erziehung und Unterricht, 44*, 185–201.

Lengfelder, A., & Heller, K. A. (2002). German Olympiad Studies: Findings from a retrospective evaluation and from in-depth interviews. Where have all the gifted females gone? *Journal of Research in Education, 12,* 86–92.

Linn, M. C., & Petersen, A. C. (1985). Emergence and characterization of sex differences in spatial ability: A meta-analysis. *Child Development, 56*, 1479–1498.

Locke, E. A., & Kristof, A. L. (1996). Volitional choices in the goal achievement process. In P. M. Gollwitzer & J. A. Bargh (Eds.), *The psychology of action: Linking cognition and motivation to behavior* (pp. 365–384). New York: Guilford Press.

Locke, E. A., & Latham, G. P. (1994). Goal setting theory. In H. F. O'Neil Jr. & M. Drillings (Eds.), *Motivation: Theory and research* (pp. 14–31). Hillsdale, NJ: Erlbaum.

Marsh, H. W. (1989). Age and sex effects in multiple dimensions of self-concept: Preadolescence to early adulthood. *Journal of Educational Psychology*, *81*, 417–430.

Marshall, S. P., & Smith, J. D. (1987). Sex differences in learning mathematics: A longitudinal study with item and error analyses. *Journal of Educational Psychology*, *79*, 372–383.

Meece, J. L., Wigfield, A., & Eccles, J. S. (1990). Predictors of math anxiety and its influence on young adolescents' course enrollment intentions and performance in mathematics. *Journal of Educational Psychology*, *82*, 60–70.

Middleton, J., & Spanias, P. (1999). Motivation for achievement in mathematics: Findings, generalizations, and criticisms of the research. *Journal for Research in Mathematics Education*, *30 (1)*, 65–88.

Midgley, C., Kaplan, A., & Middleton, M. (2001). Performance-approach goals: Good for what, for whom, under what circumstances, and at what cost? *Journal of Educational Psychology, 93*, 77–86.

Muehlum, A. (1986). Die oekosoziale Perspektive: Folgerungen fuer eine Handlungstheorie [The eco-social perspective: Implications for a theory of action]. In A. Muehlum, G. Olschowy, H. Oppl & W. R. Wendt (Eds.), *Umwelt, Lebenswelt. Beitraege zur Theorie und Praxis oekosozialer Arbeit* (pp. 208–249). Frankfurt/M., Germany: Suhrkamp.

Mura, R. (1987). Sex-related differences in expectations of success in undergraduate mathematics. *Journal of Research in Mathematics Education, 18*, 15–24.

Nicholls, J. G. (1984). Achievement motivation: Conceptions of ability, subjective experience, task choice, and performance. *Psychological Review, 91*, 328–346.

Oelschlaegellotkin, H. C. (1997). *Evolution in Mind: An Introduction to Evolutionary Psychology.* Cambridge, MA: Harvard University Press.

Olszewski-Kubilius, P., Kulieke, M. J., Shaw, B., Willis, G. B., & Krasney, N. (1990). Predictors of achievement in mathematics for gifted males and females. *Gifted Child Quarterly, 34,* 64–71.

Parsons, J. E., Adler, T. F., & Kaczala, C. M. (1982). Socialization of achievement attitudes and beliefs: Parental influences. *Child Development, 53*, 310–321.

Pintrich, P. R., & Schunk, D. H. (1996). *Motivation in education: Theory, research and application.* Englewood Cliffs, NJ: Simon & Schuster.

Plotkin, H. (1997). *Evolution in mind: An introduction to evolutionary psychology*. Cambridge, MA: Harvard University Press.

Renninger, K. A., Hidi, S., & Krapp, A. (Eds.) (1992). *The role of interest in learning and development.* Hillsdale, NJ: Lawrence Erlbaum Associates.

Rustemeyer, R. (1999). Geschlechtstypische Erwartungen zukuenftiger Lehrkraefte bezueglich des Unterrichtsfaches Mathematik und korrespondierende (Selbst-) Einschaetzungen von Schuelerinnen und Schuelern [Teachers' expectations concerning gender-specific performance in mathematics and the corresponding self-evaluation of male and female students]. *Psychologie in Erziehung und Unterricht, 46*, 187–200.

Rustmeyer, R., & Jubel, A. (1996). Geschlechtsspezifische Unterschiede im Unterrichtsfach Mathematik hinsichtlich der Faehigkeitseinschaetzung, Leistungserwartung, Attribution sowie im Lernaufwand und im Interesse [Gender-related differences in mathematics concerning the subjective evaluation of one's own competence, expectation of performance, attributions, learning effort, and interest in the subject]. *Zeitschrift fuer Paedagogische Psychologie, 10*, 13–25.

Schober, B. (2002). *Entwicklung und Evaluation des Muenchner Motivationstrainings (MMT)* [Development and evaluation of the Munich Motivational Training]. Regensburg, Germany: Roderer.

Schober, B., & Ziegler, A. (1998). *Maladaptives Verhalten von Grundschulkindern nach Misserfolgen in Leistungskontexten – die Bedeutung impliziter Persoenlichkeitstheorien* [Maladaptive behavior of primary school students after failure – The impact of implicit theories]. Paper presented at the meeting of the 39. Tagung experimentell arbeitender Psychologen, Marburg, Germany.

Schober, B., & Ziegler, A. (2001). Das Muenchner Motivationstraining (MMT): Theoretischer Hintergrund, Foerderziele und exemplarische Umsetzung [The Munich Motivational Training: Theoretical background, aims, and a first evaluation]. *Zeitschrift fuer Paedagogische Psychologie, 15*, 166–178.

Schunk, D. H., & Rice, J. M. (1986). Extended attributional feedback: Sequence effects during remedial reading instruction. *Journal of Early Adolescence, 6,* 55–66.

Seegers, G., & Boekaerts, M. (1996). Gender-related differences in self-referenced cognitions in relation to mathematics. *Journal for Research in Mathematics Education, 27,* 215–240.

Steele, C. M. (1988). The psychology of self-affirmation: Sustaining the integrity of the self. In L. Berkowitz (Ed.), *Advances in experimental social psychology* (Vol. 21, pp. 261–302). San Diego, CA: Academic Press.

Stipek, D. J., & Gralinski, J. H. (1991). Gender differences in children's achievement-related beliefs and emotional responses to success and failure in mathematics. *Journal of Educational Psychology, 83,* 361–371.

Stoeger, H. (2001). *Soziale Performanzziele im schulischen Leistungskontext* [Social performance goals in the school setting]. Unpublished doctoral dissertation, University of Munich, Germany.

Surber, C. F. (1984). Inferences of ability and effort: Evidence for two different processes. *Journal of Personality and Social Psychology, 46,* 249–269.

Tiedemann, J., & Faber, G. (1994). Maedchen und Grundschulmathematik: Ergebnisse einer vierjaehrigen Laengsschnittuntersuchung zu ausgewaehlten geschlechtsbezogenen Unterschieden in der Leistungsentwicklung [Girls and mathematics in elementary school: Results of a 4-year longitudinal study of gender differences in the development of achievement]. *Zeitschrift fuer Entwicklungspsychologie und Paedagogische Psychologie, 26,* 101–111.

Tiedemann, J., & Faber, G. (1995). Maedchen im Mathematikunterricht: Selbstkonzept und Kausalattribution im Grundschulalter [Gender differences in elementary school children's self-concept and attributions in mathematics]. *Zeitschrift fuer Entwicklungspsychologie und Paedagogische Psychologie, 27,* 61–71.

Topping, K., & Ehly, S. (1998). Introduction to peer-assisted learning. In K. Topping & S. Ehly (Eds.), *Peer-assisted learning* (pp. 1–23). Mahwah, NJ: Lawrence Erlbaum Associates.

Vollmer, G. (1983). *Evolutionaere Erkenntnistheorie* [Evolutionary Epistemology] (3rd ed.). Stuttgart, Germany: Hirzel.

Weiner, B. (1985). An attributional theory of achievement motivation and emotion. *Psychological Review, 92,* 548–573.

Wigfield, A., & Eccles, J. S. (1992). The development of achievement task values: A theoretical analysis. *Developmental Review, 12,* 265–310.

Ziegler, A. (Ed.) (2001). *Implicit theories as antecedents of motivation and behavior.* Lengerich, Germany: Pabst.

Ziegler, A., Broome, P., Dresel, M., & Heller, K. A. (1996). Physikalisch-technische Vorerfahrungen von Maedchen [Previous experience in physics and technology among girls]. *Physik in der Schule, 34,* 163–164.

Ziegler, A., Broome, P., & Heller, K. A. (1998). Pygmalion im Maedchenkopf. Erwartungs- und Erfahrungseffekte koedukativen vs. geschlechtshomogenen Physikanfangsunterrichts [Pygmalion in girls' minds: Effects of expectations and experiences in coeducative versus single-sex beginning physics instruction]. *Psychologie in Erziehung und Unterricht, 45,* 2–18.

Ziegler, A., Broome, P., & Heller, K. A. (1999). Golem und Enhancement: Elternkognitionen und das schulische Leistungshandeln in Physik [Golem and enhancement:

Parental cognitions and their children's academic achievement behavior patterns in physics]. *Zeitschrift fuer Paedagogische Psychologie, 13*, 135–147.

Ziegler, A., Dresel, M., & Schober, B. (1998). *Messung motivationsbezogener Schueler(innen)merkmale* [Measuring motivation among students]. Unpublished manuscript, University of Munich, Germany.

Ziegler, A., Dresel, M., & Schober, B. (2000). Praediktoren des Selbstvertrauens von Maedchen und Jungen vor dem erstmaligen Chemieunterricht am Gymnasium [Predictors of self-confidence among girls and boys attending college preparatory schools prior to initial chemistry instruction]. *Psychologie in Erziehung und Unterricht, 47*, 66–75.

Ziegler, A., & Heller, K. A. (1998). Motivationsfoerderung mit Hilfe eines Reattributionstrainings [Enhancing motivation through attributional retraining]. *Psychologie in Erziehung und Unterricht, 45*, 216–229.

Ziegler, A., Heller, K. A., & Broome, P. (1996). Motivational preconditions of gifted and highly gifted girls in physics. *High Ability Studies, 7*, 129–143.

Ziegler, A., Kuhn, C., & Heller, K. A. (1998). Implizite Theorien von gymnasialen Mathematik- und Physiklehrkraeften zu geschlechtsspezifischer Begabung und Motivation [Implicit theories of gender-specific giftedness and motivation of mathematics and physics teachers from the German Gymnasium]. *Psychologische Beitraege, 40*, 271–287.

Ziegler, A., & Schober, B. (1996). Geschlechtsbezogene Unterschiede in mathematikbezogenen Kognitionen zum Zeitpunkt des Gymnasialeintritts [Gender differences in cognitions related to the subject of mathematics at the time of transfer to secondary school]. In K.-P. Treumann, G. Neubauer, R. Moeller & J. Abel (Eds.), *Methoden und Anwendungen empirischer paedagogischer Forschung* (pp. 145–153). Muenster, Germany: Waxmann.

Ziegler, A., & Schober, B. (1999). Der Zusammenhang von Eltern- und Kindkognitionen bezueglich des Faches Mathematik [Cognitions of parents and their children concerning their mathematical ability]. *Familienforschung, 11*, 72–95.

Ziegler, A., & Schober, B. (2001). *Theoretische Grundlagen und praktische Anwendungen von Reattributionstrainings* [Theoretical foundations and practical application of attributional retrainings]. Regensburg, Germany: Roderer.

Ziegler, A., Schober, B., & Dresel, M. (2005). Primary School Students' Implicit Theories of Intelligence and Maladaptive Behavioral Patterns. *Education Science and Psychology, 6,* 76–86.

Knowledge – Experience – Action

A new model to analyze their mutual relation

André Büssing†, Britta Herbig, & Annika Latzel

Introduction

It is not an achievement of modern times to realize that knowledge has to be transformed into action in order to be useful for mankind. Indeed, Confucius (551–479 BC) had already stated that "the crucial point of knowledge is that one bears it in mind and applies it". Or, as Goethe put it, " To know is not enough, one also must apply. To want is not enough, one also must do." It is as well known since then that this gap between action and knowledge is the crucial point for causing trouble: In literature and philosophy, a series of examples is described where knowledge is not applied or even worse where it is acted against better knowledge. This divergence between knowledge and action is not only a point of frustration but is also a research topic for psychologists. Frustrating insofar as research shows again and again a persistently low correlation between knowledge and action; and a research topic in that people expect that psychology will find ways to deal with this problem.

For example, in health psychology: At least in western society, everybody knows the risks of smoking, the consequences of an unhealthy lifestyle for problems like cardiac infarction, or the dangers of infection with HIV; nonetheless, people do smoke, eat too much fat, do too little exercise, or have unprotected sex. The same holds true for environmental issues: People are concerned about the exploitation of nature, the destruction of the ozone layer, or the diminishing resources of drinking water on earth, but again, people do not recycle natural resources as much as possible, drive cars even when it is not necessary, and use drinking water in abundance (see Mandl & Gerstenmaier, 2000, for an overview).

Common to all these phenomena seems to be a gap between the knowledge and the actual subjective "beliefs" that the persons might consciously or non-consciously have.

In the case of health hazards, these beliefs may consist of a too low probability estimation regarding the risk of becoming ill. For environmental problems, a resigned attitude may exist, namely "The problems are too big and my effort can change nothing. Others, like politicians are better suited for dealing with these problems." In many cases, these beliefs have their roots in personal experiences, like "My grandfather smoked his whole life and was in good health all his life" or "I did without my car the last year but the ozone layer became even thinner."

Starting from an overview of some common conceptualizations of knowledge and behavior, we will outline in this chapter a model that might explain the divergence between knowledge and action, and integrate, as exemplified above, the role of experience for this gap. We propose that the often missing correlation between knowledge and action has its basis in the type of conceptualization used to measure them. In order to provide preliminary evidence for this model, we will present results from our studies showing that relations between knowledge and action can be found if adequate conceptualizations and empirical measures are used.

Knowledge and action

Conceptualizations of knowledge

There are many different ways for considering the concept of knowledge. As we are interested in the relation between knowledge and action some theories and differentiating conceptualizations of knowledge will be roughly presented that are also explicitly or implicitly concerned with action. First, dimensions of knowledge are presented that allow the classification of every type of knowledge. Second, some more specific theories on knowledge are outlined, and third it is shown that the dimensions explicit vs. implicit knowledge can combine several important aspects of other dimensions and theories on knowledge. Namely, the dimensions "global vs. specific" (e.g., Doane, Sohn & Schreiber, 1999; Higgins & Baumfield, 1998), "declarative vs. procedural" (e.g., Kihlstrom, 1999; Ryle, 1993) and "explicit vs. implicit" (e.g., Seger, 1994) as well as theories on situated knowledge (e.g., Greeno, 1998; Menzies, 1998), inert knowledge (e.g., Renkl, 1996), and knowledge compilation (e.g., Anderson, 1982, 1992) are outlined regarding their proximity to action.

The dimensions of knowledge we will present here are "global vs. specific knowledge" and "declarative vs. procedural knowledge." The distinction between global vs. specific knowledge describes the discrimination of general thinking and problem solving skills (global knowledge), on the one hand, and domain-specific knowledge that is useful only for certain problems or situations, on the other hand. As Higgins and Baumfield (1998) discuss, recently, attention to global knowledge has been neglected in favor of specific knowledge, although global knowledge might be very important for our understanding of transfer achievements. Regarding the question of proximity to action, specific knowledge is by definition closer to action than global knowledge.

One of the most common knowledge dimensions is that of declarative vs. procedural knowledge (Kihlstrom, 1999). Declarative knowledge as knowledge about facts and procedural knowledge as knowledge about procedures are associated with the distinction between "knowing that" and "knowing how" made by Ryle (1993) or Dreyfus and Dreyfus

(1986). Regarding their closeness to action, many researchers have come to the conclusion that growing expertise goes along with an increase in non-formal elements in work (e.g., Benner, 1984). Or, as Dreyfus and Dreyfus (1986) stated, expertise excels with an intuitive reliability of activity. Professional expertise involves more of the intuitive "knowing how" and less of the theoretical, and thus formalized, "knowing that." A person with a great deal of professional "knowing how" may not be able to translate it into "knowing that" (Ryle, 1993). The impact of "knowing that" or declarative knowledge may decrease during the acquisition of expertise but never ceases to play a role.

Besides these dimensions of knowledge that can be used to differentiate all kinds of knowledge several theories of knowledge exist that deal with the question of action. Situated knowledge is defined as knowledge that is principally bound to a situation (Greeno, 1998) and, therefore, to certain antecedence conditions in order to put it into action. That is, situated knowledge has a close relation to action only if the environmental surroundings are very similar to those in which the knowledge was learned (Greeno, Smith, & Moore, 1993). The theory of situated knowledge is closely related to the global vs. specific dimension insofar as situated knowledge seems to describe specific knowledge. Situated knowledge might at least in parts explain the low correlation between knowledge and action as a transfer problem between learning and using conditions, since successful transfer depends on structural invariance of the interaction between actor and situation. It also offers one possible explanation for the phenomenon of inert knowledge (Renkl, 1996) – existing knowledge that is explicitly defined as being not used to solve problems, thus knowledge that is not put into action. Other explanations for inert knowledge consider deficient meta-processes and structural problems. The notion of deficient meta-processes refers to problems in controlling the application of knowledge in such a way that conditional knowledge for use, which normally controls the access of certain knowledge parts, is missing (Alexander, Schallert, & Hare, 1991; Brown, 1984). The notion of deficient structures refers to the problem that knowledge is not stored in a format which would allow its use. Thus, both theories, the theory of situated knowledge and the concept of inert knowledge, attribute the divergence between knowledge and action to problems in the access of knowledge, whereby the concrete knowledge contents are not taken into account.

A third theory, the ACT model by Anderson (1982, 1992), deals with knowledge content and the increase of efficiency in the use of knowledge. In this model, Anderson describes the acquisition of cognitive skills. In a series of steps, declarative knowledge is transformed into procedural knowledge through continuous use. In this so-called compilation process, different processing steps in the form of production rules (if-then) collapse into one production. A necessary precondition for this is that all productions are available in a certain sequence and that they all serve the same overall goal. The so developed compiled knowledge might become implicit, and thus difficult to verbalize. It allows, on the one hand, faster performance but, on the other hand, the difficulty to name this knowledge can contribute to a low correlation between knowledge and action since most measures of knowledge depend on the ability of persons to verbalize their knowledge.

The common characteristic of the outlined theories is that they all describe special types of knowledge and, therefore, have a limited area of application. The dimensions global vs. specific and declarative vs. procedural knowledge are defined by knowledge contents in contrast to the presented theories, which are more or less defined by processes. Each of the dimensions and theories may contribute in part to explain the gap between knowledge and action, but they do not consider the content and process character of knowledge simultaneously. The distinction that tries to combine these two aspects is that between explicit and implicit knowledge (see Herbig, 2001; Herbig & Büssing, 2003, for a detailed comparison of the two forms of knowledge). Explicit knowledge describes the common notion of conscious, verbalizable and formalizable knowledge whereas the results on implicit knowledge are more heterogeneous. The following definition of implicit knowledge comprises various fundamental findings we understand to be essential for this type of knowledge (Büssing, Herbig, & Ewert, 1999):

> Implicit knowledge contains declarative as well as procedural knowledge (Lewicki, 1986; Moss, 1995). It is acquired and strengthened by concrete and sensual experiences (Polanyi, 1966). Acquisition of implicit structures does not depend on attention or awareness for learning (Reber, 1997), moreover – as a direct consequence of this –, its contents are not reflected and examined. One of the most prominent features of implicit knowledge is that it is not consciously perceived as guiding ones' actions, i.e., it works below a subjective threshold (Dienes & Berry, 1997). It also has a complex structure (Berry & Broadbent, 1988) and contains "naive," sometimes wrong theories that can be examined and changed (Fischbein, 1994; Lee & Gelman, 1993) through explication (Gaines & Shaw, 1993).

This definition of implicit knowledge shows firstly that a very close relationship between implicit knowledge and action exists, and secondly how both knowledge contents and processes can account for the missing correlation between knowledge and action. First, as implicit knowledge is acquired in the course of experience, action is antecedence and consequence of knowledge at the same time. Second, as the processes involved are not conscious or, more precisely, are working below a subjective threshold, knowledge contents cannot be reflected. That is, although the measures of explicit knowledge might be adequate, measures of implicit contents can find new or even contrasting action-guiding knowledge. In the reminder of this chapter, we argue that if adequate measures for implicit knowledge are used, the gap between knowledge and action will decrease considerably. Moreover, it is necessary to look at different conceptualizations of action in order to determine which type of knowledge influences which type of action. Some conceptualizations of action are outlined in the next section.

Conceptualizations of action

In the following, we will present two theories of action which comprehensively consider the role of knowledge – German action regulation theory by Hacker (1992a; see also Engeström, Miettinen & Punamäki, 1999) and the concept of experience-guided working (e.g., Böhle & Milkau, 1988; Carus, Nogala, & Schulze, 1992).

In German action regulation theory, action is divided into three stages of regulation: the planning phase, i.e., goal setting and designing of a plan for reaching the goal; the monitoring phase, i.e., the supervision of plan execution, whereby plan and sub-plans must be remembered; and the feedback phase, i.e., evaluating if the goal has been reached. Furthermore, actions are divided into different levels of regulation. At the level of intellectual regulation, conscious analysis and synthesis processes take place for the regulation of complex activities for which no ready pattern of activity exists, that is explicit knowledge has to be processed and used. The level of flexible activity pattern builds on already existing basic patterns for the required activity that only have to be adapted for the situation. At this level, thus, knowledge and processes are conscious; they are not automated, but already mastered. At the sensor-motor level, highly automated activities take place. Because they are no longer conscious, no planning or feedback loops are detectable (Frese & Zapf, 1994). The matrix of stages and levels of action regulation in this theory shows that knowledge (except for the senso-motor level) has to be conscious and readily available in order to plan all actions in advance and monitor goal achievement closely. This theory would not expect a divergence between knowledge and action on the intellectual level or the level of flexible activity pattern. Only highly automated behavior should not necessarily relate to reported knowledge. Therefore, the action regulation theory cannot sufficiently account for the gap between knowledge and action.

The model of experience-guided working (Carus et al., 1992) and the sub-concepts of subjectifying and objectifying action (Böhle & Milkau, 1988), however, allow for better insight into why reported knowledge and actual action may not correlate. Before the model of experience-guided working is outlined, an overview of the features of objectifying and subjectifying action is given in Table 1.

Table 1. Objectifying and subjectifying action

Subjectifying action	**Objectifying action**
Points of reference: • concrete and unique qualities and variations	*Points of reference*: • objective findings and universally valid, generalizable rules
Emotions: • important for the structuring of action • object-related feelings	*Emotions*: • subordinate or disturbing elements of practical action
Sensuality: • perception by complex sensuality and by movements of the whole body • emotions are an important part of perception	*Sensuality*: • Exact, objective sensual perception only by one sense • Emotions are disturbing for objective perception
Environment: • No separation between subject and environment • Environment has subject character	*Environment*: • Separation between subject and environment • Environment has object character
Type of action: • Dialogic-interactive action • Experience of simultaneity of action and reaction	*Type of action*: • Action either influences the environment one-sidedly or takes up influences and information reactively from the environment
Course of action: • Goals and results as well as the concrete procedure develop only during the action process	*Course of action*: • Planning of action steps and goals precedes action

Both forms of action cannot be compensated for or replaced by each other since they achieve different things. In experience-guided working a mutual crossing and completion of these two forms is assumed.

Especially results from research in advanced manufacturing systems show that human experience is necessary when it comes to reacting flexibly and effectively in unpredictable, critical situations (Carus et al., 1992). Experience in the context of experience-guided working is not only seen as a precondition for and a product of action but also as a process that can produce new patterns and insights in the moment of realizing the gap between real and expected situational conditions. This perspective highlights the active dealing of the individual with conditions of the environment during the course of experience development. The notion that experience is bound to the action process, therefore, focuses not only on the subject of experience but also on the field of experience and the respective conditions of experience (Böhle & Milkau, 1988). Relying on this assumption, the following characteristics of experience-guided working can be summarized:

- Complex sensual perception through several senses and perception of relations; senses are not particularized they are used simultaneously.
- Attention is distributed, i.e., it is focused on symbols as well as on objects, processes, and movements.
- Perception of diffuse, not exact defined information.
- Vivid and associative thinking.
- No separation between planning and execution; pragmatic stepwise procedure and practical testing.
- Holistic images or patterns render the sequential-analytic interpretation of essential information partially unnecessary. Therefore, they allow for a time-critical development of strategies and evaluations of system states even in unpredictable, chaotic situations.

Subjectifying action and experience-guided working depend on the development of holistic and flexible anticipation characteristics. That is, holistic mental images about how a situation should look like, which then are compared with the actual situation. They differ from situational images in objectifying action insofar as the comparison uses a similarity principle rather than an identity principle. This allows mental simulation with several diffuse variables. Therefore, in experience-guided working, two different types of knowledge can be found: First, objective rules and exact information for use in the comparison for identity. This type of knowledge is codifiable and can, therefore, be reported. Second, diffuse information in various combinations for use in the comparison for similarity. This type of knowledge might be difficult to report and can therefore lead to an apparent mismatch between knowledge and action.

Knowledge and action in expertise

In this section, we will address the relationship between knowledge and action in expert performance. Although expertise is a quite heterogeneous concept (Sloboda, 1991), researchers agree that experts usually work faster, more precisely, and more efficiently than novices and need fewer resources (Sonnentag, 2000; Speelman, 1998). Differences between novices and experts are found above all in qualitative aspects – in the organization of performance prerequisites for a flexible, situation-, and goal-orientated use of resources as well as in meta-knowledge and strategies (Hacker, 1992b). Action-guiding psychological images have a special position in this organization of performance prerequisites as they reduce the working memory load by compressing the knowledge, whereby capacities to deal with complex characteristics of a situation are released. This concept of psychological images is quite similar to the term of "holistic anticipation characteristics" in experience-guided working. Both notions imply that implicit experiential knowledge achieves special results in working situations that cannot be solely accomplished by routine.

An obvious relation between implicit knowledge and expertise consists of a lack in the ability to verbalize the knowledge (e.g., Dreyfus & Dreyfus, 1986). This circumstance especially influences the development of expert systems in a negative way. A problematic factor in the elicitation of expert knowledge is that experts master rules in such a way that they recognize situations in which the use of the rules is not appropriate (Reber, 1993). This constitutes a serious restriction for the codification of expert knowledge and therefore a problem for the development of expert systems. When experts report about their knowledge, the verbalized rules often do not correlate with their actual doing. Similar results were found in research on implicit knowledge (Gazzard, 1994). Such incorrect or incomplete reports can cause immense problems when used in expert systems, e.g., financial losses in industry or health hazards in medicine. Kirsner and Speelman (1998) report an example of an important French cheese manufacturer who developed, at great expensive, an expert system to estimate the ripeness of soft cheese. It was concluded from the experts' information that the important variables to determine ripeness were the surface tension and the necessary pressure for denting the cheese. However, the implemented expert system failed. Later on, it was shown that the actual important information was the olfactory impression that was gained by the lesion of the cheese rind. Similar experiences can be found in several other areas where experts use complex sensual perception and information, but, at the same time, are not aware themselves of the complex nature of their knowledge and action.

Another important relation between expertise and implicit knowledge lies in the form of its acquisition. Expertise as well as implicit knowledge is generated mainly in concrete (working) situations, that is they are not abstractly imparted but acquired through concrete actions in relevant contexts (Myers & Davis, 1993, Polanyi, 1962, 1966). Experience-guided working therefore determines the acquisition of expertise. Regarding the mental representations in expertise and implicit knowledge, there are indications that knowledge representations that experts have in their domain differ from those in other domains or from those of novices (Rouse & Morris, 1986).

Model of implicit knowledge, experience and action (MIKEA)

In the following section, we will integrate the action model of experience-guided working with the distinction between explicit and implicit knowledge in order to show that the gap between knowledge and action is at least partially due to methodological problems. One preliminary remark is necessary on the range of application of the model: Sometimes knowledge is referred to as implicit, which in fact is only automated (like the ACT theory, see above). This type of knowledge is excluded from the model; only implicitly acquired knowledge is looked at. Moreover, as already implied in the previous section with the framework of experience-guided working, by "expertise" we refer to adaptive expertise, i.e., expertise in dealing with critical or new situations, and not to routine expertise, which develops in dealing with the same situation over and over again (Hantano & Inagaki, 1986).

As Figure 1 shows, we differentiate on the knowledge side between implicit and explicit knowledge, meanwhile on the action side, objectifying and subjectifying action is

Figure 1. Model of implicit knowledge, experience, and action (MIKEA).[1]

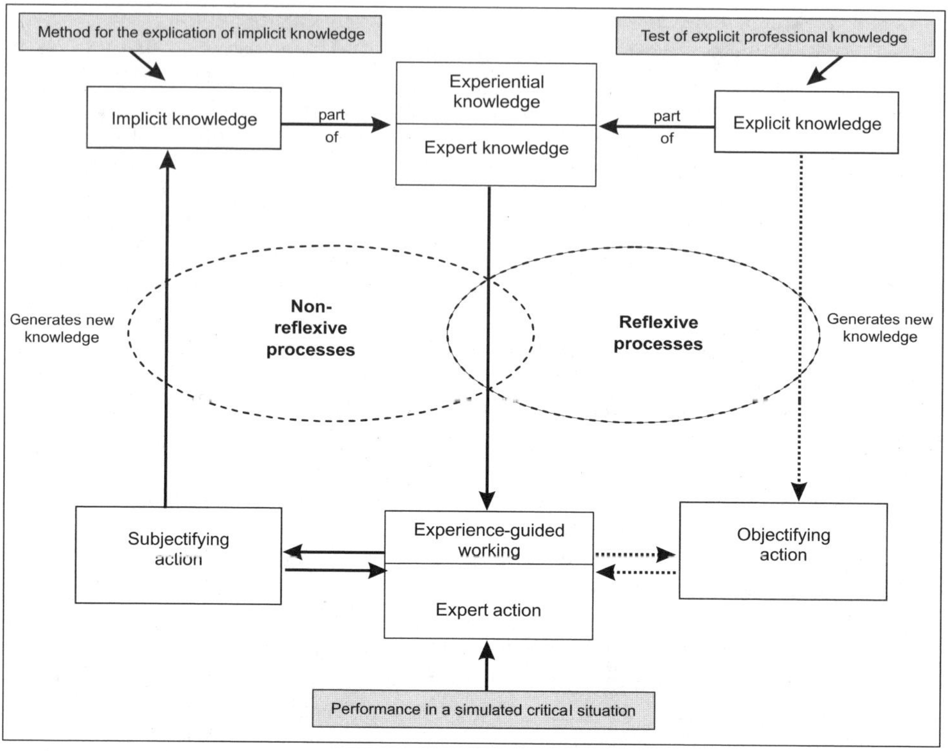

[1] Shaded fields refer to the methods used for measurement (see Method section)

contrasted. Explicit and implicit knowledge is a part of expert knowledge, with subjectifying and objectifying action being part of expert action, whereby the focus is laid on implicit knowledge and subjectifying action. The same assumptions apply to experiential knowledge and experience-guided working. The separation of experiential knowledge and expert knowledge, respectively experience-guided working and expert action, demonstrates that the concepts have different theoretical origins and are not completely equivalent. That is, not every person who has lots of experience becomes an expert (e.g., Ericsson, Krampe, & Tesch-Römer, 1993).

Experiential and expert knowledge are put into action through reflexive as well as non-reflexive processes. Even if a person is not always sure about the knowledge base that led to the action, the activity itself is always a potential object of reflection. Information and associations, which are generated in the context of subjectifying action, are digested through non-reflexive processes and build up implicit knowledge. This way of generating implicit knowledge in working stresses the central function of subjectifying action for this type of knowledge. Every new experience in the same domain extends this knowledge. Eventually, it influences actions as implicit experiential knowledge without being consciously perceived as guiding ones' actions. Under the premise that this knowledge is adequate for a situation, an increase in performance can be observed. With growing seniority, implicit knowledge is accumulated that entails at least parts of expertise.

The model also gives some information on the development of explicit knowledge (dotted lines in Figure 1) that is not at the center of our presentation. In general, we assume that a certain amount of reflexive processes is a necessary precondition for the acquisition and use of explicit knowledge. The model does not claim to describe or explain all phenomena in the area of explicit knowledge. Other models may be better adapted to do this (e.g., Anderson, 1982, 1992; Logan, 1988). However, the model is well suited to demonstrate why consistently low correlations between knowledge and action are found in various research areas: With growing experience, experiential knowledge in different domains of life accumulates and influences the actions. Due to the implicit mode of knowledge acquisition, the protagonist has no chance for conscious knowledge reflection. As most measures of knowledge depend on conscious and verbalizable knowledge, people will fall back on explicit knowledge that makes up only a small part of the real action-guiding knowledge. In the following section, we will present our study in which – as far as we know – for the first time implicit and explicit knowledge are measured and tested separately for their respective impact on action.

The study

The following section begins with an outline of our research method with its approach for explication of implicit knowledge in an ecologically valid situation, followed by a summary of empirical evidence for the model. The important aspects of our research design are firstly the applied context and secondly the unique method for assessing implicit knowledge. Our research has the goal of studying implicit theories and knowledge bases that have been shaped in the course of experience. We argue that in finding access to this implicit knowledge our understanding of actions can be enhanced. When methods can be developed that are capable of explicating more unconsciously proceeding action causes, stronger relations between actions and knowledge can be found. Several preconditions have to be fulfilled when implicit knowledge is to be investigated. There is consensus that implicit knowledge, in the sense outlined above, can be best studied in a non-routine task; thus a critical non-routine working action has to be constructed. Furthermore, a measure for implicit knowledge and an independent measure of explicit knowledge has to be developed allowing explicit and implicit knowledge to be contrasted.

We present empirical evidence for our model based on the results from a laboratory study, in which various measures for the different kinds of knowledge important for experience-guided action were used, which allowed us to analyze the different modes of knowledge in their relation to experience-guided action.

Research questions

Specifically, our research is guided by following goals and hypotheses: While numerous measures for explicit knowledge exist, the investigation of implicit knowledge until now has focused on artificial tasks (see Seger, 1994, for an overview). To broaden this scope of research, our goal is to first explicate implicit action-guiding knowledge in a valid natural working context, and second, to relate this implicit knowledge to differences in performance. Based on our definitions of implicit knowledge and experience-guided working, we assume that differences in performance are due to different experiences and, therefore, differences in implicitly acquired knowledge, while the amount of explicit knowledge should not help to explain these differences in performance. Therefore, as proposed in MIKEA our **main hypothesis** is that a relation between knowledge and action can be found when implicit knowledge is compared with subjectifying action, but a lower or no relation when explicit knowledge is compared with subjectifying action.

Methods

Boundary condition: Creating an ecologically valid working situation

The working simulation used for the explication of implicit knowledge was chosen from the domain of nursing. The simulation of a critical situation served two purposes within the frame of MIKEA: First, to measure experience-guided working in a standardized situation, and second, to set the precondition for measuring implicit knowledge as the situation can help activate this knowledge. The following six criteria were considered in the process of developing the nursing simulation.

First, the situation had to be of sufficient solvability. This ensured that all participants have had relevant experience about the nursing field with which they are confronted in the laboratory. Second, the situation had to make an immediate intervention necessary so that the time and decision pressures experienced hindered participants in engaging in explicit problem solving. Third, the information with which participants were confronted with should be ambiguous and complex – a condition in which subjectifying working can evolve and in which implicit knowledge can be studied. Especially in critical situations with a complex structure, implicit knowledge can contribute to the successful management of a situation (Griffin, Schwartz, & Sofronoff, 1998; Reber, Kassin, Lewis, & Cantor, 1980). Fourth, the effect of the actions should be directly observable to allow for dialogical-interactive action and an objective criterion for judging successful performance. Fifth, the situation should enable nurses to make use of sensual information as part of experience-guided working. Sixth, for pragmatic reasons, the successful management of the situation should be possible with the help of only a few technical devices.

The nursing situation which finally was used for the working simulation was "hypoglycemia." In this situation, nurses had the task of dressing a small wound on the forearm of a patient resulting from a motor-bike accident. Documentation indicated that the patient was suspected of closed head trauma. Indeed, the patient had no closed head trauma, but showed symptoms of hypoglycemic shock. The difficulty inherent in this situation was to differentiate the symptoms of the closed head trauma from the actual diagnosis, the symptoms of hypoglycemia (e.g., both involve symptoms like weakness and trembling).

Nursing experts ensured this situation fulfilled the above criteria. The participants' impressions also indicated that we were successful in creating an ecologically valid working situation in the laboratory. Items about the realism of the situation and the patient behavior showed a high ecological validity of the situation (situation $M = 4.0$, $SD = 0.82$; patient $M = 4.56$, $SD = 0.51$, on a five point scale).

Testing explicit knowledge

To compare the effects of explicit and implicit knowledge on action, as proposed in MIKEA, an independent test for explicit professional knowledge was needed. The form of the explicit knowledge test used here is a semi-structured interview with questions, which were generated on the basis of the relevant literature and with the help of expert interviews. Questions cover theoretical and practical aspects of relevance for dealing successfully with the nursing simulation. Besides these nursing topics of primary interest, nurses were asked about additional topics in order to avoid priming effects. The interviewer read the questions in a standardized format and asked participants to recall all information that spontaneously came to their minds when hearing the question.

The form of a semi-standardized interview deliberately was preferred against a fully standardized interview as the latter could potentially hinder idiosyncratic information being detected and could imply that nurses realize their gaps in knowledge. Therefore, it was felt that a completely standardized test bears the risk of nurses referring to explicit knowledge in the time interval until the implicit knowledge test, causing a Zeigarnik effect of enhanced availability of explicit knowledge. To further lower the possibility of priming effects to a minimum, a time span of 7–14 days between the knowledge test and the laboratory session was chosen. Thus, the flexible form of the test provides the possibility of making inter-individual different forms of knowledge apparent, while ensuring maximal standardization.

Explicating implicit knowledge with the repertory grid method

We were guided by the assumption that implicit knowledge only can be found in a practical context, in which direct action has to be taken. This is analogue to the mode of acquisition for implicit knowledge through experience. Thus, performing a simulation before the explication of implicit knowledge should help the participants to recall action-guiding implicit knowledge. Explicating knowledge was done in the form of a repertory-grid interview on the basis of the elements participants mentioned as action guiding.

Kelly (1969) invented the technique of repertory-grid. This technique bears a resemblance to the considerations about tacit knowledge by, e.g., Polanyi (1962) from a constructivist perspective, that each person constructs his or her world with idiosyncratic constructs that are not easily accessible inter-individually. It can be used to describe in detail relevant knowledge as well as help to generate action-guiding constructs that are not conscious while being in action. According to Kelly (1955) people use constructs to make forecasts about future events. Actual events allow people to approve or to disapprove their constructs and consequently to revise their constructs or to confirm them. This process of anticipation of events and the evaluation of the constructs on the basis of anticipation is comparable to the process and use of experience in our comprehension of experience-guided working. The constructs persons use are of dichotic nature serving a differentiating and an integrating function of their construction of the world.

In research about implicit knowledge, the same processes are mentioned, even with a similar terminology. Polanyi (1962) describes the function of differentiation and integration as fundamental processes of our construction of the world. He considers differentiating as a rather explicit process, which is subject to conscious attention, while integration is assumed to occur without attentional resources on an implicit level. By doing the repertory-grid interview participants were asked to differentiate their action-guiding elements and to name action-guiding constructs. This procedure has the potential to shed light on people's implicit knowledge in its integrated form.

Elements were generated by means of asking nurses about their action-guiding elements supported by the videotape of the action and by questions like "What was important for you in the situation?" In a second step, nurses did the repertory grid interview following this procedure: They were asked to decide if they – from their own subjective point of view – perceived each of two action-guiding elements as similar or different, and were asked to formulate the nature of this difference or similarity. At the end of this process of differentiating, nurses had generated idiosyncratic dichotic constructs of importance for their just performed action and had rated each element on each construct, meaning that they judged if they perceived one element more on the side of this pole of the construct or the other.

A data matrix from a repertory-grid interview, thus, consisted of elements and constructs, whereby each construct had two dichotic poles. Analyses of these matrices were done for the grid data of a single person and for grid data combined from several persons (e.g., Büssing & Herbig, 2003a; Büssing, Herbig, & Ewert, 2002; Herbig, Büssing & Ewert, 2001). Both modes of analysis are based on content analysis of the elements and constructs, with the possibility of a following visualization in the form of correspondence analyses (Benzécri, 1992) or multidimensional scaling (Young, 1985). By comparing these data with responses in explicit knowledge testing, verbalizations, and quality of action, implicit knowledge dimensions were revealed.

Experimental procedure

In order to find empirical evidence for the MIKEA the three measures reported above were used. One to two weeks before the actual laboratory study, participant's explicit knowledge was tested. The laboratory study began with the critical incident, followed immediately after by the method of explication. In detail, the procedure of the laboratory study was as follows:

1. Familiarization of participants with the ward and the medical and care supplies in the laboratory.
2. Reading the patients case history and studying the nursing task.
3. Watching the videotaped simulated nursing situation.
4. Cued recall to generate the action-guiding elements.
5. Repertory-grid interview to generate action-guiding constructs.

To assess possible effects of moderator variables, questionnaires were given to the participants. Finally, biographic information and questions about participant's impression of the realistic nature of the setting and situation were included.

Sample

The results of the study presented here are based on a sample of fifteen registered nurses (11 female, 4 male) from three different hospitals. Average job tenure was 14 years and 9 months (average age: 34 years). The participants worked on thirteen different wards. Current work positions were: Five nurses, nine assistant ward nurses, one ward nurse, and one nursing advisor. Participation was voluntary and additionally paid for.

Measures: Measure for the quality of action

The performance score was based on expert statements listing the central nursing actions which are necessary for the successful accomplishment of the situation. Two independent observers rated the videotaped performance along these criteria in the following four areas: Information of the doctor, dressing of the wound, symptoms check for a closed head trauma, and hypoglycemia. The aspects were weighed differently according to their importance before they were computed to an overall score. To differentiate successful from non-successful action, the cut-off point of 3.5 was chosen, considering a performance that neither endangers the patient nor involves serious complications. With this score, nine nurses were considered as performing successfully, while six nurses were considered as performing non-successfully.

Measure for explicit knowledge – Analysis of the data from the explicit professional knowledge test

Data of the professional knowledge test were compared against a checklist of correct answers (generated with the help of nursing experts and the relevant professional literature), from which a performance score of explicit knowledge can be computed (maximum score: 312 points). Besides an overall score of available explicit knowledge, specific scores were generated for the different nursing areas, e.g., "diabetes" or "wound dressing." To be able to get an exact fit between responses of explicit knowledge in the domains and the sufficient knowledge for successful management of the situation, another score can be computed containing only responses that are directly of use for a successful simulation accomplishment. Thus, aspects of importance in everyday hospital life (e.g., items like "ask visitors to leave the room before doing the dressing of the wound") were removed because they do not bear meaning for the specific nursing simulation. The maximum score possible here is 86.5.

Measure of implicit knowledge

From the repertory-grid interview, data about action-guiding elements and constructs and their relation were obtained. The absolute amount of generated elements and generated constructs could be computed. For our purpose of contrasting implicit and explicit knowledge, however, the focus was more on the number of elements/constructs generated newly with the method of explication, thus on those aspects that did not have an equivalent in the test for explicit knowledge.

Relation between the different modes of knowledge and action – Quantitative results

With MIKEA we propose that implicit knowledge should be related to subjectifying action while explicit knowledge should be related to objectifying action, whereby in the concept of experience-guided working, subjectifying action should make the difference in the successful performance of critical situations. The following paragraph presents quantitative results on this assumption.

In order to investigate differences in implicit knowledge, as a precondition it has to be assured that participants possess comparable amounts of explicit knowledge. In our study (Büssing & Herbig, 2003a; Büssing, Herbig, & Ewert, 1999, 2000), indeed, no systematic differences the explicit knowledge of successful and non-successful performing nurses were found. Table 2 shows the result of Mann Whitney U tests comparing the total scores in the explicit knowledge test for both groups. Comparisons regarding only the specific knowledge of use for the concrete simulation also did not reach significance.

Table 2. Group comparisons of explicit knowledge

Dependent variable	Groups	*M*	Exact *p* value
Total score in the test of professional knowledge	Successful Unsuccessful	111.50 125.00	.11
Explicit knowledge specific for use in simulation	Successful Unsuccessful	39.39 41.00	.98

Separate analyses for the sub-domains "diabetes" and "wound dressing" also revealed no differences in both groups regarding their explicit knowledge (p value for "diabetes" = .76; p value for "wound dressing" = .15). Overall, these results for specific knowledge domains suggest that there is no relation between specific explicit knowledge in one area and the actual performance in this area (see Büssing et al., 2001). It can be interpreted, in line with MIKEA, that explicit knowledge is not sufficient to explain performance differences in critical situations. What results are obtained, when the relation between implicit knowledge and the quality of action is analyzed?

Before conducting this analysis, it had to be assured that the knowledge generated with the help of the method of explication is of an implicit nature. Thus, implicit knowledge found by the method of explication was compared with the explicit knowledge stated by nurses in the explicit knowledge test. Guided by the assumption that the method for explication detects implicit knowledge which can not be collected by an explicit professional knowledge test, we held the hypothesis that the method for explication reveals different implicit knowledge dimensions. Indeed, the results from our study were that 66.3% of the explicated knowledge was not mentioned in the test of professional knowledge. We expected a certain overlap between the aspects mentioned in the knowledge test and the aspects generated with the method of explication, since action-guiding implicit knowledge cannot be assessed independently of the explicit knowledge necessary for dealing with a critical situation. Therefore, we did a separate analysis for elements and constructs comparing new explicated constructs and elements with the knowledge already mentioned in the explicit knowledge test, expecting an overlap mainly on the level of the elements. Since elements are assessed by verbal questioning similar to measures of explicit knowledge, they are expected to be of a more explicit nature than the constructs. For our sample, the percentage of elements mentioned in the method of explication and already mentioned in the explicit knowledge test (M = 48%) is higher than the percentage of constructs (M = 18%). Computing a Wilcoxon Test for dependent samples the difference is significant (p = .001). There are significantly more elements than constructs that already have been mentioned in the explicit knowledge test. Thus, the generated constructs mainly seem to be the knowledge bases carrying implicit dimensions. For further validation studies and the discussion of the implicitness of the knowledge generated with the method of explication, see Büssing et al. (2002).

According to MIKEA, if implicit knowledge is assessed using the method of explication, a relation between this knowledge and experience-guided working should be found, which indeed was the case (see Table 3). Successful nurses held a higher amount of implicit knowledge than non-successful ones on the construct level in two respects: They, first, generated more constructs in the method of explication than the non-successful nurses, and second, they transferred fewer explicit constructs from the explicit

Table 3. Group comparisons of aspects of knowledge stated with the method for explication

Dependent variable	**Groups**	***M*** [1]	**Exact *p* value** [2]
Number of elements first stated in the grid	Successful Unsuccessful	0.23 –0.50	.090
Number of constructs first stated in the grid	Successful Unsuccessful	0.53 –1.04	.001
Number of elements first stated in the knowledge test	Successful Unsuccessful	0.37 0.58	.13
Number of constructs first stated in the knowledge test	Successful Unsuccessful	–0.18 –0.40	.069

[1] For the comparisons of elements and constructs designated in each case the absolute size of the grid matrix was kept constant by studentized residues. The number of elements/constructs was determined by comparisons between elements/constructs named in the knowledge test and those named in the grid method. Those elements and constructs with identical contents to the ones mentioned in the respective knowledge test were evaluated as already designated.

[2] Mann Whitney U Tests for two independent samples.

knowledge test to the knowledge stated in the method of explication of implicit knowledge.

The same analysis for the area of elements also shows a significant difference: The number of elements mentioned for the first time in the implicit knowledge test is higher in successful nurses than in non-successful nurses, indicating more implicit knowledge at the level of the elements in successful nurses. Concerning the transfer of knowledge aspects from the explicit knowledge test to their statements as elements in the method of explication, the same trend is apparent; the comparison, however, does not reach significance. Non-successful and successful nurses did not differ in the number of elements (generated by the explication method) that they had already mentioned in the explicit knowledge test. Thus, differences in performance can be related to differences in the implicit knowledge bases of the participants; the implicit knowledge of successful and non-successful groups especially differs at the level of the constructs (see Table 3). To summarize, as proposed in the model, when measures for implicit knowledge are used, quantitative relations between experience-guided action and knowledge can be found, where a measure for explicit knowledge does not show a relation to action.

Relation between the different modes of knowledge and action – qualitative results

The finding that there is a quantitative dissociation in the knowledge mode between successful and non-successful nurses does not sufficiently help to conclude about the nature of the differences. What are the qualitative knowledge dimensions that might enable nurses to act successfully? Or, more specifically, are the differences in knowledge in line with the different acting modes as proposed by MIKEA? To elucidate this qualitative distinction in the implicit knowledge, a multi-dimensional scaling procedure (MDS) for both groups of successful and non-successful nurses was conducted. Only comparable elements and constructs in each group were entered in the MDS in order to visualize similarity judgments in the form of geometrical distances. The stress indices and RSQ values[1] obtained in the two-dimensional solutions for our both groups (see Figures 2 and 3) show a satisfying fit. For the group of successful nurses, stress = 0.159, RSQ = 0.978. For the group of non-successful performing subjects, Stress = 0.183, RSQ = 0.972.

For the group of successful performing nurses, axes were rotated. Interpretation of the solutions was done in terms of finding meaningful groupings of elements and constructs along the two dimensions. The bases for the interpretation in accordance with MIKEA are the following expectations:

First, both groups should display a certain amount of explicit knowledge regarding medical diagnosis, and second, as subjectifying action is essential for dealing with critical situations, the group of successful nursed should show more features of this action type in their action-guiding knowledge than the group of non-successful nurses.

Figure 2. Knowledge in the group of successful nurses

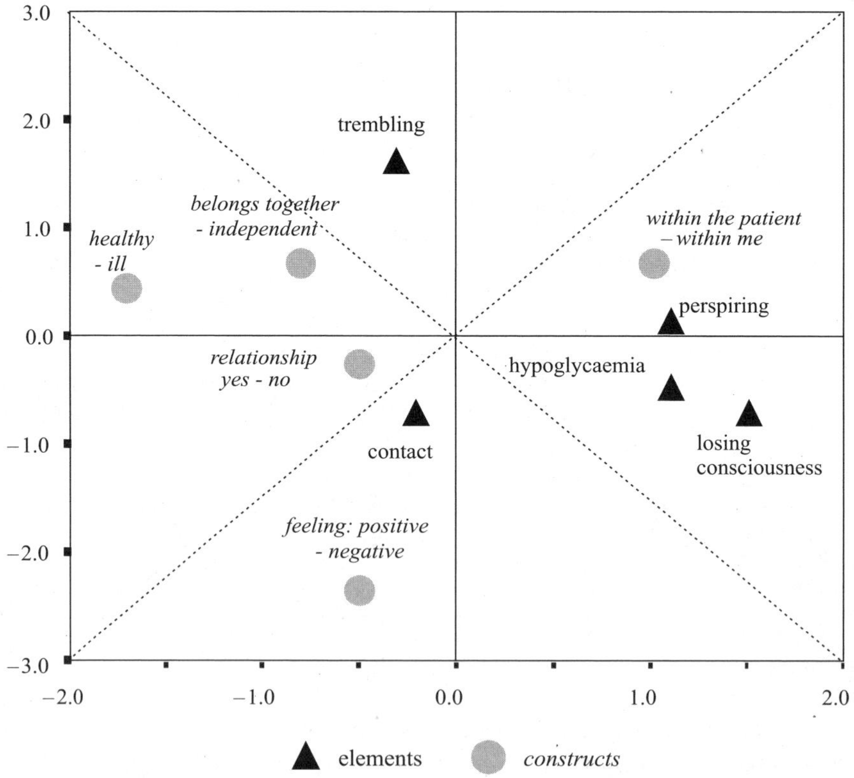

[1] Stress values between .1 and .2 indicate a satisfying fit. The nearer the RSQ values are to 1, the better is the fit of the solution (Bühl & Zöfel, 1996).

Regarding the first assumption, figures of both groups show a distinction between groupings of objective medical symptoms used for diagnosis and more "soft" features. The explicit medical knowledge cluster of good performers contains "hypoglycemia," "perspiring," and "losing consciousness" (see Figure 2), while for poor performers a cluster with "closed head trauma," "changed vital signs," and "losing consciousness" is found (see Figure 3). Differences, however, appear in the following aspect: Although "perspiring" as the distinguishing symptom between hypoglycemia and closed head trauma was perceived by both groups, the non-successful group associated this element with a feeling of uncertainty, and thus with a disturbing content that didn't have diagnostic value (geometrical distance between perspiring and the "medical" cluster).

As outlined in Table 1, feelings as disturbing elements of action are a feature of objectifying action, which, in turn, is not sufficient to deal with critical situations. But what about feelings in the group of successful nurses? Well performing nurses mentioned the construct "positive and negative feeling" that belongs to the same dimension as the diagnostic information, i.e., feelings are seen as valuable information in this group. This constitutes an essential feature of subjectifying action. To summarize this result in line with the theory of experience-guided working and MIKEA: Successful nurses tend to use feelings for diagnostic purposes and working decisions, whereas non-successful nurses

Figure 3. Knowledge in the group of unsuccessful nurses

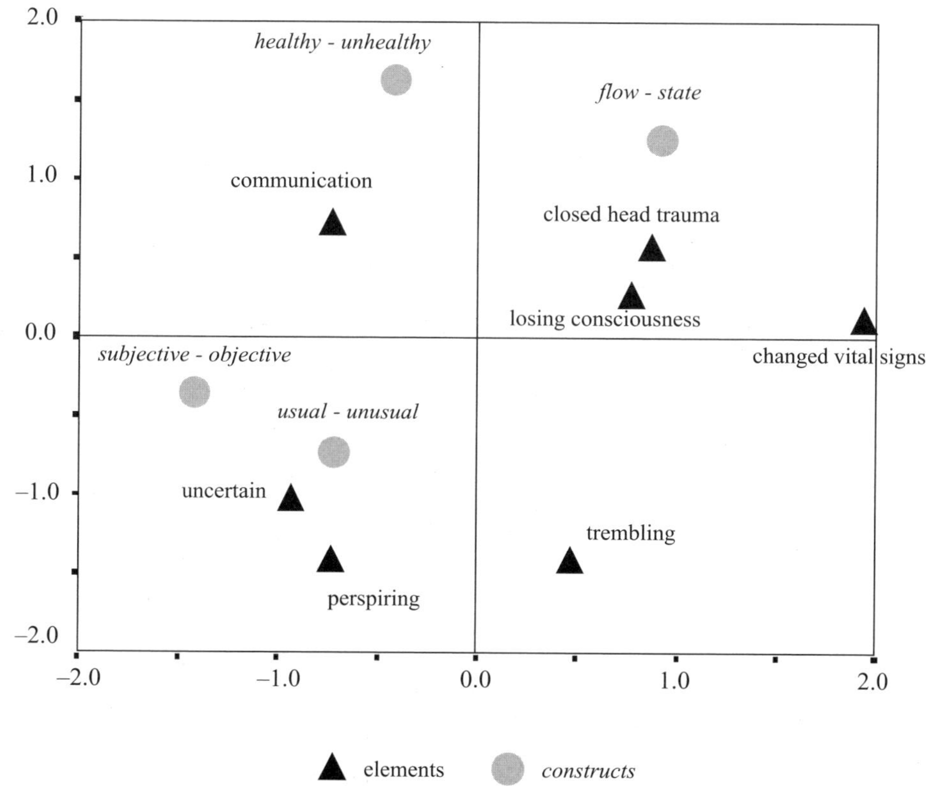

do not consider feelings as meaningful for working action, and instead attribute feelings with a disturbing quality, suggesting that they perform in an objectifying working modus.

Another important result from MDS refers to the dialogic-interactive action in subjectifying working modus vs. a unidirectional (active or reactive) type of action in objectifying working modus: In both groups, the construct of "healthy-ill/unhealthy" appears in proximity to the element "communication." Both groups, thus, consider social interaction as an important means of getting a first impression of the patient's state of health. However, the group of successful nurses differentiates between the element "contact" and the construct "relationship yes-no". The construct "relationship yes-no" takes into account actions of the nurse as well as actions of the patient. Thus, where successful nurses consider their own actions as well as those of the patient as important, i.e., engaging in dialogic-interactive action as part of subjectifying action, non-successful nurses seem to proceed from a more limited reactive view, focusing only on their own activities, which is a feature of objectifying action.

Two further differences related to the action types can be found in the visualizations: The perception and use of diffuse information by the good performers and the time-sequential structure of knowledge of the poor performers. The use of diffuse information as a feature of subjectifying action can be outlined with the position of the element "trembling" in both groups. For the non-successful group, the element "trembling" is in an isolated position from the bunch of symptoms and the other clusters suggesting that it was not used for diagnostic purposes. For the successful nurses, "trembling" as well is not associated with the medical symptoms; however, its position is near to the construct "belongs together-independent". This indicates that successful nurses perceived "trembling" as an important, although unspecific, sign. "Trembling" cannot be understood in the bunch of medical symptoms, but seems to be taken into account by successful nurses as an unspecific warning signal indicating something is wrong. Moreover, in the visualizations of the non-successful nurses, a time-sequential order of the knowledge along the simulation can be found that indicates an objectifying working modus. Starting (see Figure 3) with the first symptoms the patient displayed ("perspiring" and "trembling"), the course of diagnosing ("unusual" up to "closed head trauma") and subsequent action ("communication") can be followed. No such sequence can be identified in the MDS of the successful nurses, which might hint at a holistic and thus subjectifying action.

To sum up, the results of this study provide initial confirmation of the validity of the MIKEA model. First, it was presented that successful nurses held higher amounts of implicit knowledge than non-successful ones, while the groups did not differ in their amount of explicit knowledge. Second, the comparison of the contents of the action-guiding knowledge bases revealed qualitative differences, which suggest that actions of successful nurses are based more on a subjectifying working mode, while non-successful nurses seem to use an objectifying modus of working.

Discussion

Turning back to the questions posed above: Were we successful in demonstrating that our model can shed light on the divergence between action and knowledge? And, were we able to develop measures that adequately capture the different conceptualizations of knowledge and action in the model? Our research on these questions was guided by the assumption that specific data only can be collected when a specific situation is under scrutiny in an ecologically valid context. The situation should allow for complex working action and interactive, dialogic action in which the use of senses contributes to successful performance. Thus, subjectifying working should be made possible. Expert opinions as well as the subjective impressions of participating nurses indicate that we were successful in recreating a critical work situation with high ecological validity in the laboratory. On this basis, implicit and explicit knowledge could be collected. In doing so, special importance was given to the explication of implicit knowledge using the repertory-grid method as a new approach in the struggle to tap action-guiding implicit knowledge. Knowledge data were collected immediately after the action to activate relevant knowledge features, and to reduce the possibility of memory faults. Quantitative and qualitative results were reported that describe how different modes of knowledge relate to successful performance: As proposed, implicit knowledge showed a relation to action, while for explicit knowledge no correlation was found.

Besides the quantitative differences observed between successful and non-successful nurses in our study, the method for explication allowed qualitative differences to be described. The repertory grids depict specific, presumably action-guiding elements. Besides their capacity to shed light on the different action-guiding elements, more implicit, i.e., more unconsciously connected knowledge elements with the action, e.g., feelings or strategies, could be detected.

In constructing this research paradigm with a focus on qualitative as well as quantitative knowledge differences, we follow a new approach in implicit learning research (e.g., Neuweg, 2000) that suggests that instead of the focus on a quantitative dissociation between the explicit and implicit modes of knowledge, more meaningful results can be obtained if the qualitative dissociation between explicit and implicit learning modes come under scrutiny. Our method has the potential to explain correlations between action and knowledge in using newly revealed idiosyncratic implicit knowledge that cannot be detected by many of the other experimental procedures used in current research. However, our results are based on a specific situation characterized by certain criteria in a complex critical situation. Thus, the results cannot simply be generalized to other action domains; this is not within the scope of this study. However, for an important expert domain, i.e., for critical situations, our research was able to detect characteristics of implicit knowledge. It would be a challenge to broaden the scope further to other working domains and to other kinds of tasks.

The theoretical approach outlined in our model, that implicit knowledge acquired in the course of experience can account at least in part for the gap between knowledge and actions, was strengthened by the results presented here. We found evidence that implicit knowledge and experience-guided working are closely related, while explicit knowledge offers no explanatory value for actions. According to our model, the determinants of these actions can be understood as having been unconsciously shaped in daily experience by similar situations and interactions. In these experiences, the senses incorporate information and integrate it with already formed experiential knowledge to come to a new understanding of a situation involving maybe slightly different attributions than experiences before this. Our model (see Figure 1) illustrates this process on the left side: experience in working situations is transformed by non-reflexive processes into implicit knowledge. Because many of these new understandings of situations have been acquired unconsciously, the holder of these implicit theories might not be aware that she/he is holding these theories, and, still more importantly, is not aware that this implicit knowledge might also direct her/his actions.

To sum up, the results indicate that our model can be used to explain the divergence between knowledge and action by introducing adequate conceptualizations and new measures for the respective concepts. Moreover, the measures developed in our research have some practical implications for learning and facilitating change in performance (see also Büssing & Herbig, 2003b). As shown in the introductory examples from health psychology, implicit knowledge acquired by experience is not necessarily correct or adequate for all situations. However, as they are not usually subject to reflection, changing implicit contents is difficult. The presented method for explication can be used as a tool to make implicit knowledge available for reflection. In being confronted with a detailed and integrated cognitive depiction of their working action, a person can become self-aware and can gain new understanding of her/his experiences and knowledge. Implicit theories that developed in the course of daily action can break through the border of consciousness offering their holders the possibility to revise these theories or to find evidence for them. In a current follow-up study with a controlled test-retest experimental design, the effects of such an explication are being investigated, answering question such as, does the explication of implicit knowledge change the quality of action and what is the nature of these changes (Büssing, Herbig, & Latzel, 2004)?

As outlined in the theoretical section, several theories and conceptualizations offer possible explanations for the divergence between knowledge and action. However, many of them deal with specialized types of knowledge or action. All things considered, the model presented in this chapter can be employed with a broader range of situations, where knowledge and action are seemingly divergent. In addition to this theoretical explanatory value, the measures developed on the basis of this model (e.g., the method of explication) constitute practical tools usable for the promotion of implicit learning processes in ongoing education.

References

Alexander, P. A., Schallert, D. L., & Hare, V. (1991). Coming to terms: How researchers in learning and literacy talk about knowledge. *Review of Educational Research*, *61*, 315–343.

Anderson, J. R. (1982). Acquisition of cognitive skill. *Psychological Review*, *89*, 369–406.

Anderson, J. R. (1992). Automaticity and the ACT* theory. *American Journal of Psychology*, *105*, 165–180.

Benner, P. (1984). *From novice to expert: Excellence and power in clinical nursing practice*. Menlo Park, CA: Addison-Wesley.

Benzécri, J. P. (1992). *Correspondence analysis handbook*. New York: Marcel Dekker.

Berry, D. C., & Broadbent, D. E. (1988). Interactive tasks and the implicit-explicit distinction. *British Journal of Psychology*, *79*, 251–272.

Böhle, F., & Milkau, B. (1988). *Vom Handrad zum Bildschirm. Eine Untersuchung zur sinnlichen Erfahrung im Arbeitsprozeß* [From steering wheel to screen. An examination of sensual experience in the working process]. Frankfurt: Campus.

Brown, A. L. (1984). Metakognition, Handlungskontrolle, Selbststeuerung und andere, noch geheimnisvollere Mechanismen. In F. E. Weinert & R. H. Kluwe (Eds.), *Metakognition, Motivation und Lernen* [Meta-cognition, motivation, and learning] (pp. 60–109). Stuttgart: Kohlhammer.

Bühl, A., & Zöfel P. (1996). *Professionelle Datenanalyse mit SPSS für Windows* [Professional data analysis with SPSS for Windows]. Bonn: Addison-Wesley.

Büssing, A., & Herbig, B. (2003a). Tacit knowledge and experience in working. *Psychology Science, 45*(3), 142–164.

Büssing, A., & Herbig, B. (2003b). Implicit knowledge and experience in work and organizations. In C. L. Cooper & I. T. Robertson (Eds.), *International Review of Industrial and Organizational Psychology, 18*, 239–280.

Büssing, A., Herbig, B., & Ewert, T. (1999). *Implizites Wissen und erfahrungsgeleitetes Arbeitshandeln: Konzeptualisierung und Methodenentwicklung* [Tacit knowledge and experience-guided working: Conceptualizing and method development]. Munich, Germany: Technische Universität München, Lehrstuhl für Psychologie.

Büssing, A., Herbig, B., & Ewert, T. (2000). Intuition als implizites Wissen. Bereicherung oder Gefahr für die Krankenpflege? [Intuition as implicit knowledge – An enrichment or danger for nursing?] *Pflege, 13*, 291–296.

Büssing, A., Herbig, B., & Ewert, T. (2001). Implizites und explizites Wissen – Einflüsse auf Handeln in kritischen Situationen [Implicit and explicit knowledge – influences on action in critical situations]. *Zeitschrift für Psychologie, 209*, 174–200.

Büssing, A., Herbig, B., & Ewert, T. (2002). Implizites Wissen und erfahrungsgeleitetes Arbeitshandeln: Entwicklung einer Methode zur Explikation in der Krankenpflege [Implicit knowledge and experience-guided working: Development of a method for explication in nursing]. *Zeitschrift für Arbeits- und Organisationspsychologie, 46*, 2–21.

Büssing, A., Herbig, B., & Latzel, A. (2004). Explikation impliziten Wissens – Verändert sich das Handeln? [Explication of implicit knowledge – Is there a change in action?]. *Zeitschrift für Psychologie, 212,* 87–106.

Carus, U., Nogala, D., & Schulze, H. (1992). Experience-guided working: An undervalued resource for advanced manufacturing systems. In P. Brödner & W. Karwowski (Eds.), *Ergonomics of hybrid automated systems III.* Proceedings of the Third International Conference on Human Aspects of Advanced Manufacturing and Hybrid Automation (pp. 423–428). Amsterdam: Elsevier.

Dienes, Z., & Berry, D. (1997). Implicit learning: Below the subjective threshold. *Psychonomic Bulletin & Review, 4*, 3–23.

Doane, S. M., Sohn, Y. W., & Schreiber, B. (1999). The role of processing strategies in the acquisition and transfer of cognitive skills. *Journal of Experimental Psychology: Human Perception and Performance, 25*, 1390–1410.

Dreyfus, H. L., & Dreyfus, S. E. (1986). *Mind over machine: The power of human intuition and expertise in the era of computer*. New York: Free Press.

Engeström, Y., Miettinen, R., & Punamäki, R.-L. (Eds.). (1999). *Perspectives on activity theory*. Cambridge, UK: Cambridge University Press.

Ericsson, K. A., Krampe, R. T., & Tesch-Römer, C. (1993). The role of deliberate practice in the acquisition of expert performance. *Psychological Review, 100*, 363–406.

Fischbein, E. (1994). Tacit Models. In D. Tirosh (Ed.), *Implicit and explicit knowledge: An educational approach* (Human Development, Vol. 6, pp. 96–110). Norwood, NJ: Ablex.

Frese, M., & Zapf, D. (1994). Action as the core of work psychology: A German approach. In M. D. Dunnette, J. M. Hough, & H. C. Trinadis (Eds.), *Handbook of industrial and organizational psychology* (Vol. 4, pp. 271–340). Palo Alto, CA: Consulting Psychologists Press.

Gaines, B. R., & Shaw, M. L. G. (1993). Knowledge acquisition tools based on personal construct psychology. *Knowledge Engineering Review*, *8*, 49–85.

Gazzard, S. (1994). *On implicit learning of sequential and conceptual rules*. Sydney: University of Sydney, Department of Psychology.

Greeno, J. G. (1998). The situativity of knowing, learning, and research. *American Psychologist*, *53*, 5–26.

Greeno, J. G., Smith, D. R., & Moore, J. L. (1993). Transfer of situated learning. In D. K. Dettermann & R. J. Sternberg (Eds.), *Transfer on trial: Intelligence, cognition, and instruction* (pp. 99–167). Norwood, NJ: Ablex.

Griffin, T., Schwartz, S., & Sofronoff, K. (1998). Implicit processes in medical diagnosis. In K. Kirsner, C. Speelman, M. Maybery, A. O´Brien-Malone, M. Anderson, & C. MacLeod (Eds.), *Implicit and explicit mental processes* (pp. 329–341). Mawah, NJ: Erlbaum.

Hacker, W. (1992a). Action regulation theory and occupational psychology – Review of German empirical research since 1987. *German Journal of Psychology*, *18*, 91–120.

Hacker, W. (1992b). *Expertenkönnen. Erkennen und Vermitteln* [Expert skill. Detecting and imparting]. Göttingen, Germany: Verlag für Angewandte Psychologie.

Hantano, G., & Inagaki, K. (1986). Two courses of expertise. In H. Stevenson, H. Azuma, & K. Hakuta (Eds.), *Child development and education in Japan* (pp. 262–272). San Francisco: Freeman.

Herbig, B. (2001). *Vergleichende Untersuchung von Struktur und Inhalt expliziten und impliziten Wissens im Arbeitskontext* [Comparative study of structure and content of explicit and implicit knowledge in the work context]. Aachen, Germany: Shaker.

Herbig, B., & Büssing, A. (2003). Comparison of explicit and implicit knowledge in the work context. *Psychology Science*, *45* (3), 165–188.

Herbig, B., Büssing, A., & Ewert, T. (2001). The role of tacit knowledge in the work context of nursing. *Journal of Advanced Nursing*, *34*, 687–695.

Higgins, S., & Baumfield, V. (1998). A defense of teaching general thinking skills. *Journal of the Philosophy of Education*, *32*, 391–398.

Kelly, G. A. (1955). *The psychology of personal constructs*. New York: Norton.

Kelly, G. A. (1969). A mathematical approach to psychology. In B. Maher (Ed.), *Clinical psychology and personality: The selected papers of George Kelly* (pp. 94–113). New York: Wiley.

Kihlstrom, J. F. (1999). Conscious vs. unconscious cognition. In R. J. Sternberg (Ed.), *The nature of cognition* (pp. 173–203). Cambridge, MA: MIT Press.

Kirsner, K., & Speelman, C. (1998). Introduction and overview. In K. Kirsner, C. Speelman, M. Maybery, A. O´Brien-Malone, M. Anderson, & C. MacLeod (Eds.), *Implicit and explicit mental processes* (pp. 3–12). Mawah, NJ: Erlbaum.

Lee, M. G., & Gelman, R. (1993). *Contributions of developmental and cognitive psychology to education* (Education and Technology Series monograph). Paris: United Nations Educational, Scientific, and Cultural Organization.

Lewicki, P. (1986). *Nonconscious social information processing*. London: Academic Press.

Logan, G. D. (1988). Toward an instance theory of automatization. *Psychological Review*, *95*, 492–527.

Mandl, H., & Gerstenmaier, J. (Eds.). (2000). *Die Kluft zwischen Wissen und Handeln – Empirische und theoretische Lösungsansätze* [The gap between knowledge and action – Empirical and theoretical attempts for solution]. Göttingen, Germany : Hogrefe.

Menzies, T. (1998). Toward situated knowledge acquisition. *International Journal of Human-Computer Studies*, *49*, 867–893.
Moss, E. (1995). *The grammar of consciousness. An exploration of tacit knowing*. London: Macmillan.
Myers, C., & Davis, K. (1993). Tacit skill and performance at work. *Applied Psychology*, *42*, 117–137.
Neuweg, G. H. (Ed.). (2000). *Wissen – Können – Reflexion – Ausgewählte Verhältnisbestimmungen* [Knowledge – skill – reflection. Selected approaches to define their relations]. Innsbruck, Austria: Studienverlag.
Polanyi, M. (1962). *Personal knowledge: Toward a post-critical philosophy*. Chicago: University of Chigaco Press.
Polanyi, M. (1966). *The tacit dimension*. New York: Doubleday.
Reber, A. S. (1993). *Implicit learning and tacit knowledge. An essay on the cognitive unconscious*. New York: Oxford University Press.
Reber, A. S. (1997). Implicit Ruminations. *Psychonomic Bulletin & Review*, *4*, 49–55.
Reber, A. S., Kassin, S. M., Lewis, S., & Cantor, G. (1980). On the relationship between implicit and explicit modes in the learning of a complex rule structure. *Journal of Experimental Psychology: Human Learning and Memory*, *6*, 492–501.
Renkl, A. (1996). Träges Wissen: Wenn Erlerntes nicht genutzt wird [Inert knowledge: When what is learned is not used]. *Psychologische Rundschau*, *47*, 78–92.
Rouse, W. B, & Morris, N. M. (1986). On looking into the black box: Prospects and limits in the search for mental model. *Psychological Bulletin*, *100*, 349–363.
Ryle, G. (1993). *Aspects of mind*. Oxford, UK: Blackwell.
Seger, C. A. (1994). Implicit learning. *Psychological Bulletin*, *115*, 163–196.
Sloboda, J. (1991). Musical expertise. In K. A. Ericsson & J. Smith (Eds.), *Toward a general theory of expertise* (pp. 153–171). Cambridge, UK: Cambridge University Press.
Sonnentag, S. (2000). Expertise at work: Experience and excellent performance. In C. L. Cooper & I. T. Robertson (Eds.), *International Review of Industrial and Organisational Psychology*, *15*, 223–264.
Speelman, C. (1998). Implicit expertise: Do we expect too much from our experts? In K. Kirsner, C. Speelman, M. Maybery, A. O'Brien-Malone, M. Anderson, & C. MacLeod (Eds.), *Implicit and explicit mental processes* (pp. 135–147). Mawah, NJ: Erlbaum.
Young, F. W. (1985). Multidimensional Scaling. In S. Kotz & N. Johnson (Eds.), *Encyclopedia of statistical sciences* (Vol. 5; pp. 649–658). New York: Wiley.